ARCHITECTURAL ACOUSTICS

A GUIDE TO INTEGRATED THINKING

© Raj Patel, 2020

Published by RIBA Publishing, 66 Portland Place, London, W1B 1AD

ISBN 9781 85946 636 0

The right of Raj Patel to be identified as the Author of this Work has been
asserted in accordance with the Copyright, Designs and Patents Act 1988
sections 77 and 78.

British Library Cataloguing-in-Publication Data
A catalogue record for this book is available from the British Library.

Commissioning Editor: Elizabeth Webster
Assistant Editor: Clare Holloway
Production: Richard Blackburn
Designed & Typeset by Zoe Mercer
Printed and bound by Short Run Press

Cover image: © Doublespace

www.ribapublishing.com

ARCHITECTURAL ACOUSTICS

A GUIDE TO INTEGRATED THINKING

RIBA ✛ Publishing

RAJ PATEL

Contents

Preface

One of my earliest and most enduring memories is of the interaction between sound and architecture. In my early years I lived on a wide street with a parade of shops topped by houses on both sides. Our front door was behind the shops, reached via a long narrow alleyway that connected the street to the rear shop delivery area. The alley was five storeys tall, plastered brick on both sides. Just by stepping into it, the sound of the world changed. If I clapped my hands or stamped my feet a loud ringing would fill the space. Years later I would learn that this phenomenon is called a 'flutter echo' – common in spaces with parallel, sound-reflecting walls, and especially pronounced when spaces are tall and narrow.

You could feel it traveling up and along the walls. It could be activated by whistling (I would run down it trying to 'catch' the sounds I made), banging sticks or bouncing balls. I found this ability to manipulate my sonic landscape fascinating and engaging; it was my first experience of playing with architecture. I can still hear that sound clearly in my mind.

I was always fascinated by the sounds and noises things made, and the tactility of it – from the satisfying 'click' of turning on an old radio dial (not to mention the music coming from it), to setting a turntable needle down on a vinyl record. I learned to play musical instruments, both classical and modern, listening to myself and others play in concert halls and rock clubs, subconsciously thinking about the relationship between sound and space. At a crucial moment around the age of 16, I stumbled on a prospectus for the University of Southampton. Acoustics was listed first in the index. I read it, visited, and took the course. I have been practising some form of acoustic consulting, sound or multimedia design ever since.

I've had the opportunity to understand and apply creative acoustics thinking very broadly across the built environment. While there are myriad rules and criteria that can, and must, be applied, the challenge has been learning how to communicate good acoustics design to professionals with very different backgrounds who pay less attention to it. I've worked with many wonderful architects, designers and artists willing to explore and work beyond a rules-based approach to achieve successful outcomes. It has been rich and rewarding, with the great benefit of being able to see people enjoy the spaces, and take on unique characters once left to the users and visitors.

I've never been much of an academic. I tend to learn by a process of experimenting, making, learning and repeating. It was a surprise to be asked by the RIBA to write a book, and that several architects had suggested I would be a good candidate to do so, and it was even more surprising to me that I said yes. I remained daunted by the prospect down to the final words. This is primarily because I have spent most of my career developing tools and techniques to explain acoustics using sound instead of words. It seemed like the obvious way to easily convey meaning and achieve better outcomes. It was a challenge to put this into writing, but I hope that summarising some of these thoughts and experiences will be useful to others in the future.

I would like to acknowledge and thank the following people:

Elizabeth Webster, Senior Commissioning Editor at the RIBA, for her abundance of patience in getting this done. Clare Holloway, Associate Editor at the RIBA for her diligence and for keeping things moving in the final 12 months. Deanna Wallach, my assistant, for her patience, editing, photo sourcing, biscuits and cakes. Fiona Shipwright for working closely with me in the development, direction, transcription and editing of the conversations that form the backbone of the text. Solène Wolff at PLANE-SITE for direction, guidance, and assistance in the planning process and initial assembly of materials.

Daniel Imade, King of the Arup Photo Library, for all his work on the Case Studies. Willem Boning and Leah Guszkowski for assistance in developing the book format and approach. Kelsey Habla for the new drawings and figures used throughout. Brendan Smith for the visual representations of audio. Peter Grueneisen and Annette Gref at Birkhauser for use of images and text from his excellent book *Soundspace* for the Acoustic Terminology section, modified and developed by the author and Avi Bortnik.

To all my fellow acoustics, audio-visual and theatre consultants at Arup who contributed to chapters throughout, my sincere thanks for your critique and encouragement, for embracing challenges, and for making Arup an enduringly vibrant place to work.

I've had the pleasure of working with some great acoustic consultants over the years. Too numerous to mention all by name, I wish to recognise a few who have been close colleagues for 20 years or more, from whom I learned a lot at a pivotal time as our collective practice was developing, and from the many projects we shared: Finola Reid, Fiona Gillan, Helen Butcher, Sylvia Jones, Alban Bassuet, Andrew Nicol, Andy

Officer, Chris Field, Chris Manning, Colin English, Dave Anderson, Ian Thompson, Iain Clarke, Joe Solway, John Miller, Kurt Graffy, Kym Burgemeister, Malcolm Wright, Nathan Blum, Ned Crowe, Nick Boulter, Nigel Cogger, Paul Malpas, Peter Griffiths, Richard Greer, Rob Harris, Roger Kelly and Sam Tsoi.

Thanks to Ian Knowles, my friend and colleague for almost 28 years, who contributed much to this book.

Special thanks to Neill Woodger, whom I have collaborated with on countless endeavours and adventures in acoustics, and without whom many achievements would not have been realised.

To Derek Sugden and Richard Cowell – for having a vision of the transformative effect of acoustics in design, and for imparting it with their wisdom and unmatched wit to create an environment and legacy that lives on through all who have worked at, or with, the Acoustics, AV, Theatre team at Arup.

To the acoustic consultants everywhere who go out every day to spread the word, and to those who find new ways to better demonstrate and use sound proactively in the design process, elevating it above what is necessary, to what delights.

To my son Jay and my daughter Reva. And to my wife Jennifer – for everything.

Acknowledgements

Introduction

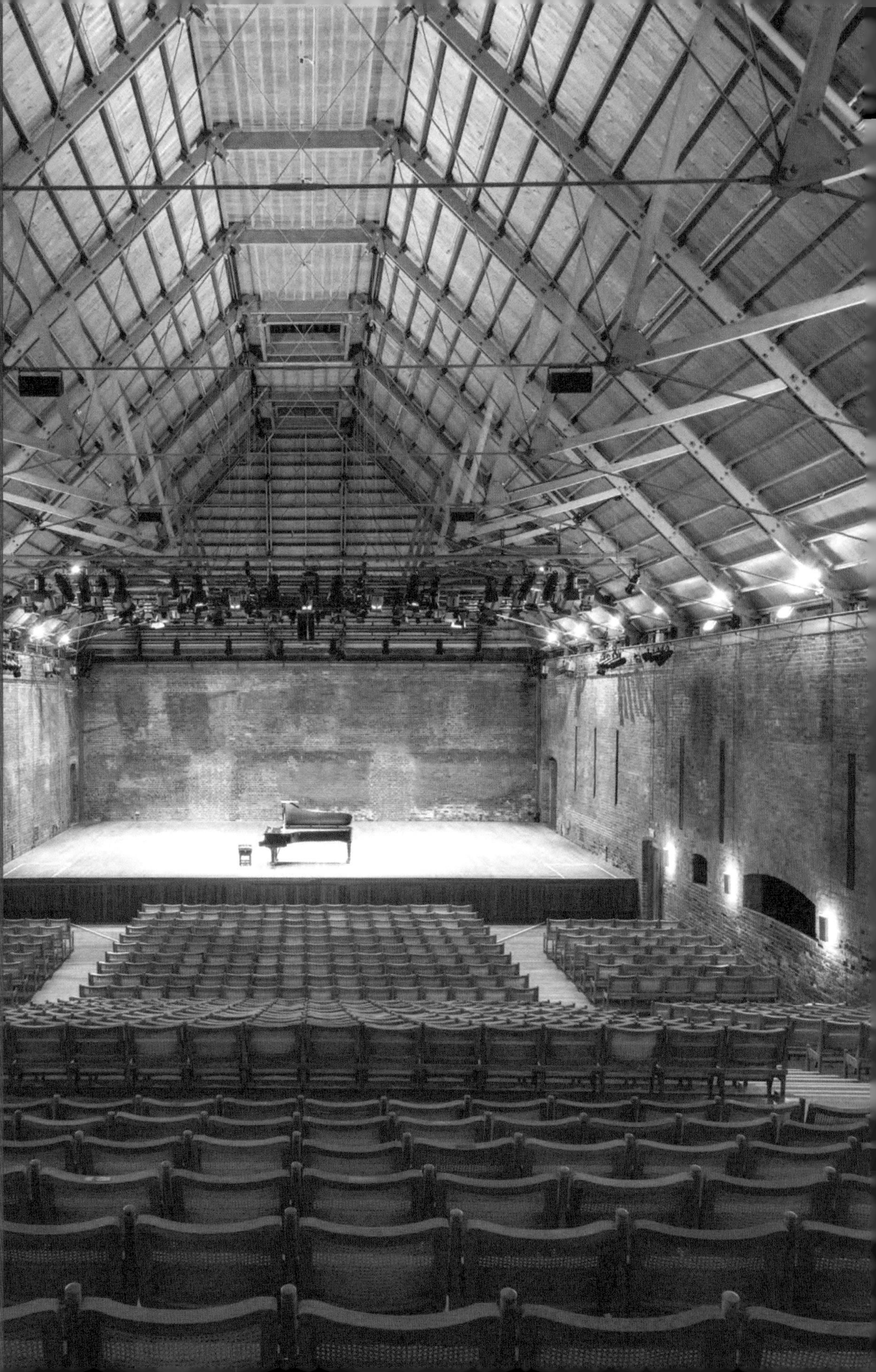

How often do you think about sound and how you want people to feel when you are designing a space? Good acoustic design is inherent to architecture. Every decision you make about shape, form, geometry, volume and materials defines the acoustics. So how do you design proactively for the right outcomes, the first time?

Architects generally receive little, if any, education in acoustics. In formulating design goals for projects, acoustics is a low priority – except when it is fundamental to a building's function (e.g. a concert hall). This is a missed opportunity. Great aural environments can be transcendental. Acoustics is the invisible art. When done well, spaces feel right – elevating one's experience. Get it wrong and it can make buildings unfit for purpose. Poor acoustics can be expensive, difficult or impossible to correct once you have them. It requires integrated thinking from the start.

Understanding acoustics – the propagation of vibration through air and solids, the conversion of vibration into sound, the range of subjective views on what constitutes pleasant sound or unwanted noise at different frequencies (low, medium, high or to use the musical analogy bass, mid, treble) is extremely complex. It requires a fundamental grasp of the physics, engineering, art and psychology of sound. Experiencing acoustics during the design process by listening is now accessible using auralisation tools. Used well, this encourages better design outcomes.

There are plenty of technical books on architectural acoustics for those who want to delve deeper into the subject. This book is intended to help those unsure why acoustics is important in design at all, approaching acoustics for the first time, or as a refresher when starting work on new projects. It aims to capture the essential information needed to design well. The opening essays provide background and insights for incorporating good acoustic thinking for design in the broadest sense. Acoustic Terminology captures key words that will likely be encountered in a working career as a designer. The Case Studies present projects by type, to quickly understand what is important and why, with project examples for guidance. The intention is to foster an approach to thinking about sound at the start of projects, the positive potential of using sound creatively, and to help engage your clients in dialogue about it. Hopefully it helps to elevate the acoustics profession and its integration with other design disciplines.

This book does *not* replace the essential role of the acoustic consultant who is needed on most if not all projects. Most impactful at the very start, a good consultant with expertise of the building type will provide invaluable advice.

We should strive to create spaces that delight all the senses. The right blend of what you see and how it feels is what creates exceptional, emotionally engaging spaces. I advocate thinking about sound in the way you design from the outset. Ask the question: 'How do I want people to feel in this space?' and consider every sense when you do.

Raj Patel, New York, February 2020

1

Acoustics and Architecture

Take a moment to think about what you hear right now. If it's helpful, close your eyes for a minute. The simple act of paying attention changes the act of hearing to listening. The skill in listening is in applying attention.

Studies have shown that conscious thought takes place at the same rate as visual recognition. This requires a fraction of a second. To notice something out of the corner of your eye, turn toward it, recognise and respond to it, can take a second. Reaction to a new or sudden sound happens at least ten times as fast.[1] This is a result of a fundamental evolutionary relationship we have with sound that is often forgotten or taken for granted. Hearing is the only one of our five primary senses that works in three dimensions. It works while we sleep and has been key to our survival

as a species. It is has always been the first sense to alert us to danger. On hearing a sound, we can quickly determine how far away it is, which direction it's coming from, how quickly, and if it's likely to cause harm. The hearing instinct is finely tuned to suppress certain sounds, and focus on others, depending on the information it receives. It is why many of us still need an alarm clock to wake in the morning.

In a world dominated by what we see, the role of sound in how we perceive, relate to, and behave in our surroundings seems vastly underappreciated, even ignored. Given the important sensory role it plays, sound should be something all designers think about in great detail. Consider the vast array of visual illusions compared to the modest number of known auditory illusions. Visual stimuli are often important in creating

Previous page:
St Pancras Station,
London, UK.

or reinforcing an aural illusion. The eye is easy to trick, the ear is not. Did we appreciate the sound of our environment, and the acoustics of our buildings, more in the past than we do today? If we did, what changed? What can we learn? What do we need to get it back?

The sounds of prehistory

In the last 20 years researchers investigating certain prehistoric sites have found notable acoustic phenomena. The Lascaux Caves in France contain fabulously preserved Palaeolithic paintings brought to life in flickering fire light. When activated by rhythmic sound, they mimic the animals depicted on the walls. It has been argued that this is not a designed result, but one of circumstance – that the best caves for painting were those that were non-

porous. Perhaps coincidentally, they are reverberant by nature. Stonehenge, the Neolithic site at Salisbury Plain in Wiltshire, UK (see above) is the subject of increasing archeo-acoustic research. The bluestones of the circle 'sing' when struck.[2] They are also highly reverberant when other sounds occur within them, such as replicas of Neolithic instruments being played. The pyramid Temple of Kukulkan, or El Castillo, in Chichen Itza, Mexico (see overleaf) has a well-known acoustic phenomenon. When one claps perpendicular to the stairs, the sound of a 'serpent' ascending the staircase can be heard followed by the 'chirp'[3] of a bird that appears to emanate from the small chamber at the top of the pyramid. The chirp is actually a descending tone, the result of sound reflections from the stairs. It is strongly representative of the Quetzal bird, whose feathers are depicted in

Stonehenge, Salisbury, UK.

El Castillo, Chichen Itza, Mexico.

the Kukulkan deity. Whether this was by design or accident remains disputed. This example is notable as chirps can be found following similar stimuli in staircases around the world. The tone is a function of the step height, width and depth. These can be designed and engineered. It would simply have required prototyping, trial and error. Given the prolific building of the Mayans, this suggests a great deal of thought went into the design process. The resulting sound was an important function of the architecture.

The great Greek Amphitheatre at Epidaurus is known the world over for its exceptional acoustics (see opposite). It is an extraordinary piece of sonic architecture. Its location, nestled into the hills and facing away from the city, would have been very

effective at limiting the amount of noise intruding into the venue. The trees around the site, with the aid of the wind, create a pleasant, ambient background noise. They quell the sounds of the city (both then and now) providing a neutral sound 'scene' against which to perform. Spoken word tradition and its propagation were paramount for Ancient Greek culture. Sustaining it was one of the primary functions of spaces like this. The curved stone steps help propagate sound around the theatre. They also reinforce sound from the performers. This creates a 'surround sound' effect for the listener. It would have required a deep appreciation of architecture and acoustics to achieve this auditory effect. Epidaurus is an excellent example of how concave shaping can be used to optimise and positively influence the

escape the enclosure thus reducing reverberance (which would have otherwise significantly reduced speech intelligibility), as well as improving natural ventilation. The Romans further advanced engineering and architecture to create increasingly impressive and bold structures. Vitruvius began to document approaches for acoustically successful design[5] in response to challenges in some of these grand spaces. Especially where domes, arches and other curved surfaces were a feature designed to create specific acoustic experiences, these examples show an advancing knowledge of how to deliver successful outcomes integrated into architecture.

Later in history, these same approaches were developed to deliver rich immersive sound experiences essential to the transcendent spiritual nature of religious spaces. As the progression of architecture and engineering allowed more complex structures to be realised in the West, these spaces were also adapted for enhanced speech and music. In Byzantine churches, half domes above the clergy helped project sound to the congregation, and over the choir to the nave, giving the impression of sound coming from above. The development of large-scale, large volume, 'grand' spaces in classical architecture was often acoustically challenging. By the Reformation, with church services being delivered in local language and dialect, the challenges presented by large-volume spaces (with respect to speech intelligibility) were quickly realised. Smaller spaces for worship were increasingly popularised as a result.

The other grandest building forms of the Renaissance and Enlightenment were typically musical. Western Classical music form and composition developed symbiotically with architecture and engineering (and the development of musical instruments). Composers usually created works for and in the spaces

acoustics of a space; a mechanism later used to great effect in both Eastern and Western spiritual and religious architecture.

Acoustics in enclosed spaces

As the first roofed theatres of classical antiquity evolved from the amphitheatre, designers encountered new acoustic challenges as they developed enclosures. In his book *Roofed Theaters of Classical Antiquity*,[4] George Izenour shows strategic openings of the Odium at Agrippa in optimal locations on the side and rear auditorium walls. These logically serve the dual functions of allowing some sound to

where they were first performed. They used the architectural acoustics to adapt their compositions; be that the cathedral, the salons, ballcourts, jewel boxes or great halls in the palaces of Europe. Listening to the works of Haydn, Mozart, Beethoven or Tchaikovsky being performed in the spaces they were designed for, and with instruments and technology available at the time of their conception, is a very different experience to hearing them played in the concert halls of the 20th and 21st centuries. The works often feel bolder, louder and more immersive, much like spectacular rock or pop concerts do in the arenas of today. The question of whether the architecture or place shaped the music[6] is a subject of ongoing debate.

Volume, scale and acoustics

Over the course of the Industrial Revolution, grand, monumental building structures became prevalent for new reasons. Factories and production lines were originally housed in buildings with cramped and dangerous working conditions. Noise was a major challenge in these spaces and hearing loss an unavoidable occupational hazard. The first train stations were built to accommodate steam locomotives, with all the noise, heat, steam and soot that entailed (see two images left).

Large volume spaces with operable windows were a necessity. As a society we have developed an emotional and historic attachment to many of these spaces. With that attachment comes a mandate to maintain them. Often this means converting them to house modern technology, converting power stations into museums, or factories into office spaces. This has been achieved with various degrees of acoustical success.

If spaces were scaled with acoustic functionality in mind they would commonly be smaller volumetrically than visual aesthetics would dictate, thus requiring fewer additional acoustic 'treatments' overall. This would lead to a more sustainable outcome in terms of the overall building size and amount of material used. We can imagine – and computers can help us design and engineer – amazing, colossal spaces. We can work out ways to construct and deliver them. But should we?

Designing a positive acoustic future

Good aural architecture considers at its heart how people experience, react to and behave in space.

In other industries, good sound is at the core of design philosophy. Manufacturers of high-quality cars emphasise a focus on great sound throughout their products. From the operation of a door handle to the closing of the door itself, the clicks produced by the stereo dial and steering wheel levers, to the purr of the engine resonating through the chassis, these audible and tactile triggers are important. The same should be true of architecture. In both passive and active states, we can feel the effects of good acoustic design decisions.

Perhaps one reason for the lack of integration in architectural design is the scepticism about acoustic design resulting from well-known projects with perceived deficient acoustics, built post-1945. The most well-known of these are a few major concert halls that were criticised for having 'poor' acoustics when they opened ('poor' meaning not having the sound of the so called 'great halls' such as Große Musikvereinssaal Vienna, Amsterdam Concertgebouw and Boston Symphony Hall). These projects variously suffered from major design

changes during their late stages. This was often because of a demand for increased seat count to meet economic expectations for revenue, and/or architectural experimentation with new shapes and forms. Acoustic consultants, applying evolving and developing analysis and prediction techniques, were not able to successfully resolve these issues at the time. In retrospect, the acoustics of some of these spaces are being reconsidered.

Acoustics are a result of room shape, form, volume and material selection. It is not possible to simply scale a building up in size and have the same acoustics as a smaller one. Over time the 'rules' developed to foster good acoustics design – or, more accurately, to avoid problems with acoustics – may have done so at the expense of creating acoustical *interest* in buildings. This makes the job of the architect one of compliance, and potentially misses the opportunity to develop delightful acoustic experiences. It is the job of the architect to champion experiences for the senses. The role of the acoustician is to develop the methods, tools and integrated design that allows for those tailored and unique experiences to happen.

Acoustics should not necessarily be uniform in the built environment. Spaces should be designed with unique, delightful, bespoke acoustics. Good acoustic design can create transition moments. It can be exceptionally useful at transitions (vestibules, stairwells, level changes) to accent, enhance and ignite architectural experiences. It can be used to guide and lead people through buildings and spaces. The auralisation tools now available to explore this during the design process allow exciting spaces to be created that do not meet conventional acoustic criteria while still being great and successful spaces to inhabit. It should be an integral part of what architects do.

St Pancras Station, London, UK.

2

Soundscapes

Wherever you go, there is always sound. Even in the quietest places, once you focus your attention and begin to listen, you will hear beyond perceived silence and recognise the underlying sounds that are integral to the world around us. Those who live in urban environments may be more likely to notice this when we are in nature. Likewise, those who live more rurally are acutely aware of noise when they are in urban environments.

As cities have grown and developed, so too have their soundscapes. Hoofbeats on cobblestones and the sounds of working dockyards have given way to food vendors on street corners and taxis in traffic, 'natural' parts of the evolving urban environment. Some cities have unique sonic fingerprints: the chiming bells of Big Ben in London or the trams of Hong Kong – sounds that define their locales. While these soundscapes are the result of conscious planning and decision making, to what extent was the resulting sound environment considered, much less designed, by its urban planners, architects, landscape designers and acousticians?

The detrimental effects of noise on health, wellbeing and cognitive function are well documented in the World Health Organization Guidelines.[1] It is a major source of complaint from the public to city authorities around the world. From the advent of the Sony Walkman in the 1980s to the development of personal digital audio devices, individuals have taken increasing control of challenging noise or acoustic conditions by simply putting on headphones and enclosing themselves in their own personalised worlds of sound. But this results in a profound loss – as the flow of people through the urban landscape changes, how they relate to each other and their surroundings, how they navigate landscapes and listen to and learn from one another is also fundamentally transformed.

Spaces used for rest, respite and immersion in positive and/or peaceful sounds have been integrated into public life for centuries. They were natural environments, spiritual sites, parks or plazas (often with water features), venues for music and entertainment – these places could be enjoyed alone or communally. They were crucially woven into everyday life. Increasingly, these places are harder to find or access; their role in social cohesion eroded. As urban concentration increases, it is important that designers proactively plan for purposefully humane conditions. Good sound integrated into holistic approaches in urban design is vital. It will impact buildings, the spaces between them, streets, transport, greenspaces and urban resiliency. Using architecture to foster the connection between a person and their environment places great responsibility on the designer, with even greater reward when it is done well.

Taking control of our sonic environment

Canadian composer R. Murray Schafer coined the term 'soundscape' and advocated its use in approach to design. In his book *The Soundscape: Our Sonic Environment and the Tuning of the World* Schafer asks:

"Is the soundscape of the world an indeterminate composition over which we have no control, or are we its composers and performers, responsible for giving it form and beauty?"

This concept has been well known within the acoustic community for many years, often advocated for in urban planning. It is now receiving increased global attention and has developed into national and international guidance documents.

In the future, soundscape design will supplement or perhaps even replace standard acoustic assessment procedure. It will be supported by a wealth of evidence-based contextual survey information (e.g. crowd-sourced, app-based data). There will be a greater emphasis on the findings of cognitive and behavioural scientists regarding the human impacts of sound (and noise). Importantly, it will define how to tune our surroundings for better environmental outcomes. We can expect this will initially be advocated as a multi-disciplinary demand for better design, followed by increasing mandates via government agencies. Soundscapes of the built environment will become conscious compositions and have far reaching impact on building forms, massing, materiality, planning and much more.

We must take collective responsibility for what our world will sound like through multi-disciplinary ownership of compositions of sound – both indoor and outdoor – and aspiring to transformational outcomes. To achieve the best results, each project should consider and benchmark goals and align them with contextual aspirations. Deviations from standard acoustic design approaches must be justified and documented throughout the design process. This is imperative from the earliest stages of project planning to set the foundations for the best outcomes. Support of soundscape initiatives must be maintained through design, construction, commissioning and delivery.

Acoustic design has traditionally focused on the prevention, if not alleviation, of unwanted sounds, e.g. noise. It favours standardised criteria which are consistently applied across a broad, diverse population. Soundscape design seeks to address the nature of perception and broaden its scope. It presents different sound sources and acoustic environments in distinct circumstances, to deliver positive results for health, wellbeing, productivity and enjoyment, among many other metrics.

Shape and form

The soundscape design approach can be broadly grouped in the following categories:

- **City** soundscape planning is fundamental to achieving preferable rather than probable future soundscapes for our urban environments. It requires proactive engagement with government agencies. It means providing education and assistance in developing frameworks that demystify the process for achieving a balanced outcome between activation and amenity via appropriate policy parameters. This approach often favours defining processes and pathways over defaulting to numerical data. It challenges the blanket assumption that quieter is better, delving deeper into soundscape character and aspirational long-term goals.

- **Precinct** soundscape design often forms a cumulative subset of city soundscape planning, often focusing on the preservation of tranquil spaces or the emphasis of especially vibrant locales within a broader cityscape. Individual precincts can also be developed as isolated experiences, either transitory or standalone. As they are well-defined areas, there is a greater opportunity to survey and understand how people currently perceive their existing environment. This helps the designer understand which soundscape elements they should introduce, retain or remove.

- **Building** design increasingly recognises positive soundscape influence on performance and wellness. Concepts such as traditional sound masking are being challenged and there is a greater focus on early involvement to facilitate sound mapping holistically throughout a building. The auditory component of indoor environments is inextricably linked to experience and brand.

Collaboration with branding consultants may be key for some clients to achieving the best outcome for a project, commensurate with other aesthetic design goals.

- **Room** design requires an even more granular level of detail during the conceptual stages of design. This level of detail responds to a growing opportunity to influence project outcomes within the controlled environment offered by rooms within buildings. Depending on application, soundscape interventions may be more overt as they are targeted to a specific function, the influence of which can be controlled to adjacent spaces.

Shaping

- **Passive** soundscape design incorporates traditional acoustic engineering approaches such as noise control, sound insulation and room acoustic design to promote a base soundscape condition.

- **Active** soundscape design incorporates audio-visual infrastructure to introduce curated and/or composed content to spaces and may include standard methodologies such as sound masking.

- **Persuasive** soundscape design incorporates analysis of naturally occurring sound sources (e.g. people, animals, water, wind in trees) and curates these sound sources as part of the overall soundscape composition.

This framework incorporates a focus on auditory components of soundscapes. It should be noted that experience of soundscape is a multi-sensory phenomenon that includes a contextual understanding of how sounds are perceived.

Challenges

One of the main challenges in encouraging soundscape design is to shift perspective and make a commitment to a nonstandard approach, which requires some risk. Balancing the need to comply with minimum standards against the proposal to deviate from standard criteria requires significant consultation and buy-in from all relevant stakeholders and continued advocacy of designers. This means all stakeholders must have investment in, and ownership of, soundscape design outcomes.

Although conceptually decades old, applying the soundscape approach is still in its infancy. There is much research and development to be done. This includes further standardisation of survey methodologies, and extensive database compilation to better understand contextual perception of sound, and noise, across cultures and environments. There are significant challenges in obtaining sufficient data points to support soundscape design aspirations for a project. These are necessary to address the aspiration for contextual understanding of how soundscapes are perceived.

World Trade Center Memorial

The World Trade Center Memorial demonstrates a good cross-section of soundscape design approaches. The project incorporates each of the passive, persuasive and active design approaches to arrive at an end experience commensurate with the gravitas of the memorial. The goal was to create a journey from outside to within the memorial building that encouraged reflection and remembrance.

The site is surrounded by busy roads which define the keynote of the existing soundscape. The level of the ground plane for the memorial plaza was lowered relative to the surrounding road network, stepping down from the noise sources with trees and other plantings (borrowed from a similar approach found in New York's Central Park). This provides an effective form of passive noise mitigation. Extensive greenery delivers natural sound masking activated by prevailing winds year-round. Two large water features are specifically designed to create a complementary natural soundscape. These persuasive design elements make the sounds of the road traffic all but disappear.

As visitors complete their journey they are led to the memorial pavilion. Curated content with active soundscape components is housed here. Coupled with appropriate sound insulation, room acoustic design and audio-visual specification, this final part of the experience was composed to provide a suitable cadence to the overall soundscape experience.

Future

The work of artists like John Cage, Pauline Oliveros, Alvin Lucier, Max Neuhaus, Bill Fontana, Steve Reich and Harry Bertoia can all be referenced as inspiration for both subtle and literal applications of the soundscape design approach. 'Times Square' (Max Neuhaus, 1977–1992, 2002–present) created a sonic moment at the heart of the famous New York landmark. The work was not identified by any maker, instead it was there to be discovered. 'Harmonic Bridge' (Bill Fontana, 2006) placed accelerometers on London's Millennium Bridge that converted the real-time vibrations (natural, wind and human) into sound played into the turbine hall at the Tate Modern. Harry Bertoia's 'sonambient' sculptures encourage tactility and foster a bond between human, material, sound and architecture. All structures have their own dynamic movement. In a future with increasing use of sensors in buildings, the availability of data to create

site-specific soundscapes should be used to great effect. The prevalence of 3D immersive technologies, both in design processes and delivered active systems, should also be embraced where appropriate to support soundscape outcomes.

We, as designers, have a surprising amount of influence over the built environment of the future. Localised sound in buildings can guide its occupants in distinct ways; either as part of a way-finding system offering directional cues, or ambiently, inviting people to listen to and appreciate the building architecture.[2] Appropriate sound design is a mark of quality. It has the potential to transform a person's entire experience. It should be varied to encourage listener awareness of experiences and textures that interrupt or support aural perception of space. At its best, this will be one part of implementing a better universal design approach that is inclusive and beneficial for all.

3

Sound and Architecture – The Future?

It was sometime in the spring of 1985 that I first questioned acoustics design in buildings. I had played in a variety of great sounding rooms as a young musician with orchestras in northwest London, where I was born and raised. Brent Town Hall, Watford Town Hall and Watford Colosseum were fantastic sounding spaces whether onstage as a musician or sitting in the audience. Good acoustics were never in question. During my first experience in the audience at the Barbican Concert Hall in London, I was struck by how remote the orchestra felt, and the lack of acoustic response of the room. A few months later, onstage at the Royal Festival Hall with the London Symphony Orchestra, a new challenge – trying to hear other sections of the orchestra, struggling to keep time and play together. I remember thinking how strange that was in a 'proper' concert hall.

At the other end of the spectrum, Sundays were spent rehearsing bass guitar with my first band. There it seemed the essence was to experiment with sounds and noise in spaces whose acoustics were different, and challenging. We did so under the watchful eye of Rastafarian TJ who ran the Brent Black Music Co-Op and Studio. He would give us tips on how to set up our gear, hear each other better, and how to best record ourselves given the space we had to work in.

All of these have proved valuable teaching and learning experiences.

Midway through my degree in Engineering Acoustics and Vibration, I was lucky enough to get an intern position at an acoustic consulting firm named after its founder, the jazz musician Sandy Brown. My first project was like stepping into a dream. I was tasked with assisting in the conversion of a Victorian church in Hampstead, north London, into the new Air Studios for the Beatles' producer George Martin. Excellent

acoustics was a fundamental aspect of the brief. In testing the main space, Lyndhurst Hall, in the months before completion, it was a thrill to watch George and his engineer Dave Harries working on mic positions to capture particular sounds in nooks and crooks, and high up in the eaves.

A few years later, I would find myself at Arup with a much broader project range including spaces for the performing arts, recording, education, transport, workplace and more. Attending meetings with architects, I would explain the importance of good acoustics to make spaces fit for purpose, and for the overall perception of architecture. Some architects would be open to seeing how this could influence their work. For others the concept was met with resistance. Acoustics was an outside force interfering with architectural aesthetics.

It was clear to my colleagues and I that trying to explain acoustics in sketches, diagrams, reports and numbers was a barrier to adopting architectural integration. We soon determined that the only way to make real progress was by allowing architects to listen to the acoustics of buildings during the design process, a process called auralisation. It took a few years for the evolution of computer processors and the right tools to allow auralisation to be realised at speeds suitable for deployment in the context of building design projects. By 1999 we had working auralisation demonstration tools in both London and New York, and our first fully fledged SoundLab prototyped and running in the New York office shortly after.

Auralisation has delivered a step change in using sound and acoustics as a proactive part of the design process, although it is sometimes approached by architects with trepidation. Many approach the process saying something like 'I'm more of a visual person, I'm not sure I'll be able to

Previous page:
Arup i|Lab, London.

hear the difference'. It is a joy to watch the lightbulb moment when they *do* hear the difference and start to engage with sound.

Of course, sound is subjective. There are occasions when everyone does not share the same opinion. But listening together is democratising. It allows empathy and appreciation of others' experiences. It breaks down barriers and allows consensus building. It helps bind teams together to appreciate acoustic design attributes, making it easier to defend (especially) when projects are value engineered. It makes us stronger as collaborators. Until recently, auralisations would be coupled with large scale projections to immerse stakeholders both visually and aurally. Now augmented reality (AR) and virtual reality (VR) are used extensively in architecture and engineering, easily coupled with auralisation. Visualisation has helped encourage its use and fostered engagement with clients and project constituents.

The future?

Speculating on the future is always challenging. The cutting edge of any design field is always shifting. Predictions are easily outdated. In the built environment ideas can only be established when someone tests them. This requires risks to be taken by design teams and clients. There is often an element of conservatism, given that buildings can stand for decades, even centuries. Yet many buildings are bespoke endeavours. Experimentation should really go with the territory, or architecture would never evolve.

The creative potential of sound is extraordinary. It has not been fully embraced as yet, at least not with sufficient commitment. We live in a revolutionary era where sound can bring radical improvements to architecture. We should encourage more design

by ear. It should be embraced the way it really needs to be. There is opportunity for architects and acousticians to explore and enjoy the creation of integrated aural experiences. We should take risks to achieve it. It challenges all of us to learn to listen more effectively – to each other and our surroundings.

Thinking about the opportunities for acoustics and architecture in the future, one could broadly consider the challenges in a series of intertwined areas.

Architecture pedagogy

Having spent time teaching in architecture schools over the last 25 years, I've been struck by the limited integration of multi-disciplinary design thinking in most courses (yes, they are courses on architecture, but great architecture requires so much to come together for the best results). Studying acoustics may make up just one or two hours in an entire degree in architecture. Some schools offer a class for a semester, which is usually an elective. Students have often commented, and it has been my observation, that architects are primarily taught from the 'outside-in', where context is the primary driver for building design. But design for the senses is a human experience. It requires thinking from the inside-out to achieve better results.

Encouragingly, I find more designers early in their careers willing to experiment across disciplines, using both 'inside-out' and 'outside-in' design approaches. They are often self-directed, seeking better ways to do things. Students are keenly aware of, and exploring, the myriad tools available to them. I am often asked about sound design tools they can use. These are currently limited in variety and geared to the trained acoustic professional. Tools to visualise sound will soon be integrated into architecture software. Gaming engines (some increasingly used in the visualisation of architecture) use sophisticated algorithms to approximate acoustic conditions in real-time. I expect these will soon be found in design software too. This offers exciting opportunities to unlock creative potential. It also presents dangers if used incorrectly. Experience is essential in interpreting if the result from a computer is representative of reality. This is precisely where the opportunity for greater collaboration exists, and one we should collectively seize.

Psychoacoustics and cognitive, behavioural and social sciences

Over the last few years sound, hearing, and noise seem to have had a zeitgeist. Several museums have held simultaneous shows on sound.[1] Books on hearing and listening have topped best seller lists around the world.[2] Research in social, cognitive and behavioural science and the physiological impacts of sound in architecture are growing rapidly. Soon the results will impact how we design. Couple this with availability of low cost, accurate acoustic and vibration sensors, and the potential to use the resulting data for design is vast.

Soon wearable devices will be able to measure our physiological and psychological response to sound. Data could be used to encourage us to change our behaviours or our environments to improve our health or performance. This data could also be shared to inform others about building acoustic performance. Spaces for silence, rest and therapy will all be designed with optimum sound in mind and be considered for inclusion in all buildings. The U.S. National Basketball League (NBA) is an early adopter of spaces like this, as many team franchises move to incorporate 'sensory' rooms (permanent accommodations for those with sensory needs) in their arenas – more than half of them will have been added by the close of the 2019 season.[3]

Before too long, architectural environments will be wired to reactively respond to sound. They will listen to us, understand what we are doing, and modify according to our needs. Some may achieve this through means of amplified sound, others through physical changes to the architecture, or a combination of the two; e.g. the Dynamic Responsive Acoustic Tuning Envelope (DRATE)/ Resonant Chamber (collaboration between RVTR, Arup and University of Michigan 2011–2013). The more time we spend in smart spaces, the more knowledgeable about us they will become. This knowledge will allow architecture to adjust its environment(s) for us, providing optimum conditions for the activity we intend to undertake. This will involve changing room acoustics, background noise, sound insulation, etc. as needed.

Sustainable development and resiliency

Acoustics plays an important role in sustainability and our environment. It will be a growing area of concern as we address rapid urbanisation in how we design. Efforts to reduce environmental noise impact have been in place since the 1970s. Economic growth and technological advancements have impacted our ability to deliver the promise of a less noisy, better sounding world. It is easy to assume, for example, that electric vehicles of the future will mean quieter cities, but this may not be the case, at least not at the outset. Electric cars are so quiet that they are having sounds added to alert pedestrians to their presence. The first 'flying taxis' are due for rollout in Dubai[4] in the early 2020s.

As yet, these are not quiet. We will likely displace a noise that we understand and have adapted to, with one unfamiliar and possibly more disruptive. If we are lucky, the pressure will be to solve noise problems before they are introduced, through more stringent standards and expectations for urban noise control.

Challenges such as this will likely impact the retrofit of existing building façades to new sound insulation standards. These will need to become greener, which can bring acoustic benefits.[5] As buildings develop the ability to listen, they will gain the ability to change dynamically. New materials will embed acoustics and vibration reactivity at the nano or meta scale, allowing unsurpassed building responsiveness.

Cities around the world battling climate change are introducing a host of features to help mitigate extreme weather events (e.g. reintroducing urban wetlands, redefining coastlines). In their passive states, many of these can be used for recreation. They can also help shape the soundscape of our cities. Sound will be a key consideration in resilient design.

Experience and digital design

The merging of digital and physical environments with a mandate to build less, and more sustainably, will allow us to deliver flexible, transformable spaces. Virtual immersive experiences for all the senses will be incorporated in all building types. Any architectural environment will have the ability to be recreated virtually. These could be experienced alone or with many other people, whether in the same place or connected virtually. The building of large volumetric spaces will become the exception not the norm.

At urban scale, we have yet to see the deployment of experience design through digital as extensively as might be expected. The future imagined in the 1920s by Fritz Lang and others – multi-tiered cities with traffic below ground and clean streets for pedestrians, surrounded by hi-rise living – may still come to pass. One can imagine, assuming we don't choose to over build, that our roads will become enclosed in lightweight, low energy OLED (Organic Light Emitting Diode) screens presenting a canvas on which digital art, information, signage and sounds will be overlaid. Traffic noise will be a thing of the past. Our journeys through cities will be enabled digitally, with sound, light and art, individually tailored to our desires or preferences.

These speculations are important in challenging the way we think about deploying our skills to achieve better design outcomes. If architects want to focus on elevating the human condition by creating experiences that inspire delight, joy, awe, wonder, and create the right conditions for human creativity, acoustics is one important factor in that process. Embracing that potential will see the partnership between architects and acousticians flourish and open the door to new design approaches and ideas that will challenge us all and most importantly, deliver positive change.

4

I and We in
Acoustics

Acoustics is the 'unsung' hero of architecture. Our most fundamental sense may be our ability to register sound. The ways in which we receive and interpret sound exist on a spectrum. Sound is experienced through more than just our ears; it is also felt through our bodies.

Our associations with certain sounds are learned and internalised, and various spaces we inhabit and construct for ourselves form the framework within which we develop these understandings. I often think of two examples of architectural space which illustrate this, which demonstrate how acoustics can either create a sense of atmosphere, or a sense of position. There are cathedrals and houses of worship, where sound travels through grand, vertical spaces – projected upwards and reflected downwards from vast, vaulted ceilings. Sound resonates, echoes, and decays in these spaces, communicating an atmosphere of grandeur or sublime wonder of the unknown. And there is our shared cultural edifice: the planned outdoor space. Plazas, sidewalks, roadways, and paths of transport. Car horns, conversations in the street, steps on the pavement. These sounds create a sense of movement from all sides and keep us aware of our position in relation to them. They do not linger so much as they follow their sources moving through space. We observe them, record them, and design spaces to showcase their unique properties and uses. These sounds are specific to their places. How we manage them in order to understand our relationship to sound comes down to the question of acoustics.

The best acoustic condition is often the most difficult to design. It is one that makes us feel we are connected to our larger environment while allowing us to be in control of our immediate surroundings. This is a place where we can hear others and understand our relationship to them in space, without

having our sense of personal agency overwhelmed – either physically or acoustically. This is tied to our cognition of sound. It allows us to create different narratives about when and where we are. When we can perceive both the source and consequence of a sound – a cymbal being struck in a concert, a faint voice coming from down the hall – we are able to develop a foundational or natural understanding of the sequence of events.

Architects must understand sound and acoustics as a time-based material: a counter-intuitive medium to a design field that thinks in concrete and steel; materials created to last lifetimes with little to no degradation or decay. Acoustics force architects to think in terms of time rather than in static, formal paradigms, and they ignore these nuances at their own risk. A space can be perfect geometrically; it can have all the important proportions, the best-looking materials and the most dramatic details. Yet if it does not resonate with our fundamental senses, it will fail.

I speak from having designed buildings that clearly demanded highly managed acoustics, and where acoustics were an equally important, but less obvious, project driver. A traditional performance hall, for example, must function as a finely-tuned an instrument in the same way as those being played on stage. Here, as an audience member, you understand that you will be asked first and foremost to listen. The space should reinforce that message and enhance that auditory experience. When Snøhetta worked on the Isabel Bader Centre at Queen's University, Canada, we looked to the traditional 'jewel-box' style of the great Western European classical music halls. Those spaces were historically symmetrical in design per the stylistic tastes of their time. In working with the acousticians at Arup, we were able to optimise the wall shaping and ceiling layout to discover an asymmetrical form

The new French Laundry Kitchen, Yountville, California, USA.

for the Bader Centre that actually improved the acoustics of the space from that of a conventionally ordered concert hall. Music, by nature, is not symmetrical, and the architecture of the Hall is suited to match.

A less obvious example would be a restaurant kitchen, and the acoustics of workplace design at large. A kitchen, whether in the heart of a home or in a Michelin starred restaurant, is an endeavour of spirit – full of energy and movement. Critical to the success of the kitchen's complex choreography is seamless communication between team members; the smooth transmission of sound and speech over the clangs and clamours of cooking. When we worked

with chef Thomas Keller to redesign his kitchen at the French Laundry in California, more than anything we wanted to create a pleasant environment for the team. A major part of this was developing unique ceiling coves, shaped to control acoustics and spread daylight evenly to the food preparation areas.

The last example I will turn to is the library. A general misconception is that these kinds of spaces should be utterly silent, a sacrosanct place for study and intellectual reflection. Yet, if we look to antiquity, to the libraries of the Ancient Near East and of the Greeks, the earliest libraries were active forums for conversation and exchange – not quiet places at all. At the main public library of Calgary in Canada,

we organised the project around a grand, vertical atrium. This meant that acoustics informed the set-up of the building, so the noisier and more bustling areas, like the lobby and children's area, are located at ground level. As you ascend the spiralling atrium, activity becomes more serene until you arrive at the reading room on the highest level. In each of these spaces, the acoustics were framed in a way that did not try to force silence into spaces, but rather encouraged a feeling of being comfortable and respectful in shared space.

Sometimes I say that acoustics are one of the last dark arts, an artform that masquerades as a science. Acousticians perform an alchemical role, turning signal into noise, noise into sound, and sound into order. At times the acoustician is a ventriloquist. At other times they are sound attenuators. Architecture is the envelope that physically surrounds us. It is the container of our memories. Acoustics, much like memory, capture the instant of creation and store its data in an ephemeral wave, perhaps losing its amplitude, but never fading out entirely. Ultimately, we rely on this art–science to improve and support our lives. If sound is an intrinsic force, then acoustics are in some manner the framework of our lives.

Craig Dykers, Founding Partner, Snøhetta, 2020

Calgary Central Library, Calgary, Alberta, Canada.

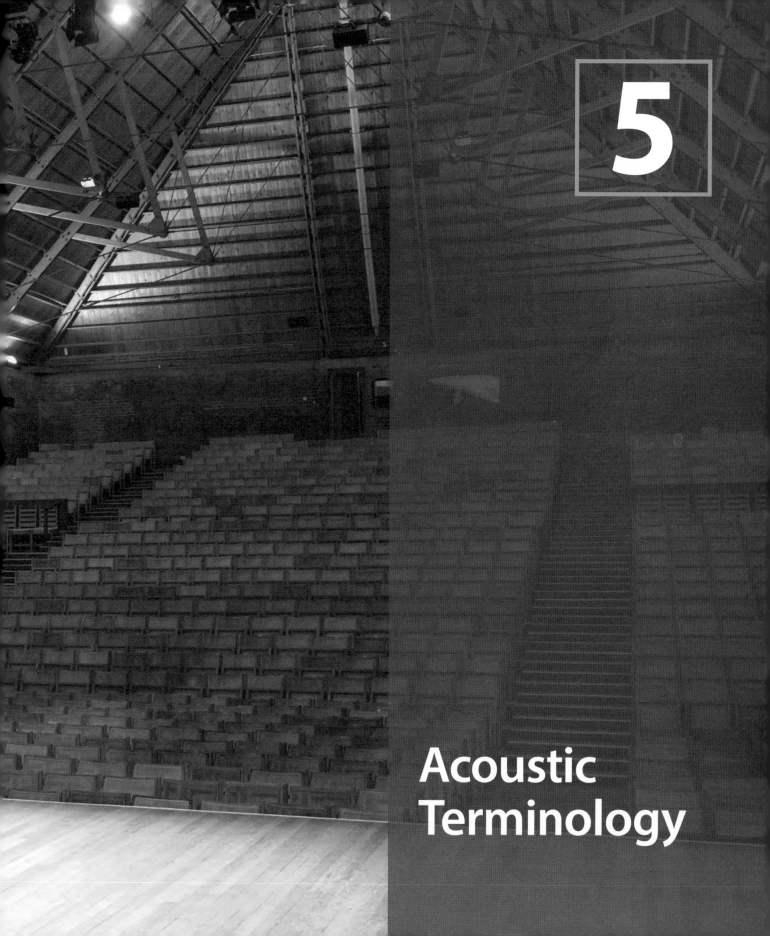

5

Acoustic
Terminology

Definition of acoustic terms

Acoustics
Science of sound

Amplitude
Strength or value of a pressure wave at a given time; usually corresponding to perceived loudness

Compression
Increase in pressure through the crowding together of particles (molecules)

Decibel (dB)
Unit of measure for sound level

dB(A) (A-weighted decibel)
Unit of measure for sound level that follows the frequency-sensitivity of human hearing

Frequency (f)
Number of cycles of vibration per second, commonly expressed in hertz (Hz) and kilohertz (kHz)

Fundamental frequency
Lowest frequency component of a complex sound

Harmonic
Sound component of a multiple of the fundamental frequency

Interference
Interaction between different sound waves

Loudness
Subjective perception of a sound pressure level

Medium
Environment through which sound is transmitted

Noise
Any unwanted sound

Octave
Interval between two sounds with double or half the frequency or wavelength

Peak amplitude
Height or maximum value of a wave crest

Previous page:
Snape Maltings, Arup
Associates, Aldeburgh, UK.

Detailed glossary

The science of sound extends to a range of disciplines.

Architectural acoustics, a small segment of the entire field, comprises two main branches.

The first, the fundamental physics of sound, deals with physical events: sound is propagated from an originating vibration source, through a medium, regardless of human presence.

The second is the human response to sound. The outer ear directs the sound to the auditory canal. The resulting auditory sensation inside the ear is translated to nerve impulses stimulating the acoustic cortex of the brain, which then interprets meaning or induced feelings (further information in the psychoacoustics section). It should be noted that the vibration caused by sound in the medium (e.g. air or through building materials) also creates a physical response.

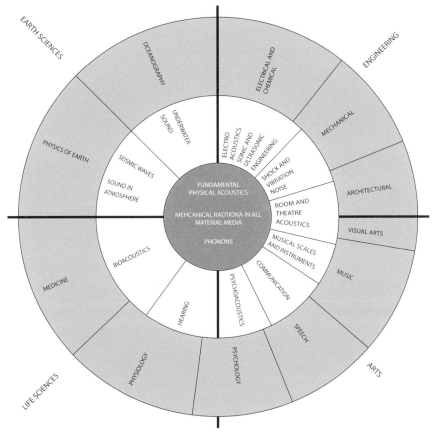

Lindsay's wheel of acoustics.

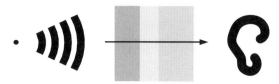

The acoustic environment.

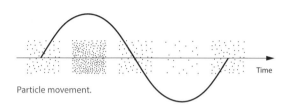

Particle movement.

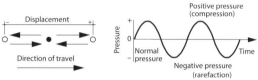

Longitudinal motion of particles.

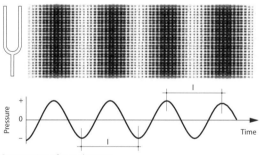

Propagation of sound waves.

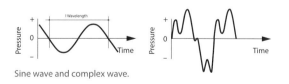

Sine wave and complex wave.

Aperiodic wave noise.

The acoustic environment

This environment consists of the sound source creating the vibration, the medium through which the generated sound waves travel, and the receiver (e.g. listener or microphone). The source may be desirable sound (e.g. music, speech, ocean waves), or undesirable noise (e.g. traffic, machinery). In the built environment, the media are usually air and building materials at a fundamental level, and there are many factors (material properties, shape, form, geometry of rooms) that influence the path from source to receiver.

Medium

The material through which waves travel. Particles in a medium (like air or water molecules) vibrate about their equilibrium positions when subject to a vibrating source, receive momentum from resulting collisions, and transfer it to surrounding particles, propagating the sound wave. Sound cannot travel in a vacuum.

Sound waves

A physical disturbance (vibration) of molecules within a medium. Sound waves move through longitudinal motion by the vibration of particles parallel to the direction of travel.

Propagation of sound waves

Occurs through particle compression and rarefaction, resulting in microscopic changes in local pressure. Although each particle moves very little from its original position, sound waves can travel long distances.

Periodic sound waves

A regularly repeated pattern of oscillation. A sine wave is the simplest form of a periodic wave, representing a pure tone at one frequency. While they do not exist in nature, sine waves can be generated electronically. Most periodic waves are more complex combinations of frequencies and pressures over time.

Aperiodic sound waves (noise)

These have no periodic frequency or oscillation and are often referred to as noise. If the noise is concentrated in a narrow range of frequencies, it is called tonal noise and may be perceived to have a pitch or hummable tone.

Period (t)
Time duration of one cycle of vibration, in seconds (s)

Rarefaction
Decrease in pressure through spreading out of particles

Receiver
Human listener, microphone, etc.

Sound
A physical disturbance, such as a vibration or pulsation of pressure in an elastic medium

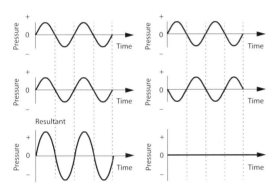

Constructive and destructive interference.

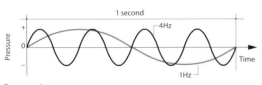

Frequencies.

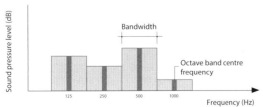

Octave bands and bandwidth.

White noise
Random, aperiodic sound with energy evenly and uniformly distributed *across the frequency spectrum*. Its amplitude is the same at every frequency, similar to white light. It generally sounds like static on a TV or tape hiss.

Pink noise
Pink noise is also random, aperiodic sound, but has an equal amount of energy *in each octave*. It derives its name from the colour spectrum resulting from light with the same energy distribution. The spectrum occurs commonly in nature and is calibrated to how we hear. It sounds more pleasant than white noise, with more perceived low-frequency content, like ocean waves.

Electronically generated pink and white noise are often used in the analysis of room acoustics and loudspeakers.

Interference
The decrease or increase of sound level at particular frequencies through the interaction of sound waves. Two or more waves may support each other through constructive interference or cancel each other through destructive interference.

Speed of sound
Dependent on environmental factors such as temperature and humidity. In air at 21°C the speed of sound is approximately 344 metres/second. This is very slow compared to light and radio waves (299,724,000m/s). The speed of sound varies in different materials, and travels faster in materials that are dense (e.g. in concrete 3400m/s, in steel 5400m/s).

Frequency
The rate of repetition of a sound wave. The subjective equivalent in music is pitch. The unit of frequency is the hertz (Hz), which is identical to cycles per second.

A 1000Hz sound vibrates 1000 times per second and is often denoted as 1kHz. Human hearing ranges from approximately 20Hz (very low bass) to 20kHz (very high treble). Frequencies are commonly divided into groups, such as octave bands. For building acoustic design purposes, the octave bands between 63Hz and 8kHz are standard. For more detailed analysis, each octave band may be split into three one-third octave bands or in some cases, narrower frequency bands.

Frequency is inversely proportional to the period (t), or duration of a cycle. The higher the frequency, the shorter the period of a sound vibration. The relationship is expressed:

$$f = 1 / t \quad t = 1 / f$$

Octave bands
The fundamental musical interval, which corresponds to a doubling or halving of frequency. Building acoustic design conventionally considers octave intervals with centre frequencies of 63Hz, 125Hz, 250Hz, 500Hz, 1kHz, 2kHz, 4kHz and 8kHz.

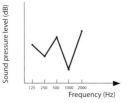

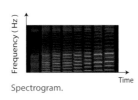

Spectrogram.

Sound spectrum analysis.

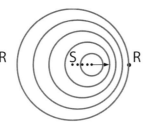

Doppler Effect.

Sound pressure
Acoustic force per unit area, in pascals (Pa),
1Pa = 1 Newton/m²

Sound pressure level (SPL)
Common acoustic measurement, using the
decibel (dB) scale

Spectrum

The range of sound frequencies, often graphically plotted to visually represent sounds and their amplitudes. This allows the detailed analysis of complex sound events.

Doppler effect

Shift in frequency (pitch) due to motion. In general, the frequency reaching a receiver is the same as the frequency at the source. When the source and the receiver are in motion relative to each other, the perceived sound frequency changes over time.

This effect can be observed when an ambulance approaches or drives away with its siren sounding. When approaching, the perceived frequency increases; when receding, the perceived frequency decreases.

Wavelength (λ)

The distance between two successive peaks of a sound wave, or the distance a wave travels during one cycle (see opposite).

A sound's wavelength is inversely proportional to its frequency, with the speed of sound as a constant:

$$f = c / \lambda$$
$$\lambda = c / f$$

Low frequency sounds have longer wavelengths than higher frequency sounds.

Sound pressure

A measure of the acoustic force on a given area. Represents an increase and decrease above and below normal atmospheric pressure. A change in sound pressure results in a perceived change in loudness.

Human perception ranges from 20 micropascals to 20 pascals (Pa), a ratio of 10^6 : 1 (one million:one).

The lighting equivalent of sound pressure is lux, the amount of light that falls on a surface per unit area.

Sound pressure level and the decibel (dB)

To more conveniently represent the large sound pressure level range, a logarithmic measurement scale is used. The resulting parameter is called the sound pressure level (L_p) and the associated measurement unit is the decibel (dB). The range of human hearing extends from the threshold of hearing, designated as 0dB, to over the threshold of pain at 140dB.

dB(A) (A-weighted decibel)

Human hearing is less sensitive to sound at low and high frequencies than it is to those in the middle speech frequency range of 500Hz to 4kHz. To make decibel measurements more meaningfully correlate to human subjective response, a 'weighting' (a strictly defined subtraction or addition) can be applied to measured levels at each frequency. This is commonly used to describe human perception of the loudness of sounds.

Wavelength and frequency.

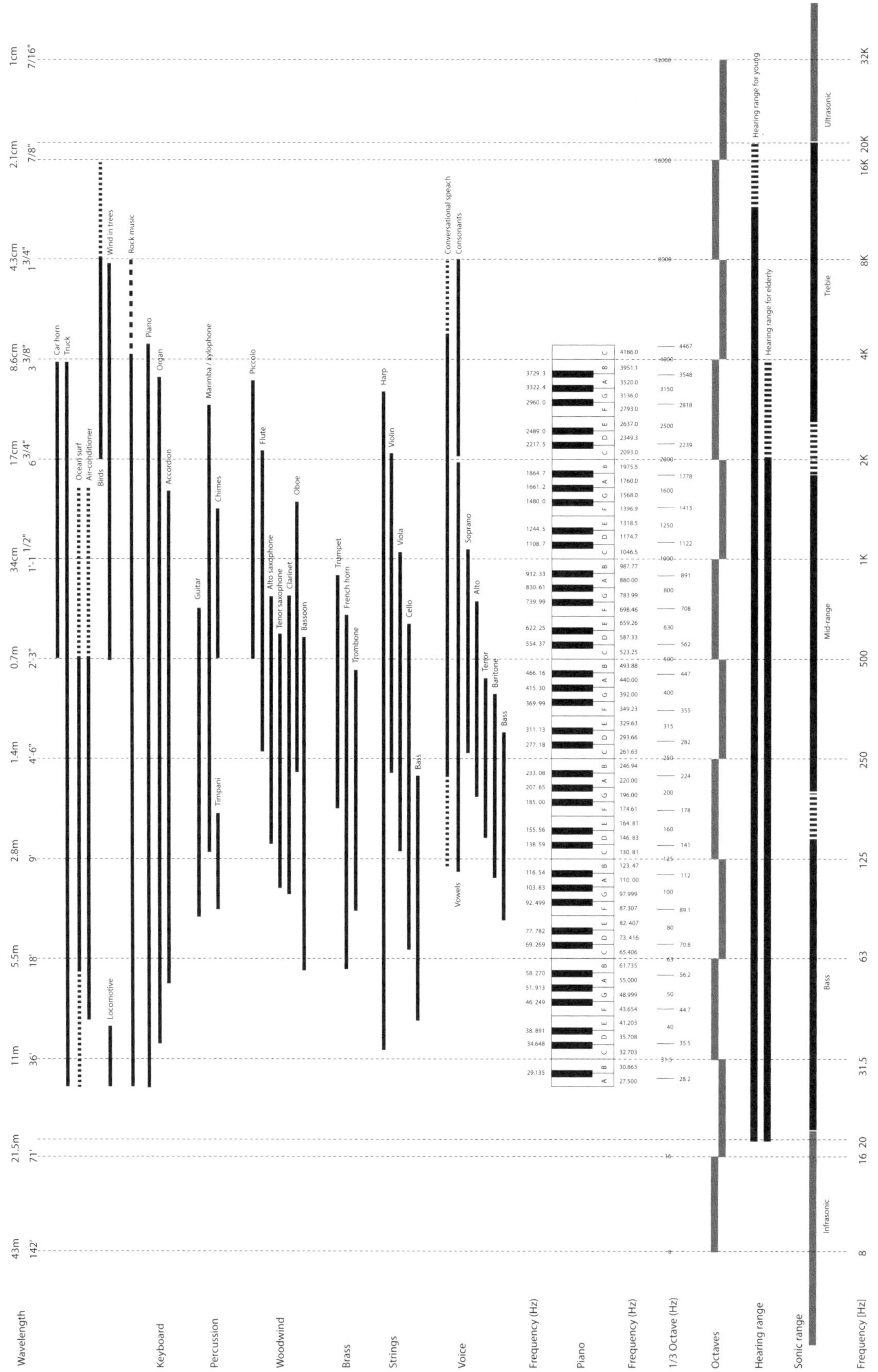

Wavelength values (left axis): 1cm 7/16" · 2.1cm 7/8" · 4.3cm 1 3/4" · 8.6cm 3 3/8" · 17cm 6 3/4" · 34cm 1'-1 1/2" · 0.7m 2'-3" · 1.4m 4'-6" · 2.8m 9' · 5.5m 18' · 11m 36' · 21.5m 71' · 43m 142'

Frequency (Hz) (right axis): 32K · 16K 20K · 8K · 4K · 2K · 1K · 500 · 250 · 125 · 63 · 31.5 · 16 20 · 8

Sound sources / instrument ranges (labels):
Car horn · Truck · Wind in trees · Rock music · Piano · Organ · Accordion · Marimba / xylophone · Chimes · Piccolo · Flute · Alto saxophone · Tenor saxophone · Clarinet · Bassoon · Oboe · Trumpet · French horn · Trombone · Harp · Violin · Viola · Cello · Bass · Soprano · Alto · Tenor · Baritone · Bass · Guitar · Timpani · Ocean surf · Air-conditioner · Birds · Locomotive · Conversational speech · Consonants · Vowels

Piano / Frequency table:

Piano note	Frequency (Hz)	1/3 Octave (Hz)
C	4186.0	4467
B	3951.1	4000
A	3729.3	3548
G	3322.4	3520.0
F	2960.0	3136.0 / 3150
E	2793.0	2818
D	2637.0	2500
C	2489.0	2349.3 / 2239
B	2217.5	2093.0 / 2000
A	1975.5	1864.7 / 1778
G	1760.0	1600
F	1661.2 / 1568.0	1480.0 / 1413
E	1396.9	1250
D	1318.5	1244.5
C	1174.7 / 1108.7	1122
	1046.5	1000
B	987.77	932.33 / 891
A	880.00	800
G	830.61 / 783.99	739.99 / 708
F	698.46	630
E	659.26	622.25
D	587.33 / 554.37	562
C	523.25	500
B	493.88	466.16 / 447
A	440.00	400
G	415.30 / 392.00	369.99 / 355
F	349.23	315
E	329.63	311.13
D	293.66 / 277.18	282
C	261.63	250
B	246.94	233.08 / 224
A	220.00	200
G	207.65 / 196.00	185.00 / 178
F	174.61	160
E	164.81	155.56
D	146.83 / 138.59	141
C	130.81	125
B	123.47	116.54 / 112
A	110.00	100
G	103.83 / 97.999	92.499 / 89.1
F	87.307	80
E	82.407	77.782
D	73.416 / 69.269	70.8
C	65.406	63
B	61.735	58.270 / 56.2
A	55.000	50
G	51.913 / 46.249	43.654 / 44.7
F	41.203	40
E	38.891	35.708 / 35.5
D	34.648	32.703
C	30.863	31.5
B	29.135	27.500 / 28.2

Octaves / Hearing range / Sonic range:
Octaves · Hearing range (Hearing range for young · Hearing range for elderly) · Sonic range (Ultrasonic · Treble · Mid-range · Bass · Infrasonic)

Row categories (bottom labels):
Wavelength · Keyboard · Percussion · Woodwind · Brass · Strings · Voice · Frequency (Hz) · Piano · Frequency (Hz) · 1/3 Octave (Hz) · Octaves · Hearing range · Sonic range · Frequency (Hz)

Sound wave
Propagation of sound through compression and rarefaction in an elastic medium

Source
Point of origin of sound/vibration

Spectrum
Data including frequency and level of complex sounds

Speed of sound (C)
344m/s in air, at 21°C

Spherical divergence
Spherically spreading sound from a point source in free space

Tone
Pure sound, sine wave

Wavelength (λ)
Distance between two peaks of a sound wave, or distance a wave travels during one cycle

Typical levels

Some typical dB(A) noise levels are given below:

Noise level, dB(A)	Example
140	Threshold of pain
120	Jet aircraft take-off at 100m
110	Chainsaw at 1m
100	Inside disco
90	Heavy lorries at 5m
80	Kerbside of busy street
70	Loud radio (in typical domestic room)
60	Office or restaurant
50	Domestic fan heater at 1m
40	Living room
30	Theatre
20	Remote countryside on still night
10	Sound insulated test chamber

Changes in sound pressure level

Because of their logarithmic nature, decibel values cannot be simply added. To predict changes in sound pressure level when additional sound sources are added, the following rules of thumb can be used:

If the difference between two sound levels is:

- 0–1dB   add 3dB to the higher value (e.g. 50dB + 51dB = 54dB)

- 2–3dB   add 2dB to the higher value (e.g. 50dB + 53dB = 55dB)

- 4–8dB   add 1dB to the higher value (e.g. 50dB + 58dB = 59dB)

- > 8dB   same as the higher value (e.g. 50dB + 65dB = 65dB)

Human sensitivity to changes in sound level

If the difference between two sound levels is:

1dB   change in loudness is usually imperceptible

3dB   difference in loudness is perceptible

6dB   clearly noticeable difference in loudness (e.g. distance outdoors is halved/doubled)

+10dB   the sound appears about twice as loud (-10dB = half as loud)

+20dB   the sound appears about four times as loud (-20dB = quarter as loud)

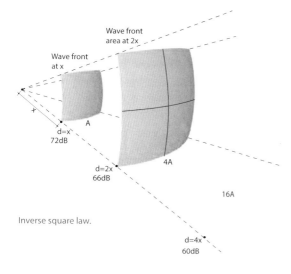

Wave front area at 2x

Wave front at x

d=x
72dB

A

d=2x
66dB

4A

16A

d=4x
60dB

Inverse square law.

Inverse square law

For each doubling of distance from a point source with a spherical sound distribution pattern there is a 6dB loss in sound pressure level.

It is used to estimate the change in sound pressure level outdoors, where there are no sound reflecting surfaces – known as the 'free-field' condition.

The inverse square law does not apply in situations where the source is on or close to a hard ground surface, or to typical rooms with sound-reflecting surfaces since room boundaries reflect sound and affect how much sound decreases with distance from a source.

When sources are close to each other in a line – called a line source – the sound radiates cylindrically rather than spherically. Each doubling of the distance reduces the sound pressure level by only 3dB. Examples of line sources are trains or road traffic when the cars are very close together.

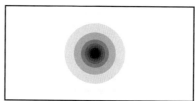
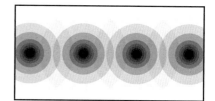
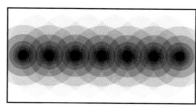
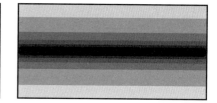

Point sources and line sources.

Sound Power Level (Lw)

A measure of the total acoustic power radiated by a source. The sound power level is an intrinsic characteristic of a source (analogous to its volume or mass) which, contrary to sound pressure level, is not affected by the environment within which the source is located.

The lighting equivalent of sound power level is lumens, the amount of light emitted by the source of light.

Definition of acoustic terms

Auditory canal
Ear canal or meatus; part of outer ear

Basilar membrane
Splits the cochlea along its length; seat of the hair cells

Binaural
Hearing with two ears

Cochlea
Spiral organ of the inner ear; transforms pressure changes into neural impulses

Eardrum
Tympanum; airtight seal between outer and middle ear

Interaural difference
Time or level difference experienced between the two ears

Localisation (spatial)
Determination of the location of a sound source

Loudness (phons, sones)
The perception of sound pressure level

Ossicles
Hammer, anvil, stirrup; small bones in middle ear

Perception
Subjective human experience of the physical aspects of sound

Pinna
External portion of the ear; helps to capture and localize sound

Pitch
The perceived frequency

Precedence effect
Helps one determine the location of a sound source via the relative arrival times of direct and reflected sound; also known as the Haas effect

Psychoacoustics
Interaction between physics and the auditory system

Threshold of hearing
Lowest perceptible loudness level: 20mPA, at 1kHz

Threshold of pain (feeling)
Upper limit of hearing before permanent damage to ears

Timbre
Tonal quality, harmonic composition of a sound, influenced by the design of a space and materials in it

2 – PSYCHOACOUSTICS

Human hearing
Involves the physiology of the auditory system, and the processing of sound information in the brain. The resulting perception of sound is not easily measurable and does not always relate to physical events in a linear fashion.

Perception
Psychoacoustics is concerned with the perception of sound. It is not an isolated discipline, but closely interconnected with psychology, physiology, biology, medicine, physics, music, engineering, architecture and other fields. The relative and subjective nature of perception and the complexity of the involved processes are the subjects of much ongoing research.

Human hearing and perception are complex, highly evolved systems. They can detect a wide range of stimuli and identify them by pitch, timbre, loudness and location.

Pressure range
At the threshold of hearing, the lowest perceptible sound pressure level, movements of the eardrum can be as small as one tenth the size of a hydrogen atom. But the ear can also respond to sound pressures a million times greater, with an energy content of a trillion (10^{12}) times more.

Selectivity
The auditory system can select and recognise different sounds by their frequency and timbre, or pick them out of an array of other sounds.

The auditory mechanism
The ear is divided into three parts: the outer ear, the middle ear and the inner ear. Each fulfils a distinctive function, from gathering sound to forwarding information to the central nervous system.

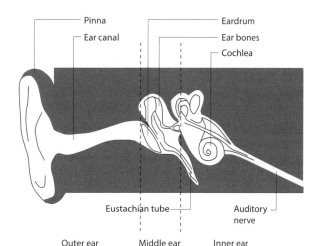

Human auditory system.

Outer ear.

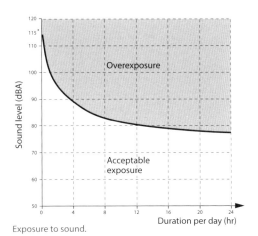

Exposure to sound.

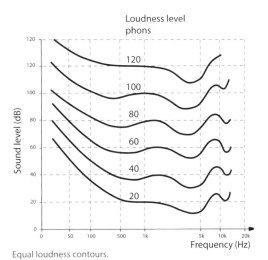

Loudness level phons

Equal loudness contours.

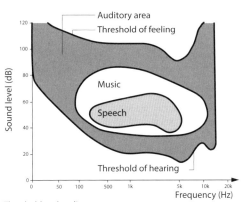

Threshold and auditory area for human hearing.

Health and occupational noise

Upper frequency hearing naturally diminishes with age. Exposure to noise can cause stress and irreversible or permanent hearing loss at any age. In the workplace this is usually subject to regulations limiting loudness and overall duration of exposure per day. Employers are required to provide hearing protection, and noise exposure training to workers. Hearing protection must be offered to workers who are exposed to sound levels over 80dB(A) for 8 hours. When the level exceeds 85dB(A) for an 8-hour day, hearing protection is mandatory. For louder sounds much shorter durations of exposure are permitted and hearing protection is mandatory.

Perception versus physics

While measurements of the physical aspects of sound are repeatable and allow an accurate prediction of its variables, human perceptual responses are less predictable.

Pitch

The subjective perception of frequency, the characteristic of a sound that makes it sound higher or lower, or that determines its relative position on a musical scale.

For pure tones, pitch is determined mainly by frequency, but also by sound level. The pitch of complex sounds also depends on the timbre of the sound and its duration.

Absolute pitch (or perfect pitch) is the ability to recognise the pitch of a tone without the use of a reference tone. Less than 0.01% of the population have this ability. Most people have a degree of relative pitch recognition, the ability to tell whether one tone is higher or lower than another.

Loudness

The relationship between sound pressure levels and loudness perception is not linear. Equal loudness contours show the average perception of loudness of a wide array of test subjects.

For example, using the lower 20 phon curve, for a sound level of 20dB at 1kHz to be perceived the same loudness at 100Hz it must be approx. 40dB. At 4kHz it is closer to 10dB. This also shows how the ear is less sensitive at low frequency, and particularly sensitive in the frequency range of most information content in speech: approximately 500 Hz to 4kHz.

Human hearing occurs between two threshold curves: The *threshold of hearing* is the minimum audible limit; the *threshold of feeling* indicates the beginning of the sensation of pain.

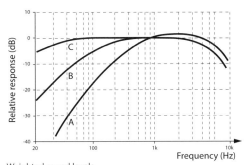
Weighted sound levels.

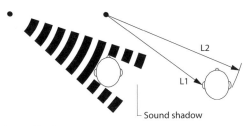
Binaural hearing.

Decibel weighting

When measuring sound levels for specific applications, weighted curves (A to E) are commonly used. A-weighted sound levels dB(A) are adjusted to more meaningfully correlate to human subjective response (note in the image below the A-weighted curve looks like the equal loudness contour inverted). B and C weightings were commonly used in the analogue sound recording and reproduction industry.

Timbre

A term describing the subjective tonal quality (or colour) of a sound; similar to spectrum in physics. It is a multi-dimensional attribute of sound, often applied to the sound of musical instruments, or the perception of sound within an architectural space.

Timbre has been defined as the attribute of auditory sensation whereby a listener can judge that two sounds are dissimilar using any criteria other than pitch, loudness or duration. For example, it is the difference you hear between a trumpet and a clarinet when they both play the same note, and how sound reflections in a room made predominantly from glass, is different to one made of wood, when you listen to the same note.

Spatial localisation

Besides the frequency filtering effect of the outer ear, binaural hearing is the main factor in localising sound sources.

Intensity level differences allow localisation at higher frequencies. At frequencies below 1.5 kHz, localisation is achieved mainly due to the different arrival times (interaural time difference) of sound to the ears.

The precedence effect

By emphasising direct sound and suppressing reflections, the precedence effect of the auditory system helps with the localisation of sounds, even in the presence of strong sound reflections or reverberation.

The ear uses the first arriving sound to locate the source. Early sound reflections contribute positively to speech intelligibility, even if some of these early reflections are louder than the direct sound.

Sound reflections arriving at a listener within 20–40 milliseconds of the direct sound, providing they are no louder than +10dB over the direct sound, will help reinforce the localisation of the original source. Sounds that are louder, or loud and later than 40 milliseconds, will likely reduce the ability to localise and may also be detrimental to perception of the direct sound, and/or perceived as echoes or other artefacts.

3 – ENVIRONMENTAL ACOUSTICS

Environmental acoustics is mainly concerned with noise, or undesirable sounds. Noise levels generally increase with greater population density.

Noise and vibration surveys

To help inform acoustic design decisions in the design process, surveys are usually performed to understand the ambient noise and vibration environment at a site. These allow proper consideration of how existing or future conditions might impact design, or how design must be developed to mitigate impact to the environs. It is important to visually and aurally assess a site, as well as look at all relevant existing building and transport data, to understand potential issues in advance. Not all sources of noise and vibration will be visible, so it is important to look at all relevant data and also to listen.

Codes and standards usually dictate the type and quality of equipment to be used for a valid survey to be undertaken. Surveys should take place over representative time periods (e.g. 24-hour periods on weekdays or weekends) to quantify conditions appropriately and document the types of sources, their frequency and duration.

Data is commonly collected and recorded for more detailed analysis as needed (e.g. for frequency-specific data). This is especially important as some sources of disturbance may be very infrequent yet still significant and may not be identified through visual or aural inspection, but clearly identifiable in measured data.

Natural sounds

Naturally occurring sounds are rarely considered bothersome and are widely accepted as part of the environment. Research indicates that certain natural sounds – waves on a beach, wind in trees, a babbling brook – are relaxing and offer health benefits. This is considered a result of the frequency content of these noise sources, which overlaps with where the ear is most sensitive (speech frequencies), so they perform a function of 'masking' speech sounds, enabling the brain to switch into relaxation mode.

Man-made sounds/noise

Perception of sound is subjective. What one person may consider a pleasant sound, another may interpret as noise. Noise is the number one complaint in many cities and can come from many sources – neighbours, traffic, construction activity, building systems, etc. Noise pollution is often regulated by governmental and private organisations via codes and standards.

Traffic

Street noise from cars, trucks, buses and motorcycles is the most common source of environmental noise. Engine and exhaust noise are prevalent at lower speeds, tyre and wind noise at higher speeds.

Subways and surface trains create vibrations that transmit through earth and structures and re-radiate in buildings as noise. Surface rail systems also create noise propagation.

Near waterways, boats can generate low-frequency engine noise, both airborne and underwater. Wave movements can cause structural vibration and structure-borne noise; whistles and horns must also be considered.

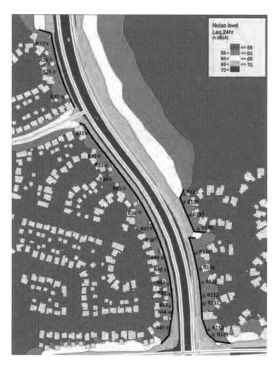

Propagation of rail noise and vibration.

Rail noise contour map.

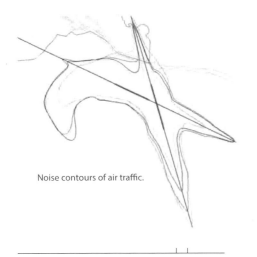

Noise contours of air traffic.

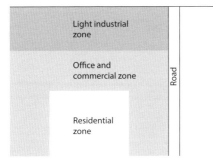

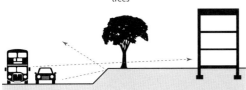

Land use and zoning.

Aircraft traffic around airports is a large-scale, long-term issue. Although updated aeroplane designs have led to significant noise reductions, increased air traffic accounts for ongoing community disturbance.

Sound propagation

Sound is attenuated with increasing distance from a source. Factors like topography and atmospheric and wind conditions greatly influence propagation.

Zoning laws

Zoning laws and maps often provide for the separation of quiet and noisy areas. Where inconsistent uses occur (e.g. a factory in a residential area, a residential area near a motorway) special precautions must be taken.

Noise mitigation measures

Noise can be reduced at the source or along the path to the receiver through barriers, terrain shapes and specialist acoustic products. In the planning stages, location and relative proximity to potential sound sources is a key factor in determining expected noise levels and whether mitigation measures might be necessary.

Terrain shapes

Natural or man-made topographic shapes or barriers can be very effective in shielding people from unwanted sound.

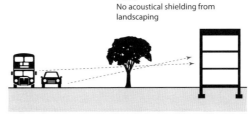

Topography poor.

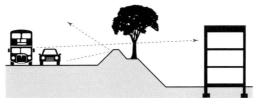

Topography better.

Topography best.

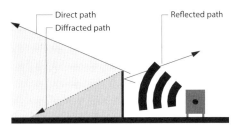

Barriers.

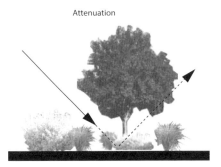

Attenuation

Minimal shielding

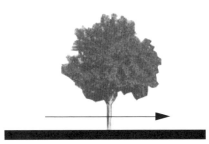

Effect of planting.

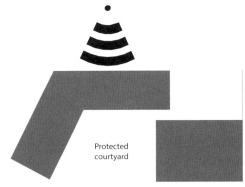

Building orientation and shapes.

Outdoor barriers

Freestanding structures and buildings can deflect, absorb or reflect sound, especially higher frequencies. Diffraction around barriers occurs for lower frequencies, making them less effective at greater distances.

Vegetation

Surface vegetation can help attenuate propagated sound. However, the shielding effect of trees and shrubs is often overestimated. A thin visual barrier of greenery has a negligible effect as a sound barrier.

Green facades and roofs are being increasingly deployed in sustainable design. They can offer some acoustic benefit in sound reduction but are less effective in close proximity to a noise source. For example, green walls in dense urban environments have limited acoustic benefit during the day but have been shown to be more effective at night. There is some psychoacoustic benefit that can be derived from increased natural sounds or birds, insects and other wildlife both inside and outside buildings due to these interventions.

Building placement

The orientation and overall shape of buildings can block or propagate undesired noise and affect sound levels.

Building features

Barriers, balconies, overhangs, atriums, recesses and surface treatments in building designs can be used to improve acoustical protection from outdoor noise. Shadow zones out of the acoustical line of sight from nearby sources can reduce sound levels at windows and other building openings. Diffraction around barriers and unwanted reflections from hard surfaces need to be considered.

The correct detailing and construction of building elements like windows, doors and mechanical systems are further steps in blocking unwanted noise.

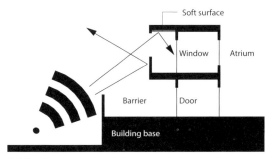

Building features.

Definition of acoustic terms

Absorbing (absorption, absorptive)
Ability of a material to reduce sound reflections incident on it

Absorption coefficient (α)
Percentage of sound energy absorbed by a surface, commonly expressed as a number from 0 to 1

Anechoic
Without significant sound reflections

Anechoic chamber
Room without significant sound reflections; for acoustical testing and measurements

Axial mode
Most dominant room mode, between two parallel walls

Coloration
Audible acoustic distortion of a sound

Decay
Decrease of sound energy over time

Diaphragm
Resonant, vibrating panel

Diffraction
The bending of sound waves around an obstacle

Direct sound
Non-reflected sound, directly from the source

Diffusing (diffusive, diffuser)
Scattering or random redistribution of sound due to surface modulation of material

Echo
Delayed reflection perceived as a distinct repetition of the original direct sound

Flutter echo
Repetitive echoes in quick succession, usually between parallel hard surfaces

Helmholtz resonator
Volume resonator; sound absorber designed to absorb specific (usually low) frequencies

Initial time delay gap
Time delay between the direct sound and the first reflection from a surface, usually in milliseconds (ms)

4 – ROOM ACOUSTICS

Room acoustics is the determination of the planning, evaluation and design of sound within a space. Like great architecture, great acoustics requires an understanding of the science and the art of the discipline, and is enhanced by experience, knowledge, skill and intuition. It also benefits from using the best processes and tools available to analyse, test and think about design throughout the process.

It is also essential to ask one fundamental question at the start of a design process – what do you want the space to sound like, and why? This will be key to achieving the right outcome.

Room properties

Getting the desired acoustic result is incumbent on the right room shape, form, geometry and material selection. If this is not achieved at the outset, then correcting acoustic issues can be difficult or impossible later.

Size/volume
The volume of a room influences its acoustic properties. Most people instinctively understand that the sound of large spaces is different from small spaces.

As sound propagates in rooms, it is weakened and reduced in level when it encounters a room boundary, surface or object where the sound-absorbing, diffusing or reflecting properties of the material primarily dictate the amount of sound level reduction. The more surfaces encountered per second, the quicker the sound reduces in level.

Large rooms have long sound propagation paths from source to room boundaries. Sound reflections have the opportunity to spread out more evenly in the space, they encounter less surface per second than in smaller rooms, and the time taken to weaken to the point of inaudibility is longer. Depending on dimensions, some sounds can be perceived as echoes. The most common experience of this is usually in churches, cathedrals and large historic buildings.

In small rooms, sound reflections encounter a room boundary more times per second, weakening every time they do, resulting in much faster decay and lower reverberance. However, they can have audible resonances (known as modes or standing waves) related to their proportions. A resonance is perceived as an amplification of certain frequencies. A common example is the vocal-range resonance you hear in the shower.

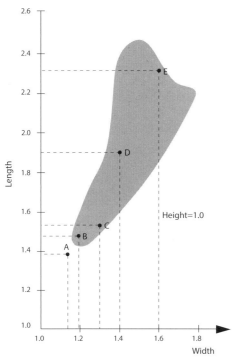

Bolt's range of
favourable proportions.

Proportions

Room proportions impact perceived acoustics. A room with a small plan area that is very tall sounds very different to a space with a large plan area that has a low ceiling.

In small rooms where length, width and height are similar, pronounced resonances are common, and can vary significantly at different positions, and with frequency. This can be acoustically problematic, particularly in rooms for music production or rehearsal, video conference, speech, etc. Desirable room proportions resulting in a favourable even distribution of room modes have been identified by investigation and empirical derivation.

	LENGTH	WIDTH	HEIGHT	SOURCE
A	1.00	1.14	1.39	Sepmeyer
B	1.00	1.28	1.54	Sepmeyer
C	1.00	1.40	1.90	Louden
D	1.00	1.60	2.33	Sepmeyer

Desirable Room Proportions.

Geometry

Room shape determines the sound reflection patterns and modal response. Shaping spaces in 3D is fundamental to creating the right sound reflection patterns in a room and key to achieving optimised acoustics.

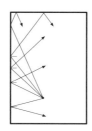

Reflection of patterns in
different room shapes.

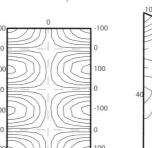

Modal distribution in
different room shapes.

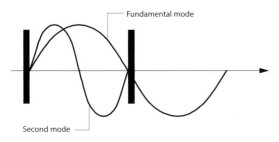

Standing wave.

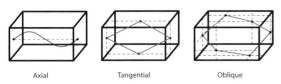

Axial   Tangential   Oblique

Possible room modes.

Reflection of patterns in different room shapes.

EQUAL
EQUAL

Angle of incidence = angle of reflection.

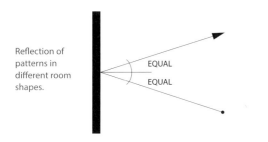

REFLECTION

DIFFUSION

DISPERSION

FOCUSSING

Reflections from different surface shapes.

Room modes

Also called standing waves or room resonances, room modes are due to parallel room boundaries reflecting sound waves back and forth. Modes can be problematic when there is an audible (and unexpected) increase or decrease in the volume level of specific frequencies. Audible room modes occur when the distance between a room's boundary surfaces are closely related to the wavelengths of sound.

The first (fundamental) axial mode between two surfaces occurs when one half of the wavelength corresponds to the room dimension. Harmonic modes occur at multiples of the fundamental frequency.

Additional, weaker standing waves exist: tangential modes between four surfaces, and oblique modes involving six or more surfaces in all three dimensions.

Generally, single dominant room modes are undesirable. They can be minimised by choosing good room proportions and by adding low frequency absorption. Angling walls and ceilings can improve the distribution of standing waves but does not eliminate them.

Room boundaries – materials and shaping

Room boundaries usually have one or a combination of the following properties: they can be sound reflecting, sound-diffusing or sound-absorbing, which can be achieved through a combination of material selection and surface shaping.

Sound reflecting

Flat surfaces with dimensions sufficiently larger than the wavelength of a sound result in *specular* sound reflections, where the angle of reflection equals the angle of incidence.

Convex shaping and articulated surfaces are sound dispersing or diffusing.

Concave shaping directs sound to a concentrated location in a space, sometimes creating an increase in the loudness of reflected sound or change in perception of where sound is coming from. This can be detrimental or unwanted if not well designed.

In classical architecture, this is often used for positive purposes. It can enhance specific sounds in a space, often focused above or behind the listener area to enhance spatial impression, or to create a specific effect – for example, in creating 'whispering galleries'. If not carefully designed, especially when the focusing is toward the listener area, it can mean uneven sound (areas of higher or lower loudness), audible echoes, or other undesirable results.

Echoes

Strong sound reflections between surfaces in rooms can be undesirable. A common manifestation of this can be in large conference or lecture spaces, where the sound from a stage is reflected from the back wall directly back to the stage, often referred to as a 'slap back' echo, and can be uncomfortable or disarming for the presenter or listener. A pattern of echoes in rapid succession, known as flutter echoes can occur in rooms with parallel hard surfaces and are also usually undesirable.

Sound diffusing
surface – monastery
chapel, Melk, Austria.

Diffraction.

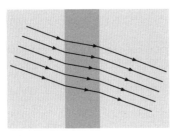

Refraction.

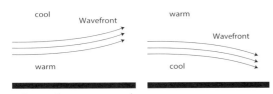

Refraction due to
temperature.

Sound diffusing

To avoid strong sound reflections from a room boundary or to create more even sound distribution in a space, it is often desirable to randomly redistribute sound energy to create a 'diffuse' sound field. To achieve this, surface irregularities are required at approximately the scale of the wavelength of the sound you want to diffuse.

To make surfaces sound diffusing across the audible frequency range of listening, a wide range of wavelengths must be scattered, which requires varying degrees of articulation, of a dimension that is one quarter of the wavelength of the frequency you want to diffuse. In historic buildings this is achieved through the visible primary and secondary layers of architecture (walls, columns, coves) that scatter low to mid frequencies, and decorative details that scatter mid and high frequencies (surface decoration, material roughness and texture). In modern monolithic design, this is generally not achieved inherently and must be planned into design or added to the material.

Most surfaces have some, even if minor, irregularities and as a result reflect sound (specular reflections) and diffuse sound, but it can be very frequency dependent, especially when the irregularities are very small.

Diffuse sound fields

A perfectly diffuse sound field across the audible frequency range exists when sound pressure levels are the same at every point in a room; the direct sound is not particularly prominent over the reverberant sound, reflected sound cannot be easily localised, and modal resonances do not exist. This is rarely achievable in practice. But achieving reasonable diffusion in certain frequency ranges, depending on the use of the room, can be important so this must be determined for any particular design situation.

Diffraction

This occurs when sound waves encountering an obstacle bend around it. The extent to which it is achieved depends on the size of the obstacle or opening in relation to the wavelength of the sound – if the sound is of similar dimension or larger than the obstacle, diffraction is more likely to occur. Longer wavelengths diffract more easily: so lower frequencies can be heard even when the source is hidden by an obstacle (for example, when a helicopter passes behind a building you can hear the low frequencies but less so the mid to high frequencies).

When waves pass through an opening in a surface, they may spread out spherically beyond it.

Refraction

This occurs when the speed of propagation changes and results in a change in the direction of travel of waves. Refraction can happen either abruptly at a change of medium (e.g. air to solid), or gradually, when sound waves travel through air of different temperatures. A similar effect can be experienced in winds of varying speeds.

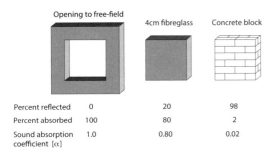

	Opening to free-field	4cm fibreglass	Concrete block
Percent reflected	0	20	98
Percent absorbed	100	80	2
Sound absorption coefficient [α]	1.0	0.80	0.02

Sound absorption coefficient.

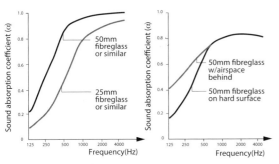

Porous absorbers' performance variance with thickness and airspace.

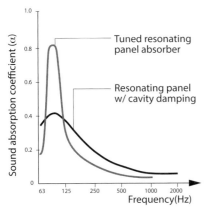

Panel absorber.

Sound absorption

When sound waves encounter a material, a portion of the sound is reflected, and a portion is absorbed. Sound absorption involves both the transformation of sound into heat energy via frictional interaction of moving particles with a material, and the passing of energy through the material. The level of sound absorption in a space has great effect on reverberation time, speech intelligibility, music quality, sound build-up and loudness. Sound absorption is highly frequency dependent.

Sound absorption coefficient (α)

This is an indicator of a material's absorption capacity. It describes the efficiency of absorption of the incident sound energy at a given frequency.

One square foot of perfect (100%) sound absorption equals 1 sabin; one square metre of perfect (100%) sound absorption equals 1 metric sabin.

Materials with a high coefficient (over 0.5) are considered sound-absorbing, materials with a low coefficient (below 0.2) are sound reflecting.

Porous absorbers

Porous materials such as mineral wool, glass fibre, felt, cellulose, wood wool and open cell foams are commonly used as sound absorbers. Performance varies with thickness and density of materials, as well as mounting condition (with or without airspace). Manufacturers' data needs careful checking for conditions of the laboratory test to ensure performance is applicable to the situation in which the designer intends to use it.

Charts or graphs with the sound absorption coefficients for various materials across the spectrum are available. Manufacturers of acoustical specialist products often provide sound absorption values derived from standardised laboratory tests.

Panel absorbers

Mounting a lightweight panel or diaphragm over an airspace allows the creation of a tuned absorber which is usually most effective at low frequency and requires careful design to ensure the required performance is achieved.

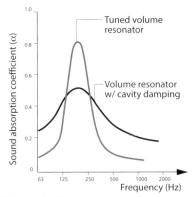

Volume absorber.

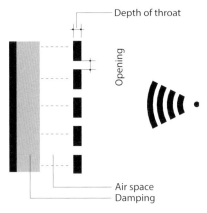

Volume absorber detail.

Volume resonators

Similar to the effect of blowing over the top of a bottle which creates a tuned note, these absorbers, also referred to as Helmholtz resonators, can be constructed with slotted or perforated surfaces over a specifically sized volume, with a defined throat length. Again, careful design is needed to ensure they can be effective.

Total room absorption

The sum of the area of all room surfaces multiplied by their respective absorption coefficients:

a = total room absorption (sabins)
S = surface area (sq. ft. or m^2)
a = sound absorption coefficient at a given frequency
$a = \Sigma\,(S \cdot a)$

Absorption by air

In large spaces, sound absorption by air becomes a significant factor for higher frequencies, resulting in a reduction of sound energy above 1kHz.

Absorption by people

In occupied spaces, sound absorption by people is a factor. Sonic differences between empty and full spaces can be significant.

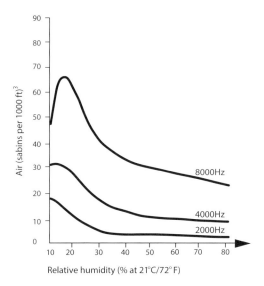

Absorption by air.

Definition of acoustic terms

Absorbers
Soft or other porous materials that absorb rather than reflect incident sound

Noise rating (NR) curve
Single number value to describe the background noise level in a space

Ray tracing
Geometric tracing of high-frequency ray patterns

Reflection
Change in the direction of a sound wave at a surface

Refraction
Change in the direction of wave travel at a change of medium

Resonance
Vibration occurring at the natural frequency of a system

Reverberation
Decay of sound within an enclosure, depending on reflections from the room boundaries

Reverberation time (RT)
Time it takes for a sound to decay by 60 dB

Room acoustics
Sound within an enclosure

Room modes
Resonances of discreet low frequencies in a space, determined by room dimensions

Standing waves
Synonymous with room modes

Speech transmission index (STI)
Numeric descriptor of the speech intelligibility in a room

Room acoustic design

The broad acoustical design goals for any space where sound is important may include reducing or eliminating echoes, controlling reverberance, promoting good speech intelligibility, limiting the transmission of sound from one space to another, and controlling the background noise from ventilation systems and other building services.

Acoustic treatment

This refers to specialist finishing materials that have sound-absorbing, sound diffusing or sound reflecting properties.

Noise criteria

Quantitative criteria are used to describe the level of desired or acceptable background noise in a room, either to evaluate an existing situation, or to specify a design value.

Noise rating (NR) curves

A set of internationally agreed octave band sound pressure level curves based on the concept of equal loudness. NR curves compensate for the lower sensitivity of the ear at lower frequencies. The curves are mathematically derived and defined in BS 8233 and commonly used to define building services noise limits. The NR value of a noise is obtained by plotting the octave band spectrum on the set of standard curves. The highest value curve which is reached by the spectrum is the NR value.

Reverberation

The build-up and decay of sound is one of the most important aspects of room acoustics. Reverberation times that are too long make understanding speech difficult or impossible, and music muddled. If reverberation is too short, rooms can sound 'dead', and sound propagation is limited.

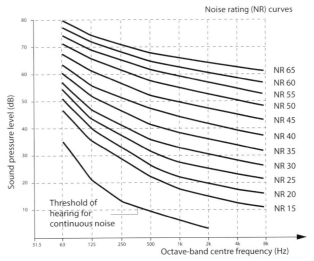

Noise rating curves.

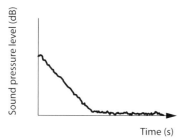

Reverberation time – smooth.

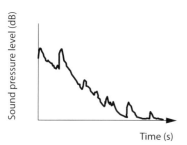

Reverberation with
pronounced reflections.

Reverberation time (RT)

Reverberation time is the duration it takes for the sound in a room to decay by
60dB, i.e. for a loud sound to become effectively inaudible. Reverberation is a useful
indicator of the subjective acoustics within a space.

It can be calculated empirically if one knows the room volume (V), surface area (S),
and the absorption coefficients (α) at each frequency band. But the formula is only
accurate for general acoustic calculations in relatively diffuse conditions, and with
regular room proportions (rectilinear), at about 500Hz, and therefore should only be
used as a high-level guide.

*However, it does not provide any information on where sound is coming from
(see importance of **Geometry** and **Proportion**). RT is a useful high-level indicator
of reverberation in the early stages of design. In detailed design and for complex
architectural spaces, better methods should be used to understand acoustics more
holistically (see **Computer Models** and **Auralisation**).*

Reverberation is directly related to room volume; a greater room volume results in
proportionally more reverberation. Reverberation time is frequency-dependent and
should be checked for each octave band.

Different room uses require different reverberation times in order to achieve their
intended functionality.

Reverberation time can also serve as a guide for the required room volume at the
early stages of a project.

Reverberation time
indicative design guide.

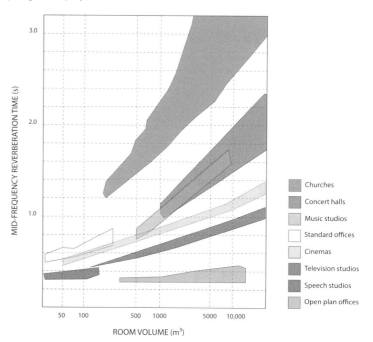

RT and volume guide.

<0.40	0.40 - 0.50	0.50 - 0.60	0.60 - 0.75	0.75 - 1.00
Poor	Fair	Good	Very Good	Excellent

Speech transmission
index (STI).

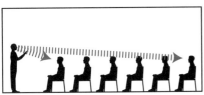

(a) Adequate loudness is essential, direct sound must have
a clear unobstructed path.

(b) Loudness of direct sound towards rear is increaased
with raked seating.

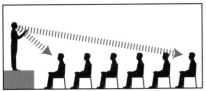

(c) Loudness of direct sound can be increased by putting
the speaker on a platform.

(d) Reflected sound enhances direct sound if time delay is
less than 50 miliseconds.

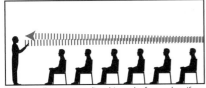

(e) Rear wall can cause a disturbing echo for speakers if over
8.5m away. Rear wall should be absorbing or diffusing.

Room acoustics
for speech.

Reverberation Time and Volume

For rooms with an audience of 150 people or greater, a general rule of thumb for early guidance is that $1m^3$ per seat provides 0.2s of reverberation time.

Based on the uses in the graphs, the room volume can be determined by multiplying the seat count by the volume per seat below for the given RT (e.g. a 2 sec RT in a 1000 seat room requires 1000 seats x $10m^3$ volume = $10,000m^3$).

$1m^3 = 0.2s$
$2m^3 = 0.4s$
$4m^3 = 0.8s$
$8m^3 = 1.6s$
$10m^3 = 2.0s$

Early decay time (EDT)

Similar to reverberation time but considering sound decay only during the first 10dB of decay (and the time then multiplied by six). The EDT is considered to correlate better than RT with the subjective impression of 'running' reverberance (e.g. reverberance during music) and also for the assessment of speech intelligibility in non-diffuse environments where a distributed loudspeaker system is the source – e.g. long tube station platforms.

Reverberant level

Sound levels in a room build up due to reflections from enclosing surfaces. The size of the room and the amount of absorption in it determine the build-up of sounds. Changes in reverberant levels due to the addition or removal of absorbing material can be predicted. Since absorption varies with frequency, calculations can be made for all frequencies where absorption coefficients are known.

Speech transmission index (STI)

A common method for quantifying the intelligibility of speech in a room. The STI is measured using specialised equipment, as defined in IEC 60268-16. STI uses a scale of 0 to 1, where 0 = unintelligible, and 1 = perfect intelligibility. In any space of large public occupancy where people are unfamiliar with the building, the desirable target is STI = 0.5, with a minimum of STI 0.45. For spaces that are speech critical e.g. classrooms, auditoria etc. STI-0.6 or higher should be expected.

Rooms for speech

In rooms for speech, good intelligibility is key. Consider carefully the relationship between the person speaking and those listening to achieve the optimum acoustic conditions.

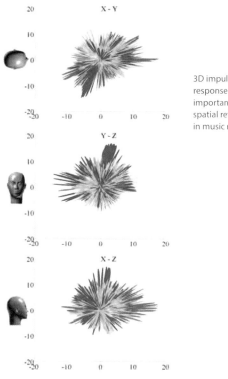

3D impulse response – importance of spatial reflections in music rooms.

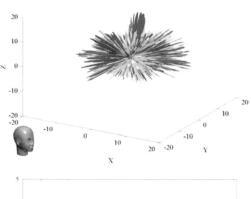

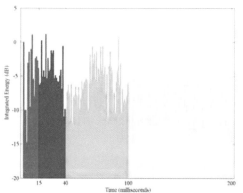

Rooms for music, opera, theatre

Quantitative values and descriptive parameters for acoustic performance for different music styles have been derived through significant research since the early 1900s, and this is an area of ongoing research that continually adds new insights and increased knowledge.

Reverberation time, loudness, early-to-late sound ratio and the initial time gap can be measured objectively. Other benchmarks exist and more are being developed in an effort to quantify more of the factors contributing to rewarding and enjoyable acoustics.

Intimacy, clarity, spaciousness, envelopment, warmth, liveness, balance and blend are some of the terms used to describe the subjective attributes of a space for music.

The understanding of the importance of listening in 3D is being discovered through research, and many of the highest rated concert halls in the world show that sound coming from all directions, but at specific timing or arrival relative to direct sound, is crucial to heightened perception and enjoyment.

In rooms used mainly for amplified music, the requirements differ from rooms with natural acoustics, and in some cases the room needs to be highly sound-absorbing for the sound system to be the main information delivery system.

Contemporary venues frequently incorporate variable acoustical features, sometimes including electronic reverberation systems, to provide a flexible environment that accommodates the sonic requirements of a wide range of musical styles.

Variable acoustics

Acoustic conditions in a space can be varied through many different means, ranging from deployable sound-absorbing curtains or banners, to moving ceiling and wall elements (to vary room volume or shape/geometry), to surfaces that change properties from sound-absorbing to diffusing, or reflecting. They can be manually controlled or computer adjustable. These do not, however, negate the need to pay attention to room acoustic design: in many respects it makes it even more critical.

Variable acoustic elements concert hall, Harpa, Reykjavik, Iceland.

Spatial Audio Systems
Audio reproduction approach that allows the recreation of the exact timing, strength, and direction of sound in full 3D, from all directions, front to back, side to side, above and below, as experienced in real-life.

Loudspeaker Performance –
Directivity and Frequency Response
A wide range of different loudspeaker types are available for different uses. Three parameters are essential in determining what type of loudspeaker type to use in any given situation.

Directivity
The pattern of sound, variable by frequency, produced by the loudspeaker. Low directivity is when sound has wide horizontal and vertical dispersion (like a bare lightbulb). High directivity devices are designed to exhibit control in vertical and/or horizontal dispersion (like a spotlight).

Frequency Response
Describes the ability to reproduce quality sound at a particular frequency; for example, a loudspeaker for music use is usually required to have a wider frequency response than one that is used only for speech.

Sound Power Rating
Describes the overall sound level the device can produce (which is usually normalised to the performance achieved at 1m for 1 Watt of power).

Active acoustics or active architecture
Active acoustics is a broad term that may refer to several electronic methods of acoustic enhancement.

Electronic sound masking systems are sometimes used in office environments to provide an artificial background noise level and to improve speech privacy where ambient noise levels are too low.

Active noise cancellation systems reduce unwanted sound through electronics by listening to sound with a microphone and instantly playing back the recorded signal through a speaker that is in the opposite phase to the signal at the microphone. At the time of publishing, this is feasible for small-scale applications like noise-cancelling headphones, equipment racks for fan noise reduction, and in some high-end cars. It is an area of constant research and development.

Active architecture systems use arrays of microphones to measure the sound in a room and use signal processing of these sounds to add early sound reflections and reverberation, which is then delivered to the room through distributed loudspeakers. These methods can be useful in multi-purpose rooms; for example, changing the sound of a room from speech lecture mode to chamber music or orchestral music mode. These systems are heavily reliant on room acoustic conditions being right to get the best result.

Audio system design
Use of loudspeakers in buildings is normally for the following purposes:

- Voice alarm (VA) systems for the broadcast of emergency announcements and crowd control building-wide.

- Public address (PA) systems for the broadcast of routine messages building-wide.

- Speech and media amplification systems – systems used to amplify people speaking, or programme media such as presentations, video, video conferencing, etc.

- Sound reinforcement systems – the primary mechanism of sound delivery in medium, large and very large spaces.

The function and need will dictate a wide variety of variables (power, infrastructure, frequency range, performance, etc.). It is important that these are well understood early in the design process.

Audio system design arrangement generally takes two forms:

1. Fully distributed systems – multiple smaller loudspeakers located in the space.

2. Distributed clusters – fewer loudspeakers in number than fully distributed systems, often with higher power ratings and higher directivity.

The primary goal of any audio system is to deliver natural-sounding, undistorted audio signals, free of feedback, with a frequency balance that reproduces music and speech sounds faithfully for the majority of listeners.

Audio systems hidden in architecture

Architecturally it is often considered preferable to hide loudspeakers behind finishes. If this is decided as an approach for the project, metal grilles or fabric finishes in front of loudspeakers must have a very high level of acoustic transparency. Design should also consider dimensional considerations and additional space required, such that maintenance and future upgrading of technology can be easily accommodated.

Loudspeaker alignment

Generally, loudspeakers within a single room must all face in the same direction to ensure no overlapping of sounds or creation of echoes (the exception being surround sound systems or immersive spatial audio systems, which can face in multiple directions).

Good room acoustics and good sound system design need to work together. Shortfalls in the design of one cannot necessarily be made up with the other. The sonic deficiencies of a room with poor acoustics cannot always be overcome with a good sound system. The cost of acoustic treatment to get a sound system to work can often be more than the sound system itself. Using a domestic analogy, you can spend money on the most expensive hi-fi sound system, but if you put it in your bathroom, it won't sound as good as it will in a space with the right acoustics.

Acoustic prediction and simulation methods

The acoustic consultant has a wide range of tools available to be able to calculate, predict and demonstrate the acoustic performance of spaces to clients, and also use them actively as part of the design process. Many have been around since the early 20th century; others have been developed since the mid-1990s and have become more accessible since 2010.

Room acoustic measurements

Interior acoustic surveys are performed in existing buildings to quantify and understand room acoustics, background noise, speech intelligibility and other metrics, as well as noise intrusion from the outside, etc. These are very useful in understanding existing conditions and correlating to user subjective comments on acoustics, and can be used to guide refurbishment of existing buildings and the design of new buildings (to avoid mistakes of the past, or replicate/enhance the best features).

Calculations

Empirical calculation methods, derived from many years of research and validation through real-life measurement, are another cornerstone of the profession and will continue to be for many years to come.

Architectural scale models

Before the development of advanced computer modelling, architectural scale models for acoustic testing were the closest approximation of anticipated sonic performance. Physical models are occasionally still used, especially for spaces with complex curved geometry, but with advances in computer modelling offer both speed and cost advantages, especially for making design changes.

Room acoustics
survey equipment.

Acoustic scale model,
Bridgewater Hall,
Manchester, UK.

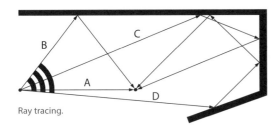
Ray tracing.

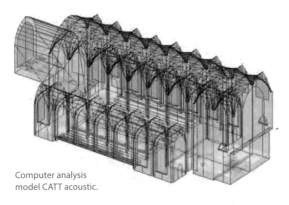
Computer analysis model CATT acoustic.

Arup SoundLab(R) auralisation studio.

Acoustic visualisation ray tracing

In the early design stages 2D and 3D ray tracing methods allow quick visual representations of sound to be made. These allow useful quick comparison between design options and macro design option evaluation, before focusing on further detailed approaches.

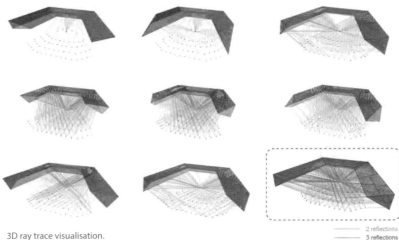
3D ray trace visualisation.

2 reflections
3 reflections

Computer models

Modelling programs of varying complexity are available for acoustic predictions, and are commercially available to the public. They require skill and experience to use effectively and interpret results appropriately.

Auralisation

Simulation of acoustic environments can be accomplished electronically with a high degree of accuracy. Simulation involves two stages, computer model analysis or measurements in an existing space, followed by processing and sound playback through a multi-channel spatial audio system in an acoustically treated room. The exact timing, strength, and direction of sound reflections is reproduced. This allows for the prediction of existing and future conditions, and the ability to evaluate architectural changes quickly. The acoustics of existing spaces can be captured and replayed in these environments, allowing refurbishment options to be accurately assessed, or using existing buildings for benchmark comparisons with those being designed. These are invaluable tools, that allow subjective evaluations of acoustics by listening.

Real-time modelling of virtual acoustic events, while moving through a virtual space, is a reality.

Room or material optimisation

New methods allow design from the inside out, by determining the desired acoustics and assembling the room design from the acoustic information. At a micro scale, parametric modelling can be used to iteratively develop the design of a surface to provide the optimum sound-absorbing, diffusing and reflecting properties.

Definition of acoustic terms

Airborne sound
Sound transmitted through air

Barrier, panel, partition
A wall, ceiling, floor, window, door or other building element considered part of the insulation assembly

Coincidence dip
Loss of sound insulation value at a panel's resonant frequency

Flanking paths
Secondary paths of sound transmission usually around the perimeter of the element in question

Impact insulation
Rating of a floor or ceiling for resisting the transmission of impact sound

Noise
Undesirable sound

Sound insulation
Resistance to passage of sound

Sound reduction index (R)
Rating of a partition for reducing airborne sound

Sound transmission loss (TL)
Sound reduction value of a partition expressed in decibels, usually at octave or one-third octave frequencies

Structure-borne sound
Sound transmitted through the solid materials of buildings

R_w rating
Sound insulation rating of a specific material or building element (measured in lab)

D_w rating
Difference in sound level between spaces (measured on-site)

Basic sound insulation problems.

5 – SOUND INSULATION

Sound insulation is concerned with sound entering or emanating from a space and can encompass a wide range of sources.

Sometimes sound needs to be prevented from escaping a room or building; sometimes prevented from entering it. Usually both are required to some degree and need to be considered carefully for internal adjacencies (vertical and horizontal) in a building, as well as impact on or from the external environment. It is important to properly evaluate sound insulation needs at the earliest stages of a project – shortfalls in design are often extremely difficult or costly to rectify, and sometimes impossible without complete reconstruction. It is also important not to over-design from a sustainability (material use) standpoint.

Providing adequate sound insulation is a basic requirement in construction and requires an understanding of material acoustic behaviour. Materials exhibit a range of acoustic attributes simultaneously. Sound insulation is mainly concerned with issues related to sound transmission through materials. This is especially important as sound insulation usually relies on mass-heavy constructions (concrete, gypsum board, etc.) which is the opposite to sound absorption which usually relies on lightweight porous material (mineral wool, fibreglass, carpet, etc.).

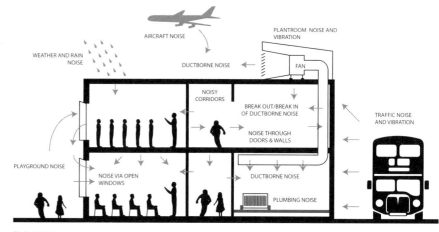

Noise ingress.

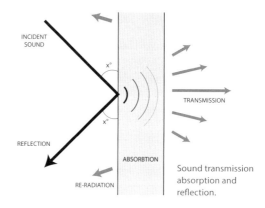

Sound transmission absorption and reflection.

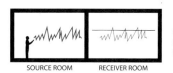

BACKGROUND NOISE CORRECT
SIGNAL BARELY AUDIBLE OVER
BACKGROUND NOISE

SOURCE ROOM   RECEIVER ROOM

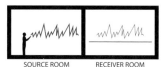

SIGNAL CLEARLY AUDIBLE
BACKGROUND NOISE TOO LOW

SOURCE ROOM   RECEIVER ROOM

Balance-sound insulation
and background noise.

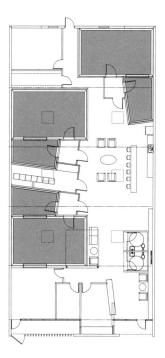

Reduction
through spatial
separation.

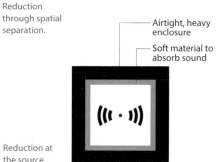

Airtight, heavy
enclosure

Soft material to
absorb sound

Reduction at
the source.

To provide interior acoustic conditions suitable for use (e.g. appropriate privacy or an environment free of distraction), sound insulation and background noise (usually from HVAC systems) must perform together. Shortfalls in the performance of one may give the impression of shortfalls in the other. For example, consider two adjacent classrooms where the sound insulation and background noise has been designed to ensure that noises from one are only barely audible in the other. If the background noise in one room is below target, sounds from other rooms will be more audible. The first reaction to this may be that the sound insulation of the room envelope is deficient. Conversely, if the classrooms are designed and achieve the correct background noise, but sound insulation is deficient, then disturbance can result. Both design criteria must be achieved for the right outcome.

A few basic strategies can be used to achieve the desired sound insulation.

- **Locate critical areas away from each other**
  Plan early to separate noise-sensitive spaces from noise-producing spaces by neutral (buffer) spaces. Consider both vertical and horizontal adjacencies. This approach will reduce the need for more complex or difficult to construct sound-insulating assemblies (which are often more costly and less sustainable as they use more material, impact other design disciplines more extensively, and can increase the construction schedule).

- **Reduce noise and vibration at the source**
  The reduction of the source sound levels is the most effective way of reducing sound transmission. Where possible, this method can produce good results at minimum cost.

- **Block the path from the source**
  Sound insulation through sound-insulating construction elements is the most common method of reducing sound transmission in buildings.

- **Reduce the noise at the receiving location using sound absorption**
  This method can sometimes reduce the effect of transmitted sound, but only modest improvements can be achieved and it is not the most desirable approach.

Types of sound transmission

Sound transmission occurs through the interaction between sound in air and sound in solids. The two types of sound transmission in buildings are airborne and structure-borne sound. Although one or the other is usually dominant, a combination of both is common. They should both be evaluated in parallel for comprehensive results.

Airborne sound

Sound waves transmitted through air. The best defence against airborne sound transmission is an airtight enclosure.

Airborne sound transmission also occurs when sound waves vibrate a panel (e.g. a wall) and the vibrating panel re-radiates sound, acting as a new, airborne sound source (like the building becoming an amplifier and loudspeaker).

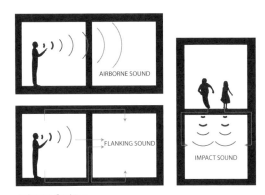

Airborne, flanking
and impact sound.

Structure-borne sound

These are sound waves transmitted through solids, such as structure, floors, walls, ceilings and building services. Examples within buildings include footfall, vibrations caused by machinery, musical instruments, etc. External sources can include underground or over-ground trains. The mechanism of hearing these sources, as above, is that vibration propagates in the structure, causing the building to vibrate – effectively turning it into a loudspeaker and amplifying the sound. If a major source of external vibration exists from a transport system, discussion with the operator can often determine whether incorporation of isolation at source can be achieved.

Factors that compromise sound insulation

Flanking paths

This is sound transmission around the perimeter of the element (wall, floor, ceiling, door, etc.). Sound, like water, will find the path of least resistance. Flanking paths around sound insulating elements can severely compromise the whole system. Secondary sound paths can easily be overlooked but must be avoided.

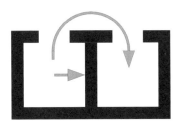

Flanking path.

Leaks

Even small gaps or holes in an assembly reduce the effect of sound insulation measures significantly. A hole or gap in only a fraction of the total enclosure area can dramatically decrease the overall level of sound insulation. The higher the basic insulation value is without an air leak, the greater the detrimental effect of any weakness. Making sure partitions are slab-to-slab where needed, penetrations from HVAC and other services are properly sealed and doors and windows are properly sealed are all essential in achieving the intended results. This is easily demonstrated by opening a door or window – opening just a little lets most of the sound or noise in; opening it much more make less of a difference.

Effect of leakage.

Weak links

The weakest link in any construction assembly will have the greatest impact on the overall level of sound insulation. A solid wall is only as good as the window, door or airduct opening cut into it. In high sound insulating constructions it is necessary to limit lower sound insulating components to less than 10% of the area of the higher performing component before sound insulation is significantly compromised.

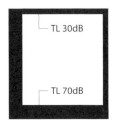

Effect of inconsistent
construction.

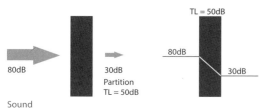

Sound
transmission loss.

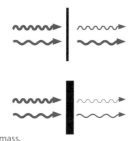

Frequency and mass.

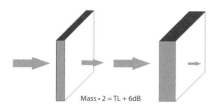

Mass • 2 = TL + 6dB

Insulation with mass.

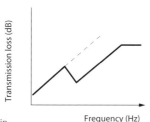

Coincidence dip.

Dual panels with
equal total mass.

Successful ways to increase the sound insulation values of a structure include the use of heavy materials, composite construction systems, structural decoupling, and airspaces between multiple construction layers. Most effective are combinations of any of the above.

Insulation with mass

- Heavyweight construction generally achieves better sound insulation values than lightweight construction.

- The insulation value of a barrier is related to the frequency or wavelength of the sound.

- A heavy barrier requires more force to vibrate; a lightweight panel vibrates more easily.

- Barriers with little mass offer limited transmission loss values; even less for lower frequencies than for higher frequencies.

- Barriers with heavy mass result in high transmission loss values, especially for high frequencies.

Mass law theory

For homogeneous building materials, every doubling of the mass adds about 6dB of sound insulation at a given frequency. For homogenous building materials, every doubling of the transmitted frequency increases the sound insulation also by about 6dB. A panel generally has a greater insulation value at high frequencies than at low frequencies.

Coincidence dip

The inherent resonant frequency of a material or assembly, which results in a reduced insulation value at that frequency.

Materials with the same mass can have varying resonant frequencies due to having different rigidity, method of attachment, connections and assembly.

Dual panel and composite partitions

Improvements over homogenous constructions can be achieved by dividing the assembly into multiple layers with air gaps, or by composite constructions of varying materials.

Coupling by rigid connections between layers reduces the effect of multiple panels. Coupling through airspace can be reduced by controlling the resonant sound in the cavity with sound-absorbing material (usually glass fibre or mineral wool).

Composite constructions with varying coincidence dips for different layers increase sound insulation.

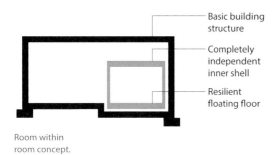

Basic building structure

Completely independent inner shell

Resilient floating floor

Room within room concept.

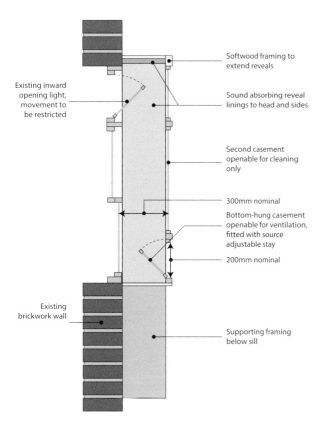

Softwood framing to extend reveals

Sound absorbing reveal linings to head and sides

Existing inward opening light, movement to be restricted

Second casement openable for cleaning only

300mm nominal

Bottom-hung casement openable for ventilation, fitted with source adjustable stay

200mm nominal

Existing brickwork wall

Supporting framing below sill

Natural ventilation and noise attenuation example.

Insulation through structural separation

A significant increase in sound insulation is made possible by structural separation. The total insulation value is greater with equal mass if the structure is separated and has no or few rigid connections.

Typical examples of separated constructions are floor slabs on rubber mounts, spring-hung ceilings and multiple wall floating 'room-within-room' or 'box-in-box' constructions.

Combinations

For high levels of sound insulation, both high mass and structural separation are required. The most effective sound-insulating enclosures are heavy, made of several layers, structurally separated and airtight.

Natural ventilation

For sustainable design, natural ventilation is becoming increasingly desirable in buildings. If windows are directly openable to exterior noise sources, façade design will normally require a convoluted path that allows air to flow freely but allows noise to be attenuated. Increasingly, products that can be inserted into the building façade or into interior partitions that allow airflow with low pressure drop are available. It is important to look at this carefully early in a design process and determine the right design approach to ensure that the right outcome is achieved.

Sound level difference (D)

A single number descriptor of reduction of sound energy between spaces. The desired difference between the noise level on one side (source) and the noise level on the other (receiver) determines the sound level difference required of the structure. A greater value indicates better sound insulation.

The sound insulation required between two spaces may be determined by the sound level difference needed between them. A single figure descriptor, the weighted sound level difference, D_w, is sometimes used (see BS EN ISO : 2013).

Sound reduction index (R)

A single number descriptor of the loss of sound through a material or construction assembly. It is a property of the tested component, unlike the sound level difference which is affected by the common area between the rooms and the acoustic of the receiving room.

The weighted sound reduction index, R_w, is a single figure description of sound reduction index which is defined in BS EN ISO 717-1: 2013. The R_w is calculated from measurements in an acoustic laboratory. Sound insulation ratings derived from site (which are invariably lower than the laboratory figures) are referred to as the R'_w ratings.

Concrete slab

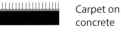
Carpet on concrete

Carpet on concrete and suspended ceiling

Floated slab, carpet and suspended ceiling

Improvements to impact noise insulation.

Impact noise

Footsteps on hard-finish floors, door slams, furniture movement and other common activities can transmit as structure-borne sound before being radiated into the air in the receiving room. Footsteps on hard floors can be mitigated through the addition of a soft surface, such as carpet or resilient underlayment, under a wood or tile floor. Impact vibrations from equipment can be reduced by the separation of the source from the structure with resilient supports such as spring mounts. Impact and vibration isolation should be included where necessary in the design stages as it can difficult to retrofit later.

Impact sound pressure level ($L'_{nT,w}$)

A single number rating to describe the impact sound insulation of floors. It is evaluated by measuring the sound pressure level in the receiving room resulting from a standard tapping machine placed on the floor of the source room. The measured values, in each of the third-octave bands from 100Hz to 3150Hz, are adjusted to allow for the acoustics of the receiving room and compared with a standard reference curve, in accordance with the procedure defined in BS EN ISO 717-2: 2013 to obtain the single figure weighted standardised impact sound pressure level, $L'_{nT,w}$. Where there are no flanking routes to modify the performance the results are described by $L_{nT,w}$. The lower the figure, the better the impact sound insulation.

Vibration

Building vibration

Structure-borne vibrations can be perceived directly either as an audible or physical sensation. Frequencies above 100Hz are typically heard as sound, while frequencies below 20Hz can typically be felt as physical vibrations. In between, combinations of heard and felt sensations are common.

Steady state vibrations

Mechanical equipment noise is the most common generator of continuous, steady state vibrations.

Random vibrations

Footfall from people walking or running, usually on a floor above, is an example of intermittent, random vibration. Floors are the most common building elements to receive these impacts.

Vibrations through the soil from trains, subways or traffic can also be a source of concern.

Vibration control

The most effective method of vibration control is at the source. Once structure-borne vibrations are present, most structures transmit them easily throughout buildings. Isolation efforts at the receiving end are typically much less successful.

To interrupt the path of vibrations in buildings, flexible suspensions and supports, resilient construction methods and floating construction methods are necessary.

6 – MECHANICAL AND ELECTRICAL SYSTEMS

Building systems such as mechanical, electrical and plumbing equipment can have significant impact on the acoustic performance of a building. Noise and vibration may be generated by the equipment itself. Ducting and piping can result in the transmission of sound from one part of a building to another.

Basic planning

Acoustic aspects should be considered in the early stages of the engineering process for building systems. Careful planning of adjacencies and exploration of layout options can improve and facilitate the final performance and is the most cost-effective form of noise control.

Sound-generating and sound-sensitive spaces should be separately located, with sufficient distances and buffer zones between them. Both horizontal and vertical adjacencies need to be considered. Sufficient space for equipment, clearances and access should be provided early on.

Establishing criteria

Establishing noise ratings (NR) for each space is required to determine appropriate layouts and connections.

Equipment noise control

Specific noise and vibration control measures for equipment rooms and distributed equipment can include room enclosures, equipment mounting systems, and vibration isolation hangers.

Ducts

Fans generate noise which propagates through attached ducts. Noise can radiate out from ductwork (called breakout noise) and can be evident at diffusers and grilles. It is usually the low-frequency component of in-duct fan sound that is most difficult to control. Low-frequency noise control strategies include sound attenuators, heavy gauge ducts, gypsum board enclosures, and large plenums with thick acoustical lining.

Airflow

Correlates with noise levels. For a given in-duct air volume flow rate, larger ducts result in lower airspeeds, and less airflow noise. Larger duct cross sections increase penetration sizes through partitions and reduce insulation values as sound travels more easily within larger ducts.

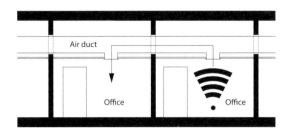

Section

Cross-talk.

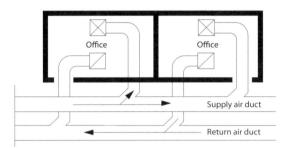

Plan

Better duct layout.

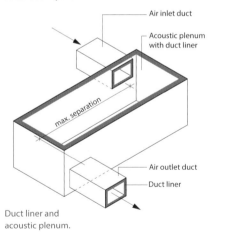

Duct liner and
acoustic plenum.

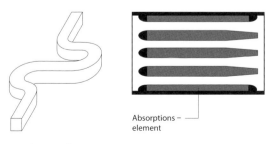

Duct looping silencers.

Noise transmission through ducts

Sound transmission between spaces via the ducted ventilation system can occur when the distance between outlets in separated rooms is short, has few intervening turns, and the duct is unlined.

Therefore, air distribution ducting, if not carefully planned, may compromise sound insulation efforts and can be a source of problems in residences and other sound sensitive structures. Transmission of equipment noise and vocal sound cross-talk via ducts can be reduced by increasing distances between inlets/outlets or adding sound-absorbing duct lining, acoustic plenums or silencers.

Duct lagging

Duct and pipe penetrations through walls should be sealed. To avoid noise breaking out through the duct walls, additional enclosures may be needed.

Air turbulence

Noise from airflow is minimised if turbulence is reduced as much as possible. Smooth transitions, rounded turns with large radii, turning vanes and Y-shaped take-offs reduce turbulence. The selection of quiet grilles and registers is also crucial.

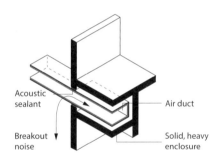

Duct lagging.

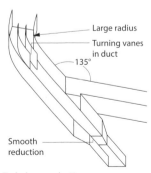

Turbulence reduction.

Vibration isolation

There are a broad array of methods and associated products that serve to limit the direct coupling of vibrating sources (mechanical equipment, lift machinery, exhaust fans, underground trains, fitness machines) with building elements. The purpose of vibration isolation is to limit structure-borne noise propagation. The isolation of equipment in a building is usually accomplished by mounting vibrating sources on carefully selected springs or rubber pads. Residential buildings near trains and roadways are sometimes erected on vibration isolation pads to reduce ground-borne vibration into the building. Sometimes it is necessary to mount sensitive lab equipment and imaging devices on their own vibration isolation platforms or in rooms with concrete slabs raised (floating) on spring isolators so that equipment can perform to specifications. Active vibration isolation systems, which can detect and counteract subtle vibrations, also exist for sensitive scientific equipment isolation.

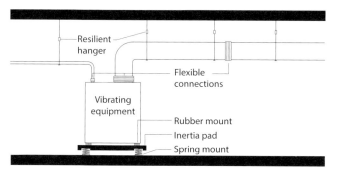

Section

Flexible equipment connections.

Pipe, duct mounting

Transmission of vibrations from equipment to the structure can also occur through connecting pipes and ducts. The use of isolation hangers and mounts, and flexible connectors to equipment, prevents short-circuiting of the equipment mounting.

Electrical isolation

Lighting, audio and general electrical systems can all be noise sources. Incoming electrical supply is normally ground-isolated as it enters a building and transformers are provided to supply the necessary systems at the incoming location. Transformers near acoustically sensitive spaces should be vibration-isolated.

In spaces with specialist audio, lighting, theatre systems/rigging, etc. separate supply is usually needed for each to avoid cross-contamination noise from one system affecting the other.

Environmental noise emissions

National, regional and local codes and standards commonly establish limits for environmental noise emission. The major areas of concern are:

- Building operations: Activity generating high sound levels that propagates to the surrounding environs may need to be limited. Codes are usually onerous (especially close to residential dwellings) and more so when the noise is from an entertainment source and/or is repetitive and/or impulsive in nature (common in entertainment/music sound and the industrial process). Criteria tend to be more stringent for events occurring at night. Retrofitting a design to increase sound insulation after the fact is extremely costly and is in some cases impossible. Consequently, this element of the design is critical to get right from the outset.

- Building systems: Mechanical and electrical systems may require equipment outside the building, or with mechanical systems venting to the building exterior. For equipment placed outdoors, select items that are inherently quiet and/or incorporate noise and vibration control to meet the required limits. Pay attention to location of equipment and screen or enclose where possible.

- Transport systems: Buildings that have high traffic, whether vehicle or by foot, require careful consideration of noise impact on the surrounding area.

7 – SUSTAINABILITY

With increasing consciousness of the impact of buildings on the climate and natural environment, acoustic consultants face the challenge of achieving acoustic design goals while minimising resource use.

Space planning

By locating noisy rooms away from noise-sensitive rooms, walls can have lighter constructions with fewer layers of gypsum board. In some cases, additional concrete and gypsum board ceilings designed for sound insulation can be avoided with space planning. Similarly, locating buildings away from noisy sites, or using terrain and other barriers to reduce noise at a site can be an opportunity to reduce glass thickness. Avoiding the need for specialist acoustical construction and simplifying construction assemblies can shorten the construction schedule, thereby reducing energy expended during construction.

Material selection

By specifying sound-absorbing materials that have high recycled content, do not require long transport distances, and require little energy to produce, the detrimental impact on the environment can be reduced.

Mechanical system noise control

Noise reduction using sound attenuators increases back pressure on fans, which increases energy consumption. Sound attenuators can sometimes be avoided by considering fan type to reduce noise or including sufficient lengths of acoustically lined duct between air handling unit fans and air terminals in receiver locations. Sound attenuators can also minimise static pressure drop and resultant energy use.

6

Case Studies

Case Study Contributors

Case study sections open with a sound wave visualisation of the author
speaking the section names.

Previous page:
National Sawdust, Bureau V,
Brooklyn, New York, USA.

Arenas

Issue	Priority	Comments
Room acoustics	H	Positive patron and performer experiences rely upon excellent acoustics. The considerations are complex and have a major impact on the architectural and structural design. High quality speech and music, via the house and touring sound systems, is usually the highest priority.
		The acoustic volume of an arena bowl is large and must be minimised as far as is practical. Sound-absorbing treatments need to be extensive in order to mitigate the issues and control unwanted sound reflections.
		These issues should also be balanced against the need for performers and audiences to 'feel' the room energy. While generally considered positive for concerts and certain sporting activities, some athletes find that crowd noise is becoming increasingly distracting, particularly in venues where temporary or permanent roofs have been added (often without acoustic consideration) to previously open-air spaces.
Speech intelligibility	H	Speech needs to be clear and understandable for PAVA announcements and live commentary. It is also critical for PAVA messages and crowd management in emergencies.
Audio systems design	H	PAVA, house sound reinforcement, and touring sound systems will need to be accommodated, both fixed and temporary. A high number of audio devices are typically integrated into the design and are often visible, especially in the bowl.
Sound insulation – external	H	Mitigating high noise levels generated by performances is critical: this can significantly impact the roof and building envelope design. Windows into the main event bowl are becoming a trend and require careful consideration.
		If frequent and significant rainfall is expected, this must be assessed to determine appropriate impact noise control.
		Building systems that penetrate the building envelope will require special attention.
Sound insulation – internal	M/H	Performance spaces need to be free of noise disturbance although they are not necessarily the most sensitive spaces. Others can require more consideration (e.g. VIP boxes, dressing rooms, broadcast areas, emergency response rooms, etc.)
		The main bowl often has openings to front- and back-of-house areas that remain ajar during events, set-up and take-down. Noise transfer between these spaces is generally tolerated, but implications should be considered during planning, and appropriate criteria developed (e.g. bowl doors may need to be closed to control noise emission).
Speech privacy	M	This aspect is most relevant to the sensitive areas noted above.
Impact/vibration isolation	H	Impact sounds on the playing or performing surfaces, and those generated by loading and unloading during set-up/take-down of touring events, have an operational impact: space-planning must take this into account.
Mechanical and electrical noise	M/H	In performance, practice and rehearsal spaces, background noise is usually in the range of NR35–45. Some noise sensitive spaces will have criteria NR25–35. Confirm requirements early.
Structure-borne noise	L/M	Background noise is usually high enough in most spaces for this not to be a concern. However, the issue still requires attention as later rectification is complex or impossible, so carefully consider major sources of possible structure-borne noise, particularly transport infrastructure.
Environmental noise	H	Controlling noise emission from loud events is a major project challenge for arenas, especially those located in urban settings or close to residential areas. Failure to achieve targets can result in forced building closure. Retrofitting design to increase sound insulation after the fact is extremely costly, if not impossible.

H – High   M – Medium   L – Low

Introduction

In the arena, both patron and performer experiences are reliant upon good acoustics. Increasingly, arenas are multi-use buildings with concerts, large-scale entertainment productions and sporting events requiring successful accommodation within the same space.

Architectural style

The evolution of the arena form can be traced back to a wide variety of historical sporting practices, with the Mesoamerican ball court and the Roman Colosseum among the most famous. These spaces were generally open-air, although the Colosseum did have a partially retractable roof of timber and canvas.

As different sports developed, they engendered their own building types and relationships between performer and spectator. Similarly, though many venues were originally built in cities where the particular sport they hosted was a core part of that city's cultural life, many were forced to move as these urban centres expanded. This had a key impact on the acoustic design approach (see later).

The multi-use arena form emerged in the USA during the 1960s. It was typically for the provision of both basketball and ice hockey facilities, with a visual focus generally on the player or performance surface – usually the lowest point in the arena – with seats arranged around it. Generally, its sightlines allowed a full view of that surface. The view of the players/performers or scoreboards/ other visual media providing information or image magnification often took priority. As a result, initially little attention was paid to the acoustics.

By the end of the 1960s, as pop music became more prevalent, arenas were typically the location of choice for big music acts to play. Acoustics were a challenge from the outset. The large volume of the spaces and insufficient sound-absorbing treatments resulted in challenging room acoustics. Large stacked loudspeaker systems were located onstage, pushing out high sound levels that struggled (in some cases) to provide coverage over large parts of the audience. This often resulted in 'echoes' of speech and music. It is easy to find historic film footage evidencing this phenomenon, or even new films mimicking the experience of that era by adding slap-back echo and reverberation to provide an 'authentic' experience.

The arena form itself usually developed to accommodate more event types, with these shaping the surface or stage: the most common being the rectilinear box, horseshoe bowl, full bowl, and large fan. In suburban locations, where noise emission was not an issue, lightweight parabolic concave roofs were cheap and efficient to build. The negative issues of the larger interior volumes and poor sound isolation were not considered a major concern given there were limited options for where events could be hosted.

Three sound system forms dominated in the bowl – the central cluster, distributed clusters, and fully distributed systems. The advantage of the latter two forms was evident in typically smaller groups of loudspeakers, that did not interrupt sightlines, which had the ability to receive a feed from the mixing desk of a live event and supplement touring sound systems in the hard-to-reach areas furthest from the stage. This format saw the central cluster almost entirely phased out by the early 1980s.

Acoustic design was still not considered the highest priority until the mid-1990s, when a confluence of issues caused a shift change to developers, owners and operators of venues:

Historical context

- Demand for live music began to increase and large venues returned to urban centres (often as regeneration projects) – multiple large venues began to compete for events.

- A statutory requirement demanded that places of public assembly have PAVA systems capable of good speech intelligibility in emergency situations.

- Advances in sound system technology resulted in house and touring systems capable of much higher sound levels, at significantly improved quality, particularly at low (bass) frequencies, which demanded closer attention to interior room acoustic design (meaning both provision of appropriate acoustic finishes and minimising of reverberant interior volume).

High concert sound levels, and the location of venues in increasingly urban areas, requires higher sound insulating building envelopes to achieve stringent noise limits in surrounding residences. This requires noise sensitive receptors (dwellings, hospitals, etc.) be clearly understood at the outset of a project so that the correct sound insulation performance can be achieved. This typically has a significant impact on the architectural and structural design of the building (especially the roof); getting it wrong is usually extremely costly or impossible to rectify once the arena is opened, unless a conscious decision is made to be able to easily add components to the primary constructions later.

Today, the acoustic experience of the interior of the arena, and its impact on the environs, are considered the paramount design concern for a successful multi-use arena. Consequently, fundamental design decisions including the site and urban fabric orientation, bowl form, height, roof shape, roof geometry, and interior finishes selection require acoustics input from the very earliest stages of a project.

Acoustic features

The main arena bowl is usually a large volume space, presenting unique acoustic challenges.

Arenas commonly have seat counts of between 5,000 and 25,000 people. The resulting geometry generally cannot be relied upon to provide a natural room acoustic to the performers – instead, this is facilitated by the audio systems. However, this does not mean that the room acoustic design can be neglected; on the contrary, controlling sound reflections (particularly late sound reflections) is critical to a successful acoustic outcome. Room volume must be minimised as far as is practical, and it is usually necessary to introduce significant areas of broadband and low-frequency sound-absorbing treatment on walls, soffits and the underside of gantries. Together these should aim to create a sufficiently controlled room acoustic that supports the sound system – rather than working against it.

Later sound reflections (beyond 50ms) should be minimised as far as is practical, as this negatively impacts speech intelligibility and music clarity. This usually requires minimising the room volume to avoid excessive reverberance (height and length should only be what is required for audio, visual, lighting and theatrical equipment to function). Arena room volumes are inherently large, with height driven by the need to achieve the right sightlines along with a safe step-height within the seating rake. For acoustic purposes, all unnecessary room volume should be eliminated. The major driving factor in this regard is roof geometry, which requires close collaboration between architect, structural engineer and acoustic consultant. Preference should be given to (as viewed from the interior) flat or convex roof forms. Concave or parabolic roof forms (that increase room height and volume, and focus sound), and interior room dimensions that extend significantly beyond the last row of seating, should be avoided.

Exposed wall areas or any significant vertical surfaces will usually need to be sound-absorbing (sometimes sound diffusing) in order to ensure that strong reflections from the sound systems are avoided. Glass surfaces require careful attention: since they cannot have an acoustic finish, they usually need to be angled to send sound energy directly to a sound-absorbing surface to avoid strong late sound reflections across the room (which will be perceived as echoes). Sound-absorbing finishes should be as effective across the audible frequency range as possible, with increasing attention required for low-frequency sound control.

The upper roof zone (typically the underside of the structural external envelope) must be highly sound-absorbing across the audible frequency range. Achieving this usually requires significant thickness of sound-absorbing material (100mm to 400mm) to be located in the zone, ideally hung two metres below the roof, with sufficient gaps so as to get maximum sound-absorbing performance from both the front and rear sides of the material, as well as additional low-frequency panel absorption from the suspension of the material. Floors usually need to incorporate some impact control, but generally do not include any carpet due to maintenance issues.

Sound-absorbing seats are typical throughout the bowl to minimise acoustic differences between the unoccupied and occupied conditions. This is advantageous for set-up, testing and sound-check for events. Some spaces may require variable acoustics to accommodate different performance types; this can be especially true in rooms where the roof is operable. The incorporation of audio and visual technology systems, control rooms and similar spaces connected to the main performance space all need to be considered very early in the process.

Future

Technology continues to be used in increasingly creative ways as part of sports, concerts and other large-scale entertainment events. As a result, arenas are likely to become much more technologically intensive. Technological infrastructure requires careful planning and must allow for easy connection or deployment of new technology in or on the architecture. The architect's challenge is how to give the space architectural character while allowing this technological overlay to happen seamlessly. Some spaces do this by making the infrastructure an explicit part of the room's design.

The use of technology, including emerging immersive audio and visual (VR, AR, etc.), as well as development of new concert and performance formats, and emerging sports (e.g. eSports) will have a continuing impact on the future development of the typology.

Velodrom, Berlin (velodrome and swimming pool)

LOCATION: Berlin, Germany

ARCHITECT: Dominique Perrault

COMPLETED: 1997

AUDIENCE: approximately 4,000–12,000, depending on configuration

FORM: classic arena bowl with 360-degree seating in plan around the central performance area

The velodrome forms part of a complex of spaces designed to Olympic standards that include a multi-use sports hall, a competition swimming pool and associated leisure facilities. The venue hosts a wide variety of events but is not home to any permanent resident sports teams.

The main roof is designed with a high level of sound insulation, given that it is overlooked by dense residential housing. This was the key impetus of the roof mass, which, in conjunction with the need to minimise room volume, results in a flat roof structure. The roof build-up consists of (inside to out) structural metal roof deck, insulation, cement board, insulation and outer finish, separated by airspaces as necessary to achieve the thermal and acoustic requirements. It should be noted that the roof contains glazing, considered beneficial for the sporting use during the daytime. This is complemented by the clerestory light at the upper seating level. The roof truss zone defines an area for technical access (catwalks) and technical systems.

Hanging between 1200mm and 2000mm below the main roof are sound-absorbing panels, consisting of high open area metal mesh with 100mm of black tissue faced mineral fibre. This system is very good at providing sound-absorbing performance across the audible frequency range. The panel system also improves low-frequency performance. Sound is absorbed as it propagates up through the panels. It also passes through gaps around the panels and reflects from the underside of the structural roof back onto the sound-absorbing treatment.

Loudspeakers are rigged from the catwalks or roof structure for accessibility and angled accordingly based on the area of seating for which they are providing coverage. A fully distributed system of loudspeakers is used, with the largest loudspeakers at the centre (the furthest distance to the audience), and concentric rings of loudspeakers, each reducing in size, sound power and directionality, to serve the upper areas of the bowl. An additional system of high-power constant directivity horn loudspeakers, optimised for speech clarity, is also provided for voice alarm purposes. This is independently powered, and battery backed up for emergency evacuation measures.

Vertical wall surfaces at each level of the building consist of perforated metal panels with 50mm black tissue faced mineral fibre behind. Sound-absorbing ceilings are provided under balconies and at each level as needed strategically. The clerestory glass is angled upwards, such that sound incidence on it is reflected onto the sound-absorbing ceilings above, rather than being reflected to the other side of the bowl, where they would be heard as echoes or degrade speech intelligibility or music clarity.

Interior view of the bowl with track in place, set up for Berlin Philharmonic concert.

Clerestory windows are angled outwards, so that sound incident on them from the bowl is directed to the sound-absorbing surfaces hanging from the roof.

View of the roof truss system from event floor, house sound system loudspeakers visible between trusses.

100mm sound-absorbing mineral fibre panels in expanded metal mesh, located 1200mm below the roof.

Pala Alpitour

LOCATION: Turin, Italy

ARCHITECT: Arata Isozaki

COMPLETED: 2006

AUDIENCE: approximately 12,000–16,000, depending on configuration

FORM: rectangular arena bowl with seats on all four sides, and one moving seat tier

Designed as the ice hockey arena for the 2007 Winter Olympics, from the outset the need for the arena to be variable to host concerts, trade shows, conventions and other events in legacy mode was imperative.

The room volume is minimised using a box truss arrangement that accommodates all catwalks, technical systems and building services. Stringent environmental noise requirements required a mass-heavy roof construction. This ensured sound insulation targets were achieved to allow unlimited concert use by a future operator.

One entire stand (on a short side of the rectangle) is movable to create a rectangular U-shape space with a flat floor.

Clear plastic seats were the architects' aesthetic preference but presented a challenge as they do not have any sound-absorbing performance. This makes sound system testing, balancing, and event sound-check in the unoccupied or partially occupied condition very difficult. Sound-absorbing treatment was added to the upstands of the terrace to compensate for this.

Hanging sound-absorbing baffles (white) are visible in the roof. Hanging baffles are less efficient than horizontal sound-absorbing treatment and usually not used as a preference – they were developed primarily for use in industrial applications where factories needed daylight coming from above. In this case, the original horizontal sound-absorbing panel design was omitted in a value engineering exercise in the construction documents phase. On completion testing, due to the unacceptable acoustic conditions for PAVA messages and broadcast sound quality, a

View of the interior bowl, during an ice hockey game.

solution needed to be implemented quickly before the start of the Winter Olympics. Although there are a much higher quantity (area) of baffles, they were easier to install by this method. They are 100mm thick sound-absorbing melamine-based foam.

The moving seating bank allows for changes in configuration and capacity. The hanging sound-absorbing baffles (white) are visible above.

Clear seats and sound-absorbing treatment to the upstands of the bowl steps.

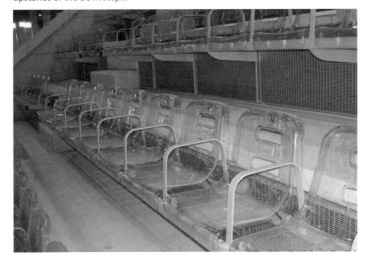

First Direct Arena

LOCATION: Leeds, UK

ARCHITECT: Arup (concept advisor) and Populous (design)

COMPLETED: 2013

AUDIENCE: up to 13,500, depending on configuration

FORM: large fan

The First Direct Arena was created from the need for a large entertainment space with secondary use for sport.

The 'super' fan shape was selected to provide excellent sightlines and bring people as close to the action as possible, reducing the furthest row to 68m compared to 98–110m in a conventional bowl or horseshoe arena. The area immediately in front of the stage can also be converted to a flat floor with 15 rows of retractable seating. This allows some shows and sporting events to come closer to the audience, and for some spectators to view those events from the side.

The arena roof height is reduced as far as practical to minimise the acoustic volume – it extends only above the upper seats to accommodate necessary technical systems, rigging, catwalks and building services. Sound insulation of the roof was crucial given close proximity of noise-sensitive receivers. The roof is multiple layers separated by airspaces with an isolated outer layer to increase the sound insulation performance (see detail).

The inner layer of the roof is a perforated, profiled metal deck with sound-absorbing treatment to the rear, consisting of 100mm thick 48kg/m³ mineral fibre and a 60mm airspace. Sound-absorbing material is provided in the stage house and immediately around the stage, from four metres above finished floor level to the underside of the roof deck, and on the walls consisting of 100mm thick melamine-based foam. It is also found on the side walls and rear walls: 50mm thick melamine-based foam. A mixture of catwalks and a tension wire grid are provided for technical access. Seats are sound-absorbing throughout.

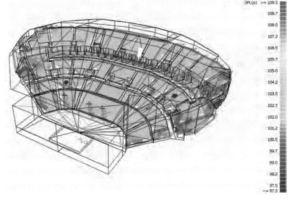

Acoustic model of the arena interior, used to optimise the design of the sound system, and distribution of sound-absorbing treatments.

View of interior fan-shaped arena. Note significant areas of white, sound-absorbing panels on concrete, increasing in density to the front (stage end).

Acoustic model of noise emission from the bowl – a very high sound insulation performance was required to ensure unlimited venue operation, and the model assesses (left) sound transmission through the building envelope (right) to adjacent buildings.

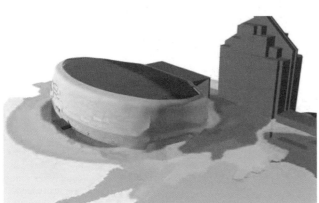

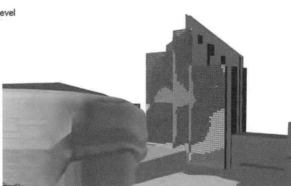

Facade Noise Level
dB(A)

- < 30
- 30 - 32
- 32 - 34
- 34 - 36
- 36 - 38
- 38 - 40
- 40 - 42
- 42 - 44
- 44 - 46
- > 46

Barclays Center

LOCATION: Brooklyn, New York, USA

ARCHITECT: Ellerbe Beckett and SHoP

COMPLETED: 2012

AUDIENCE: approximately 15,000–18,000, depending on configuration

FORM: classic arena bowl with 360-degree seating in plan

The second major arena in New York City (Madison Square Garden having been the sole arena since 1968), it was initially optimised for basketball, concerts and large entertainment events. Ice hockey was added later (and continues to have challenges regarding seating and sightlines due to audience layout).

The major acoustic challenge was the parabolic roof form – chosen for structural efficiency and being lightweight, it results in a larger than ideal acoustic volume, concave sound-focusing surface, and lower than ideal sound insulation performance, given the urban location. These issues required attention immediately after opening, given audience dissatisfaction with the resulting acoustics for events (particularly concerts) as well as noise impacts to the residential environment. A green roof was added to the exterior with optimised airspace, mass and coverage to achieve the sound insulation requirements. Interior acoustics were upgraded by the addition of high-performance sound-absorbing treatments to the roof underside, improving sound-absorbing performance across the audible frequency range. The house sound system was also optimised and improved to allow better coverage to the upper areas of the bowl (difficult to cover with a touring sound system), with signal processing to allow it to be used to supplement touring sound systems. It has since received critical acclaim for acoustic performance.

Interior view of the bowl, with the upper volume visible.

Exterior image of the green roof, added post construction to mitigate environmental noise emission.

View of upper bowl, with added broadband sound-absorbing treatment to underside of roof.

Stadia

Issue	Priority	Comments
Room acoustics	H	In modern sports stadia, the provision of a lively game atmosphere for the patrons and players is the primary aim and should be supported by an architectural form that maximises this experience. Architectural elements throughout the bowl, along with any partial roof or shading design, will have a significant impact on the acoustics and feedback levels between different areas of the crowd. Enclosed/closable roof designs require careful consideration for control of reverberance and volume.
Speech intelligibility	H	Speech needs to be clear and understandable for PAVA announcements and live commentary. It is also critical for PAVA messages and crowd management in emergencies.
Audio systems design	H	A distributed audio system is integrated within the design of most modern stadia, with loudspeaker clusters generally hung at regular intervals from the roof. Infrastructure and rigging points should be considered within the design to allow for the installation of touring systems.
Sound insulation – external	H	Noise from events (both sports and entertainment) should be limited to meet local code requirements. This is a particular challenge for open bowl stadia. Roof elements can help mitigate noise emission through their materiality, elevation and the design of natural ventilation paths.
Sound insulation – internal	M/H	Sensitive areas include VIP boxes, player/performer dressing rooms, offices and media, broadcast and critical emergency response rooms.
Speech privacy	M	Particularly relevant to the sensitive areas noted above.
Impact/vibration isolation	L/M	Vibration isolation of mechanical services equipment (which often must be located close to VIP or broadcast areas) is very important.
Mechanical and electrical noise	M	As above, the control of noise from mechanical services is primarily a concern within VIP and broadcast/media spaces.
Structure-borne noise	L/M	Background noise is usually high enough in most spaces for this not to be a concern. However, some noise-sensitive spaces may still require it. Careful consideration is still key, as rectification later is either complex or impossible.
Environmental noise	H	Control of noise emission from loud events is generally a major project challenge, especially in urban or residential settings, with limits strictly enforced. As these buildings are typically open-air, considerable attention must be paid to both location and orientation in the masterplanning phase to control noise transmitted to sensitive receivers, and to minimise unwanted external sound (e.g. major traffic sources).

H – High   M – Medium   L – Low

Introduction

From the roar that greets a goal to the tense anticipation of the starting gun, the acoustic environment within a stadium is essential to the theatre of sport. Sound systems are critical to the high-fidelity audio content delivered as part of a sporting event, and required for the communication of critical emergency information. The building envelope must mitigate noise emission to a stadium's surrounding environs.

The focus of designing for sports is increasingly geared towards the delivery of an enhanced 'gameday' atmosphere for spectators. This is partially a response to the rapidly improving quality of broadcasting standards that aim to deliver a 'close to the action' experience for those viewing at home. The acoustic environment is a key component of the unrivalled sense of scale, sheer volume and, at times, overwhelming excitement that is experienced by attending a stadium sporting event in person.

Modern-day stadia are complex buildings encompassing different types of space as they typically operate simultaneously as sporting, entertainment, broadcasting and hospitality venues. On top of this, bowl capacity can range from 10,000–120,000 seats.

While these different functions must all be considered during the design process, a stadium's raison d'être must not be forgotten: gameplay. Therefore, the primary acoustic objective concerns the aural relationship between players on the pitch, who need to be able to hear each other and officials, and the fans in the stands, who want to feel the atmosphere around them and also direct that energy towards the team or athlete they are supporting.

Designing a venue to accommodate a range of event types increases year-round revenue, generating further opportunities for the operator. The financial viability of a venue often depends on its capacity to host a range of non-sporting events in the off-season – particularly concerts and other entertainment. Promoters consequently have a detailed knowledge of the options available for touring events, and will choose venues that offer the best environment for the lowest cost in use. The benefits must be balanced against the capital cost of providing additional facilities while infrastructure must be designed to maximise use and profitability. Good acoustic design that does not require special mitigation, and provides easy-to-use sound systems, is preferable.

Architectural style

Early stadia took a range of different formats. In Ancient Greece, Olympia was the site of a stadium amongst a cluster of buildings for sporting events. Meanwhile, the Mayans developed the ball court, the most famous example located in Chichen Itza, whose influence on the space and dimensions of modern stadia can be clearly seen today. The Roman Colosseum even featured a retractable canvas roof that could be configured for a number of events, from gladiator fights to sailing races (during which the arena would be flooded).

The evolution of stadia, from groups of spectators standing close to the action to large-scale buildings, is a good way to consider their broader acoustic development. As a sport with a relatively short match duration, football was originally watched by crowds standing around the pitch. As crowds became larger, elevated stands were introduced to afford better views for these standing spectators. Over time, these stands grew taller in order to accommodate growing crowds of standing spectators and keep them close to the action. Soon roofs were added for weather protection – a development that would have a significant impact upon acoustics. The Kop stand at Liverpool FC's Anfield stadium, built in 1928, is a well-known example, where the low metal roof angled downward causes strong reflections, amplifying the crowd. The sound of the team's anthem 'You'll Never

Walk Alone' is such an important part of the club's identity that when Liverpool FC began considering the design of a new stadium, the acoustic means needed to recreate this atmosphere was a primary objective of the brief.

Steep stands afforded as many people as possible a direct view of the pitch clear of those standing in front. But they also had safety challenges. Following the 1989 Hillsborough disaster, in which spectators were involved in a crowd crush in the standing-only section of the terrace, such stands were banned in FIFA and UK League stadia. More recently, 'Safe Standing' sections have been included in several Major League Soccer (MLS) stadia and European football stadia. With typically larger capacities, these help increase crowd engagement and atmosphere. Acoustics is an important factor in their design.

The all-seater stadiums that began to emerge post-Hillsborough employ safer, more gently inclined stands. This pushes spectators further from players, making their sound as perceived on the pitch weaker. The roof, an important sound-reflecting surface, also moves further from the crowd as a result. Some of these new all-seated designs, many constructed in the mid-90s, were criticised for their lack of atmosphere; often their acoustic performance had not been considered in detail during their design. Some venues responded by installing microphones at the tops of the stands to amplify the crowd and play it back to the lower tiers (this was aided by the improved sound system designs required by emergency announcements, as defined in the UK's 'Guide for Safety at Sports Grounds'). Consequently, good acoustics soon became a design consideration in their own right.

Acoustic features

Since most stadia are not fully enclosed, acoustics should be part of the earliest planning considerations, ensuring that the building's location and orientation will minimise the impact on their surrounding environment. The form of the bowl, and the shaping and materiality of the roof/shading elements in conjunction with natural ventilation paths, will affect crowd noise both inside and outside of the stadium. These elements can also positively contribute to the acoustics and atmosphere within.

The interior of a sports stadium is designed around the seating bowl, which is typically scaled to enclose or be positioned adjacent to the field of competition. Early modern stadia were built for athletics (in many cases for hosting Olympic Games), with their final shape dictated by that of the running track. From this, grandstand seating was then devised to maximise capacity and provide good sightlines to the track. Field sports, meanwhile, were played in the centre of the track, at a significant distance from the stands.

The modern 'football' stadium, the model for most new stadia, is characterised by a much more compact seating bowl, often with multiple seating tiers to bring patrons closer to the playing field. This proximity of the stands to the field can create a more intense atmosphere for both the crowd and players. Roof elements, originally introduced for shading or protection from the weather, are important for pushing sound reflections back to the crowd and athletes. This is most pronounced at the very top rear of the bowl – a critical location for stadium acoustics as higher noise can be generated here (due to close proximity of the crowd to the roof underside), which then propagates down and forward into the crowd. The materiality and shaping of these elements can be optimised to enhance this phenomenon. Known as the '12th man' effect, many players now regard this as a potential competitive advantage.

The following elements of the architectural bowl design can provide significant improvements in the acoustics and enhance the resulting gameday experience for both spectators and players:

- **Proximity to the field of play:** the bowl geometry should be designed to bring the patrons as close to the action as possible. A compact seating bowl will also allow for different areas of the crowd to interact.

- **Shaping of interior architectural elements:** large flat surfaces such as VIP boxes with glazed fronts should be angled downward toward the field. This can provide useful reflections to the players and other areas of the crowd whilst reducing unwanted sound reflections from audio systems propagating across the stadium.

- **Roof/shading elements:** these elements can also be shaped to reflect and distribute acoustic energy back to the crowd and to the field. Careful angling and geometry should be studied early in the design to optimise shaping. The materiality of these elements is also important; lightweight materials such as canvas and ETFE can reduce the structural loads but are mostly acoustically transparent, with sound passing straight through them, except the high frequency that reflects back down. This often gives a harsh nature to the crowd sound, which can be unpleasant when sound builds up in the stands. These also affect sound system response during concert events, and on environmental noise emission.

- **Seating rake:** where feasible, the use of a steeper seating rake pushes spectators closer to the action, providing greater intimacy between the crowd and the field and maximising direct sound.

- **Balconies/tiers:** as with roof elements, the angling and height of the underside of upper seating tiers can be optimised to provide sound reflections and aid the re-distribution of sound energy back into the lower tiers and field of play.

- **Field of play:** some sports, such as cricket, require inter-player verbal communication to be clear. This means environmental noise must be mitigated to ensure this is achieved.

Challenges

A stadium's flexibility for operation as a concert venue must be considered during the project's inception phase. Creating flexible infrastructure, sufficient connectivity and access for set-up and de-installation periods is essential for enticing touring acts.

Environmental noise impact on neighbouring properties and residences represents an ongoing challenge. The limits dictated by local code requirements must not be exceeded during events.

Stadia in more challenging weather environments may require a closable roof or even, in some extreme cases, a fully enclosed/air-conditioned stadium. In the fully enclosed scenario or where the roof is closed for specific periods of time, the same acoustic challenges found within the arena typology will be experienced. Strategic location of sound-absorbing and diffusing finishes should be considered to reduce uncomfortable levels of noise build-up from both the crowd and concert events.

Opportunities

Many new stadia are being designed for ultimate flexibility to house different types of sports fields, often with removable or interchangeable playing surfaces. It is important that this kind of versatility is planned with thought as to how the bowl could also be altered to fit different sporting typologies, while ensuring the requisite crowd atmosphere is maintained.

As in the arena, technology is becoming more and more prevalent within the gameday stadium experience. This is particularly significant for more non-traditional sports, eSports being perhaps the most obvious example. Such events are already being held in large arenas and stadium operators are preparing for the arrival of these competitions in their venues as well. The operation and experience of eSports provide some unique acoustic challenges which venue designers are only just beginning to study and plan for.

City of Manchester Stadium (Etihad Stadium)

LOCATION: Manchester, UK

ARCHITECT: Arup Associates

COMPLETED: 2002

CAPACITY: 55,097

FORM: horseshoe athletics/football, bowl type

The stadium was designed to be constructed in two phases; first as an athletics stadium for the 2002 Commonwealth Games, then converted into a football stadium (becoming home to Manchester City Football Club) by excavating downward to add a lower tier around the bowl and completing the north stand.

Loudspeakers are found at the front edge of the roof, arranged in pairs; one covering the lower terrace, one the upper terrace. There is a six metre band of absorption in the roof to reduce destructive reflections from loudspeakers (optimum location determined using 2D and 3D ray tracing and CATT modelling). A roof angle was determined specifically for the rear terraces to reflect energy from the very rear of the stands down onto the lower stands and the pitch. This has the effect of providing reflected sound energy from the rear spectators to the lower terrace spectators, encouraging them to make more noise. Speech intelligibility of 0.45–0.55 STI was achieved in the unoccupied condition, with a signal to noise ratio of +15dB in the 500, 1000, and 2000 Hz octave bands. A roof curvature in both directions was designed to both focus and distribute sound energy across the stadium. Commentators on match days frequently mention the excitement of the sound in the stadium.

Stand in football mode, with lighting and sound devices discreetly accommodated in the gantry.

Shown here during the Commonwealth Games – note the addition of event and overlay lights and sound system in the roof gantry.

View of concourse areas, sound-absorbing panels (white) and loudspeakers for PAVA (black) visible above the doors.

Allianz Arena

LOCATION: Munich, Germany

ARCHITECT: Herzog and de Meuron

COMPLETED: 2005

CAPACITY: 75,000

FORM: 360-degree bowl

The home of FC Bayern Munich, the stadium is primarily used for football.

In the early concept planning phases, options were developed for the stadium roof to be enclosed in order to hold large-scale concert events without weather disruption. This, in conjunction with the need to ensure that the pitch received sufficient daylight to ensure grass growth, was a key driver in the selection of ETFE as the roof material. This was subsequently used to wrap the entire building envelope. It is vital to the stunning lighting and visual identity of the stadium.

Unfortunately, the selection of ETFE presented a significant acoustic challenge. ETFE is transparent to sound at frequencies below approximately 2000Hz, i.e. sound passes straight through it (in this regard it has a low sound insulation value and a high sound-absorbing performance since the sound escapes into the surrounding environment). The lack of sound insulation was not an issue, given that there are no noise sensitive receivers around the stadium. However, a significant concern was raised, and confirmed through analysis, that the sound of the crowd – generating the gameday atmosphere – would be lost. To counteract this, retractable sound-reflecting blinds can be deployed to the underside of the roof on game days to ensure that the crowd sound is reflected back into the stadium (these blinds are often erroneously referenced as a sun-shading device).

ETFE was a feature of the design from the competition stage, with its lighting providing unique identity, and to let daylight onto the pitch.

Retractable sound-reflecting panels in place under the ETFE to ensure that crowd noise is contained and enhanced in the bowl.

The sound-reflecting panels in the process of retraction; they are stored in the bowl at the rear of the upper stands.

National Stadium

LOCATION: Singapore

ARCHITECT: Arup Associates

COMPLETED: 2014

CAPACITY: 55,000

FORM: 360-degree bowl

Incorporating the largest domed roof in the world, with a retractable centre section roof as well as mechanised, automated retractable seating configurations, it is the only stadium custom designed to host football, rugby, cricket, athletics and large-scale entertainment events in existence.

The retractable roof is an essential component in ensuring the building can be used year round, rain or shine, given the local climate. The design of the roof was contingent on a site surrounded by no noise sensitive receivers. As a result, a mass heavy, high sound insulating roof construction was not required, allowing the dome to be built with a lightweight profiled metal deck system with the moving sections in ETFE. The dome creates a very large acoustical volume, so the underside of the solid roof was treated with sound-absorbing material incorporated into the roof design. The sound system was optimised to ensure good coverage to seats in the upper areas of the bowl, especially for touring concerts. Touring productions are given the operators' recommended sound system design guidelines to ensure that a high-quality concert experience can be achieved.

The National Stadium is part of the complex Singapore Sports Hub, which also incorporates an Olympic swimming pool, sports halls and other sports amenities.

View of stadium showing the retractable ETFE roof and solid roof areas. The roof did not have high sound insulation requirements as there were no noise sensitive receivers in the vicinity.

Stadium in concert mode; given the size of the space, it requires additional sound system infrastructure to be provided for large-scale concert events.

6.3

Concert Halls

Issue	Priority	Comments
Room acoustics	H	The quality of the sound experience for both performers and audience is vital to the success of the building. Determining the desired acoustic characteristics of the hall (reverberance, clarity, intimacy, envelopment, richness, warmth, etc.) impacts the shape and form. The degree of flexibility required to accommodate a variety of genres influences the fabric of the hall, from surface articulation to material selections, moving elements, and the integration of electronic enhancement systems.
Speech intelligibility	M	Variable acoustics and audio systems for speech reinforcement are required so that multiple uses (e.g. conferences, graduation ceremonies) can be supported without detracting from the acoustic quality for orchestral music.
Audio systems design	H	Amplified sound use is continuing to increase. Technology infrastructure must allow for easy replacement over time.
Sound insulation – external	H	The performers and audience must be free of distraction from noise generated outside the building (e.g. due to traffic, building services, rain, ambient noise specific to the site). This requires a combination of mass-heavy materials, multiple layers of lightweight constructions separated by substantial airspaces, separation of noise sensitive spaces using buffer zones, and occasionally structural isolation of the building. Acoustically treat penetrations of the building envelope (e.g. access points, building services routes), and between spaces.
Sound insulation – internal	H	The performers and audience must also be protected from noise generated outside the performance space (e.g. other performance and rehearsal facilities, front-of-house and back-of-house activities and circulation). Separate noise sensitive spaces from noise producing spaces using buffer zones, which will facilitate more efficient (and reduced cost) building construction elements.
Speech privacy	M	Some spaces (conductor, soloist, audition rooms) may require careful control of sound transmission to other spaces. Agree specific requirements early in the design.
Impact/vibration isolation	H	Vibration can propagate vertically and horizontally through the building structure, and manifest as noise in sensitive spaces. Sources include footfalls, doors slamming, building services and hydraulics, and vertical transportation. Control vibration at the source.
Mechanical and electrical noise	H	Quiet background noise levels (typically PNC15, NR15) involve significant spatial allowances for sound insulation (to control noise transfer from internal and external sources), structural isolation (to control structure-borne noise) and HVAC noise control (to accommodate low-velocity, low-noise systems and reduce airflow-generated noise). Other sources of noise include lighting equipment with integral battery chargers, transformers, dimmers, relays and ballasts, and theatre technical equipment (flying systems, moving elements, show control equipment). Acoustic testing and approval are required before use, and separate power supply is required for audio, lighting, theatre systems/rigging to avoid cross-contamination of system noise.
Structure-borne noise	H	Vibration can propagate through the ground into the building structure and re-radiate from the surfaces of the hall, where it is heard as a low-frequency rumble. Sources include rail and road traffic, movable structures, service roads and tunnels. Identify existing and future vibration sources early in the design. If affected, the building may require vibration isolation. This has space-planning, architectural, structural, building services, constructability and cost implications.
Environmental noise	M/H	Noise sources from the building include mechanical plant, music, patrons, commercial vehicles. Assess in accordance with national, regional and local codes and treat appropriately through design and planning measures.

H – High   M – Medium   L – Low

Introduction

Concert and recital halls as we know them today are auditoria primarily designed with optimal interior acoustic characteristics for unamplified orchestral and choral music performance. These are generally free of noise intrusion from the exterior, and have low internal noise from building systems (HVAC, etc.). In name, they are differentiated primarily by audience size and performer capacity. Concert halls typically accommodate orchestras of up to approximately 110 musicians and audiences of 1,600–2,000 seats. Recital halls can range in seating capacity from 200–1,600 seats, usually in the 500–1,100 range, and are often designed for smaller performer ensembles.

Increasingly, modern halls are venues for more than just a single style of symphonic or chamber music. They have branched out to include amplified music, comedy, dance and semi-staged opera and even become frequent choices for conferences and graduation ceremonies. This poses challenges in ensuring the venue is flexible enough to cope with these varying demands without detracting from the acoustic qualities required for the primary use.

Architectural style

As a building form, concert and recital halls developed over the centuries from a series of different spaces, originally designed for other purposes which were also used for music performance.

Early Western religious buildings (basilicas, churches and cathedrals) derived their plan form and height from those of Solomon's Temple. As architectural and engineering technology developed, these dimensions were often scaled up, resulting in the cube, double cube (often referred to as the 'shoebox') and quadruple cube, while keeping the overall proportions the same. The form is also the foundation for the common spaces in the great palaces of Europe; the jewel box, ball court, ballroom and great hall.

As architectural and engineering technology developed, so did the design and complexity of musical instruments, and along with these the ability of composers to create ever more intricate works. Composers were often commissioned to create works for special events, to be performed in specific places. As a result, the compositions were rehearsed in these venues, modified based on what the composer heard, and finally performed in these spaces, making the music and architecture part of the whole composition. The composer would use the architecture dynamically to push the music to the edge – something that we often forget today. Many classical compositions would, at the time of their premiere, have been the equivalent of a spectacular rock concert seen today. Did the music shape the architecture, or did the architecture shape the music? The answer is that they probably both influenced each other. What does seem clear is that the architecture and the finishes were shaped to take account of what was heard and optimised to ensure the best listening experience.

By the late 19th century, purpose-built concert halls were established as a separate building type of their own, and their design developed from precedent. Vienna's 'Musikverein' of 1870 was modelled on the 'Redoutensaal' ballroom in the Hofburg royal palace. The Amsterdam 'Concertgebouw' of 1888 was developed from the 'Neues Gewandhaus' in Leipzig, completed in 1884. These halls, still considered to be amongst the best-sounding concert halls in the world, share some basic characteristics that deliver their great sound:

- A single room – audience and performers located within the same architectural volume
- Rectilinear shoebox form of modest overall size and narrow width
- Relatively flat floor
- High performer platform

- One very shallow balcony located in the lower third of the room

- A tall unobstructed volume

- Architectural detailing that is relatively flat and sound-reflecting at low level, becoming increasingly detailed, complex and sound-diffusing towards the top – statues, mouldings, pilasters, columns, coffers and fine detailing promote strong sound reflections, creating a nicely blended (diffuse) sound that comes from the top of the room back down to the audience. The sound-reflecting and diffusing components can be matched in scale to the frequency of sound in the musical spectrum.

It is important to note that the sound is not the same in all locations in the room. It varies, and allows the listener to choose their preferred location, which is a matter of subjective taste. The characteristics of the sound are a result of where and when sound reflections arrive at the ears of the listener.

Our ears are also particularly sensitive to sound arriving from the side ('lateral sound'), which provides a sense of spaciousness or envelopment, and sound coming from behind, as well as behind and above us. A music space that achieves this optimally is not only pleasing to the brain but can also result in physical reactions (e.g. the hair standing up on the back of one's neck). Furthermore, the ear is very sensitive to sound that arrives within a short time after the direct sound emanating from a source, which increases the intimacy and clarity of music. Sound that arrives slightly later can create a sense of 'richness' and reverberance if it is blended well.

Equally important is the absence of acoustic faults. Echoes, poor timbre or tonal quality, coloration or distortion (harshness, dullness) can all detract from the quality of sound. Performers must be able to hear each other for good ensemble playing, and the audience must be free of distraction from noises outside or within the space.

There are many factors that influence our perception of music in a concert hall and individual preferences may change depending on the style of music being played. In other words, there is no such thing as a perfect acoustic any more than there is a perfect wine.

Shape and form

In smaller halls (<1,000 seats) it is generally easier to achieve good acoustic conditions, with larger halls (particularly >2,000 seats) posing greater acoustic challenges. As the seat count increases, the room must become longer, wider, or have a greater proportion of seats with balconies above (or a combination of all three). A wide room results in the important side wall reflection becoming too weak; a long room places the furthest listeners too far away from the performers and the overall sound level becomes too quiet; rooms with large numbers of balconies will create a 'distant', 'disconnected' sound quality for seats underneath the overhang. Ultimately, economic considerations around viable audience numbers will be a driving factor in determining the hall size.

Over the past 50 years, two main typologies of concert halls have emerged: shoebox (or frontal) halls where the audience is located in front of the stage in a rectangular, narrow hall with a tall unobstructed volume (typically close to a 'double cube' in shape); and 'surround' (aka 'vineyard') type halls where the audience is distributed around the orchestra in smaller seating sections and the room is shaped and sized to provide reflections to individual seating sections via a combination of the outer room boundary and intermediate dividing surfaces between seating sections.

Within these broad typologies there are variations, the key factors being the proportion of audience that is seated behind the stage, and that which is seated underneath balcony overhangs. Seats behind the orchestra have a distinctly different sound character because of the directionality of instruments; some instruments are much weaker at these seats while others (particularly French horn) are much stronger, which changes the balance between sections. Some audience members find the proximity to the orchestra and the ability to see the conductor more clearly to be exciting, while others dislike the changed instrumental balance in these seats.

Halls with no overhangs allow all seats direct access to the upper room volume. This is beneficial in terms of the perceived reverberance and immersive quality, but means that the room occupies a greater plan area for the same seat count which increases the proportion of seats that are further away from the stage. Halls with balconies decrease the average distance from audience to the orchestra at the cost of the acoustic quality of the overhung seats.

Determining the desired acoustic characteristics or 'personality' of the hall is one of the most critical early decisions to be made, as this is dependent on the form and shape. Typically, shoebox halls have acoustic reflection patterns that are dense with multiple early reflections, resulting in a clear, intimate sound with a greater sense of envelopment, but low perceived reverberance. They are suited to medium to large-sized concert halls (from around 500–2,000 seats). Surround form is better suited to very large halls because the average distance between a listener and the stage can be reduced. These halls tend to have a lower sense of intimacy and clarity. They can sound less enveloping, but the perceived reverberance is usually more audible – in these rooms the balance of direct sound to reverberant sound from the upper parts of the room is a crucial success factor.

The question of form is less important for small concert or recital halls (<500 seats), for which sufficient lateral energy typically occurs regardless of hall shape. However, avoiding excessive loudness is important for these halls, particularly if large ensembles are to be accommodated (e.g. orchestral rehearsal or recording halls), and room forms that can create significant focusing of sound, or conversely areas that lack sound, must be carefully considered.

Room geometry

The room volume is the primary location where the room reverberance develops via multiple reflections of sound. More sophisticated halls may include secondary coupled acoustic volumes in addition to the 'primary' volume containing the audience.

Choral or organ music requires more reverberance than symphonic music, which requires more reverberance than chamber, jazz, world or amplified music. The type of music with the longest reverberation requirement will usually drive the overall size of the room.

Primary sound-reflecting surfaces (mainly at lower level) are used to direct early sound reflections into the audience. These surfaces must avoid too much sound being 'pushed' onto the audience, which is sound-absorbing and will 'starve' the reverberant sound of energy.

To be useful for clarity and intimacy, sound from primary sound-reflecting surfaces should arrive at the audience within 80ms following the direct sound from the orchestra.

To achieve a sense of envelopment and spaciousness, the reverberant sound should reach seats from multiple directions. The direction from which sound arrives is important, with reflections arriving at the audience from the side (lateral reflections) being strongly preferred.

The distance from the orchestra to the audience should be kept as low as possible and no greater than 40m to the furthest seat to avoid the sound becoming too quiet.

The overall scale and shape of the room influences the degree to which the audience is exposed to the reverberant sound energy. The distribution of early sound energy from the orchestra into the audience affects the strength of sound.

The locations and angling of surfaces, such as balcony fronts and control room windows, must be carefully considered so that reflections from these surfaces do not disturb adjacent audience members or cause echoes back to stage.

Surface finishes

Typically, materials in a concert hall are sound-reflecting (except for the audience seating). Heavy surface constructions reflect bass sound energy, which contributes to the reverberant sound at low frequencies, influencing the 'warmth' of the sound.

Surface detailing and roughness of materials has a significant influence in diffusing sound – very smooth surfaces reflect sound like a mirror, while profiled surfaces redirect sound in multiple directions. It is important to ensure sufficient sound-diffusing detail, especially above the audience, to avoid harsh or strident-sounding instruments ('acoustic glare').

The physical scale of the surface irregularities determines which frequencies will be scattered, with larger-scale irregularities scattering lower frequencies, and smaller-scale details scattering higher frequencies. The required amounts and locations of sound-diffusing finishes must be driven by the desired acoustic aesthetic of the room.

The quantity of sound-diffusing surface must be carefully determined – too much can effectively have a sound-absorbing effect, weakening the sound.

The high reverberation time required for orchestral music decreases the sound quality for speech or amplified music usages. Modern halls typically include variable sound-absorbing components such as curtains or banners, tuned bass absorbers, or moving ceiling or wall components which can change the dimensions or overall room volume to tune the room to a specific performance type.

The size of the stage platform, the distribution of the orchestra on it, and the sound-reflecting surfaces surrounding the orchestra (particularly side walls) influence ensemble playing (or the ability of the orchestra to hear themselves and each other) and the ability to gauge audience perception of the sound.

Flexibility to move or resize stage elements allows a wider range of musical ensembles and repertoire to be accommodated without distorting the sound quality.

Quiet background noise levels allow a greater dynamic range of the music. This increases the impact of loud passages and allows orchestras to play exceptionally quietly while still being heard.

A low background noise level increases the requirement for sound insulation (and structural isolation of the hall) to avoid external noise disturbance to the hall.

Challenges

Achieving the right balance of architectural aesthetic and acoustic character requires close coordination and development of the shape, form and surface finishes from the very earliest stages of the project. The best-designed concert halls incorporate the acoustic finishes as an inherent part of the architecture rather than having the acoustic features appear 'bolted on'.

It is also important to consider the psychological impression certain material choices create. Halls of the late 19th and early 20th centuries, although mostly made of masonry materials, are usually rich in decoration and colours (extensive use of golds, reds, etc.). In more modern venues the increased use of wood gave rise to the adage (often used for performance spaces) that 'wood is good'. Increasing cognitive research, coupled with auralisation approaches, are investigating the impact of architectural style, colour, lighting and materials on perceived acoustics. This research will be increasingly useful to the collective design team as it develops.

Contemporary considerations including circulation space, physical comfort expectations, accessibility and inclusivity, sustainability and fire safety all have the potential to impact acoustic quality and must be integrated into the design at the earliest opportunity.

Control of unwanted noise from internal and external noise and vibration sources requires space planning for sound insulating constructions, large ductwork for low-speed air movement and attenuation treatments, and (frequently) structural isolation of the hall. Typically, a generous building net to gross ratio of 1.6 is required.

Opportunities

Advancements in contemporary computational methods, and particularly the development of tools like auralisation, which present the predicted acoustical performance in audio format, allow greater participation in the design and decision-making process. Architects, designers, stakeholders and musicians can align expectations and communicate through shared critical listening experiences.

Active acoustic systems (or active architecture systems) allow room reflections and reverberance to be generated electronically, and were initially developed to fix acoustic defects (the first being an 'assisted resonance' system to improve the poor bass reverberation in the Royal Festival Hall, London, UK). Although these systems have been resisted by more traditional arts organisations, who prefer a 'natural' acoustic sound, their sophistication and realism has

improved dramatically and they provide considerable flexibility for multi-purpose venues and those that must accommodate wide varieties of musical performance styles. They are increasingly embraced by composers as a creative tool. As a result, they are becoming further integrated as an expected audio system in certain halls.

Technology continues to increase in use and is being implemented excitingly and creatively within traditional orchestral concerts, amplified events and hybrid events (e.g. live performance of film soundtracks with orchestra). Changing demographics mean that amplified music events are likely to comprise a greater proportion of use for concert halls. Technological infrastructure must be carefully planned and must allow for easy replacement over time. The ability to easily connect or deploy new technology in or on the architecture will be a continued design challenge. Furthermore, the use of spatial sound, augmented reality (AR) and virtual reality (VR) as part of the performance experience is ever-increasing in scope and possibility. For emerging composers and creators, the boundaries between amplified, unamplified, technological and 'natural' sound are becoming increasingly blurred and will continue to have an impact on the evolution of the concert hall for many years to come.

As spaces that embody our cultural heritage – past, present and future – the success of a concert hall is increasingly more than just an architectural statement or the quality of sound for performers and audience. The question is, what experience do we want to create, and how should it sound?

The first public concert halls were built in the late 19th century in the shoebox form; the name referring to the double cube rectilinear shape. The three most well-known examples, widely regarded as the best concert halls in the world acoustically, are Vienna's Großer Musikvereinssaal, or Great Hall, sometimes also called the Goldener Saal (Golden Hall) (inaugurated in 1870, 1,774 seats and approximately 300 standing places), Amsterdam's Concertgebouw (inaugurated in 1888, 1,974 seats), and Boston Symphony Hall (inaugurated in 1900, 2,625 seats). They are celebrated for warm and rich acoustics, sounding intimate (you feel very close to the musicians even though you may be physically far away), and being enveloping (the rooms promote sound reflections coming from all around the listener). The architects for the hall in Boston conducted a tour of European halls before design began. They followed these European designs closely, except for the addition of a second balcony and angled walls around the stage to push the sound out into the audience. Re-seated at modern seating standards, these halls would reduce in capacity by approximately one-third of their seat count. Spectators are packed tightly together mainly on the floor in front of the orchestra platform and on the narrow side balconies.

After 1945, many cities around the world built new halls. Economic viability (requiring ticket sales to theoretically cover costs) was often a key factor in driving seat counts higher. New seating, comfort and safety standards required larger seats, greater row-to-row spacing and wider aisles. In these three great halls the floors are predominantly flat. Sightlines as you get further away from the stage are a challenge. At the back of the halls you can only see the head and shoulders of the musicians. This is not an issue acoustically; in fact, it is one of the key advantages. But in the new era of hall building, it was not considered appropriate as ticket buyers would expect to have much better views of the performers. As the seating rake increases, the lateral sound reflection balance in a hall is reduced. In some cases, these decisions were made after design was well underway. Avery Fisher Hall in New York is one example, where the solution was to add a third balcony and deeper rear balconies into a volume similar to the three great halls. Adding so many seats increases the amount of sound-absorbing treatment in the room, but also takes away the important upper volume, which is key for generating the rich reverberant and diffuse sound. Some halls packed too much into a volume that was too small. Some got much bigger, and the balance of direct sound, to early reflected sound, to late diffuse reverberance, began to change. Modern acoustic science was employed in attempt to bolster the richness of the acoustics. The science showed that the acoustics of a small hall could not be replicated when dimensions are increased beyond a certain point.

Many halls built in the period between 1945 and 1990 were criticised for having 'poor' acoustics in comparison to the three great halls. In the latter years of the 20th century there was a return to building smaller halls, with capacities close to 2,000 seats, where excellent acoustics can be achieved. There has also been some reappraisal of the sound of some of the previously criticised halls. By understanding that these halls do not necessarily have 'poor' acoustics, but simply a different sound to the shoebox, this allows them to be used in a way that maximises their positive acoustic features.

Generic sketches of the six general large concert hall
typologies, some example halls for each, and a comparison
of their corresponding acoustic attributes.

SHOEBOX

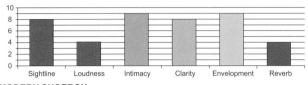

SHOEBOX
Carnegie Hall, New York, USA
Boston Symphony Hall, Boston, USA
Avery Fisher Hall, New York, USA
The Sage, Gateshead, UK

MODERN SHOEBOX

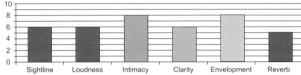

MODERN SHOEBOX
Birmingham Symphony Hall, Birmingham, UK
Bridgewater Hall, Manchester, UK

SHOEBOX – ARENA

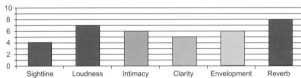

SHOEBOX – ARENA
Concert Hall, Sydney Opera House, Sydney, Australia
Suntory, Tokyo, Japan
Town Hall, Christchurch, New Zealand

ARENA – VINEYARD

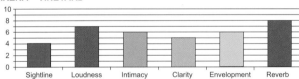

ARENA – VINEYARD
Sala Santa Sicilia, Rome, Italy
Sapporo Concert Hall, Sapporo, Japan

VINEYARD

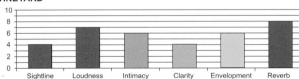

VINEYARD
Disney Concert Hall, Los Angeles, USA
Boettcher Hall, Denver, USA
Paris Concert Hall, Paris, France

FULL SURROUND

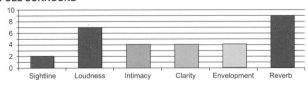

FULL SURROUND
Berlin Philharmonie, Berlin, Germany
St. David's Hall, Cardiff, Wales

Comparison of subjective
parameters for concert
hall design.

Comparison of concert
hall form evolution.

Großer Musikvereinssaal (Great Hall)

LOCATION: Vienna, Austria

ARCHITECT: Theophil Hansen

COMPLETED: 1870

AUDIENCE: 2,074

FORM: shoebox with one side balcony, two rear balconies

The first public concert hall of the classic shoebox halls, and widely considered to be one of the three best concert halls in the world acoustically.

View to front of hall, with decorative sound-diffusing surface finishes.

The room is designed predominantly in acoustically 'hard' materials – brick, plaster and wood. It is a double cube shoebox form featuring clerestory windows. An unobstructed upper volume, shallow balcony overhangs at the sides and no balcony overhang to the rear mean the majority of seats receive good sound direct from the performers, early lateral (side) sound reflections, sound reflections from the rear wall, and exposure to rich reverberant sound from above.

Wall finishes are relatively flat and sound-reflecting at low level, to promote strong lateral and rear sound energy. Higher up there are increasingly decorative sound-diffusing surface finishes scaled to the frequencies in the musical spectrum, which promote good blending of sound as it travels through the room to the listener. The coffered ceiling and finishes are highly sound-diffusing at high frequency, reducing harshness, and there are some tapestries hung in key locations to temper middle and high frequency sounds. The flat floor is good for acoustics but has some challenging sightlines as you move further back in the hall. The seats are simple with light upholstery, which minimises sound-absorbing properties. There are some tapestries hung in key locations to temper high-frequency sound reflections.

View of underside of balcony, with sound-diffusing finish and tapestries in front of parterre boxes.

Boston Symphony Hall

LOCATION: Boston, MA, USA

ARCHITECT: McKim, Mead and White

COMPLETED: 1900

AUDIENCE: 2,625

FORM: shoebox with two balconies

Symphony Hall is widely considered the best concert hall in the Americas and one of the top three halls worldwide.

View looking to the front of the hall, with minimal finishes on the walls at low level.

Modelled on the Leipzig Neues Gewandhaus of 1884, the crucial innovation at Boston Symphony Hall was the involvement of pioneering acoustician Wallace Sabine, which made Symphony Hall the first concert hall designed on a scientific basis using Sabine's research into the theory of reverberation. This allowed the required ceiling height (and thus overall volume) to be calculated rather than relying on precedent or guesswork.

The notable acoustic features are very similar to the hall in Vienna (see previous Case Study). Key differences include shallow balcony overhangs on both the sides and the rear, and sound-transparent balcony fronts. Around the orchestra, the ceiling height is lower, and predominantly sound-reflecting to improve stage acoustics. Walls are also angled in this area to help push sound towards the rear.

View to the rear of the hall, showing rear balconies and large uninterrupted upper volume.

Bridgewater Hall

LOCATION: Manchester, UK

ARCHITECT: RHWL Partnership

COMPLETED: 1996

AUDIENCE: 2,341

FORM: hybrid shoebox/surround with three balconies

Built to replace the unsatisfactory acoustics of the Hallé Orchestra's previous home, the new Bridgewater Hall has proved successful.

The hall form is an innovative blend of two typologies; a basic rectilinear shoebox plan form, with narrow balconies to the rear, sides and immediately in front of the stage, and a vineyard terrace seating arrangement towards the rear of the room, allowing a higher seat count than usual in a shoebox hall. Subdivided audience spaces have high walls surrounding them to enhance early reflections in each area. Exposed structural beams and concrete coffers in the upper room volume are sound-diffusing, and help minimise the overall external building height. An array of sound-reflecting panels above the stage provide early reflections to help the orchestra hear each other, while also allowing sound to pass around and into the upper volume to contribute to reverberant sound energy. The hall is structurally isolated from the surrounding building and noise environment (there is a surface tram system that runs on an embedded street rail in the immediate vicinity of the site, as well as traditional commuter trains close by). This provides extremely high control of exterior noise in the hall. Mechanical noise was minimised by locating the primary equipment in a 'tower' structure separate to the main building with flexible connections to all systems.

View to stage, with shallow balcony overhangs on both sides.

Detail of ventilation, provided by underfloor plenum, through slots.

View to rear; note the vineyard-style seating that can be seen within the rectilinear plan form.

Detail of vibration isolator – given the close proximity of a surface train line, the entire building is floated on vibration-isolating springs.

Detail of basement, showing that the bottom stair in the isolated structure does not touch the lower structure.

Railway Vibration Joint (RVJ)
No rigid links
Refer to Building Manager

Signage detail to ensure that maintenance does not bridge the vibration isolation joint, which would result in noise from the train being audible in the building.

Detail showing the isolation of ductwork as it enters the isolated structure.

Snape Maltings

LOCATION: Aldeburgh, UK

ARCHITECT: Arup Associates

COMPLETED: 1968, 1997
(refurbished by Penoyre & Prasad)

AUDIENCE: 826

FORM: shoebox, steep rake, pitched roof

Conversion of an old maltings house into a concert hall, undertaken by Arup Associates for Benjamin Britten.

The existing brick structure was increased in height to achieve sufficient room volume. Having had the interior grit-blasted, it retained a rough finish with good mid – high frequency diffusion. The roof was replaced and, in keeping with the malt house style, the angle was optimised to give early reflections for an increased sensation of room height. This also provided good sound diffusion at varying scales – assisted by the structure being exposed. The seating rake is steep as it was necessary to accommodate other spaces below. This decision also drove the determination of the height of the walls and room design. The seats themselves are simple with no upholstery. The room is also remarkable in that it uses a partially assisted natural ventilation approach. The heat from the audience and lights causes the air in the space to rise and it is naturally vented to the outside via the sound-attenuated chimneys on top. Cool air is drawn in from the side of the building as a result. In the summer months, the process is fan-assisted and the air can also be cooled.

Detail of grit-blasted brickwork that provides sound diffusion at mid and high frequencies.

View of hall, with
steep seating rake,
from rear stage.

View from rear seats.

Detail of the
simple seating.

Exterior view; note
roof-mounted hoods
used for the natural
ventilation system.

Sage Gateshead

LOCATION: Gateshead, UK

ARCHITECT: Foster + Partners

COMPLETED: 2004

AUDIENCE: 1,650

FORM: modified shoebox

The Sage Gateshead is the primary home of the Royal Northern Sinfonia (a chamber orchestra of up to 80 musicians), and it also serves a diverse community, both economically and sustainably.

The design brief for the hall required the capability to accommodate a full symphony orchestra and chorus, as well as conferences, rock and pop, jazz, and folk music, in addition to the Royal Northern Sinfonia itself. The shoebox form was selected as optimal. The primary inspiration of the room dimensions and form, and key aspects of the design, take their cue from the three great halls, delivered in a modern architectural style.

The building contains three performance spaces and a music school, and is close to an adjacent rail line. The individual halls are not structurally isolated; however, they are separated from each other by two structural breaks that run the entire height of the building. The external shell is connected only at the basement slab.

The ceiling consists of six individual panels that can be moved independently. These are used to change the ceiling reflection sequence and adjust support on stage, or are brought together to reduce the room volume for smaller-scale performances or those requiring less reverberance, while maintaining the architectural consistency of the room design. Sound-absorbing curtains consisting of two layers of wool serge drapes are spaced 500mm from the wall. They can cover 85% of the wall area, located in pockets located at either side of the doors in each level of the hall. These systems are all operated with a series of pre-sets for different hall configurations. The in-house sound system can support all performance types and is deployed through doors in one of the ceiling panels, so they can be removed for unamplified events.

Loudspeakers deployed through ceiling panel.

View of the isolation joint from level 3 looking down; cut in the balustrade and floor, visible adjacent to the fire extinguisher.

View to stage, showing sound-absorbing curtains deployed.

View from the stage to the rear of the hall.

National Forum of Music

LOCATION: Wrocław, Poland

ARCHITECT: Kuryłowicz and Associates

COMPLETED: 2015

AUDIENCE: 1,800

FORM: shoebox with three balconies and coupled volume chambers

One of the most highly regarded modern concert halls, the National Forum of Music is gaining widespread acclaim for its acoustics.

The 1,800-seat concert hall was designed to have a recognisable 'signature sound' inspired by the musical history of Wroclaw and its traditions of Baroque and ecclesiastical music.

Secondary acoustic volumes located behind the stage and on the upper side walls allow the intensity and spatial character of the reverberant sound to be adjusted. This is done by changing the degree to which the 34 motorised doors (that connect the secondary volumes to the main room) are open. Twenty-two suspended reflector panels above the stage and audience act as 'valves' that allow the amount of coupling between the lower room volume and the upper room volume to be adjusted, providing further variability to the amount and location of reverberation. These reflectors also allow the balance and support between sections of the orchestra to be adjusted.

The narrow room shape and stacked balconies provide a rich sequence of lateral sound reflections to seats, and provide clarity and immediacy to the sound. A motorised system of sound-absorbing curtains and banners can be deployed to cover part, or all, of the wall surfaces and change reverberation and surface reflectivity, allowing the room to be used for either smaller-scale or amplified performances.

A variable-sized orchestral platform and hydraulic lifts allow flexibility in the size of the stage, allowing use of the hall for dance and semi-staged opera performance as well as a 'reverse mode' for small-scale performances, where audience members are seated on stage and in the choir stalls. An extremely quiet background noise level (approximately at the human threshold of hearing) and high-performance sound insulation constructions preserve the impact of musical performances.

View to the rear of the hall.

There is sound-diffusing
treatment to the wall
of the lower stalls, and
each seat has a pedestal
diffuser with air supplied
from a plenum below.

View to the front
of the hall.

Appel Room,
Jazz at Lincoln Center

LOCATION: New York, USA

ARCHITECT: Rafael Viñoly Architects

COMPLETED: 2004

AUDIENCE: 483

FORM: amphitheatre

One of New York's most iconic venues, the Appel Room at Jazz at Lincoln Center features a glass wall behind the performers providing views out over Central Park.

Flexible seating systems provide an immersive performance and broadcast experience for audiences of between 300 and 600 people. An electroacoustic enhancement system allows the performance environment to be adjusted to suit the repertoire, and provides ensemble support for musicians. Mechanical seating risers allow the venue to convert from flat floor to tiered seating modes. The acoustically transparent balcony fronts prevent focusing from the concave room shape. Large airgap double glazing prevents external noise from being audible within the venue. Suspended acoustic panels concealed above an acoustically transparent visual ceiling absorb late sound energy, to prevent disturbing echoes and improve clarity.

View to the front of the hall, with a glass wall behind the stage.

View from the side of the amphitheatre arrangement.

Angela Burgess Recital Hall, Royal Academy of Music

LOCATION: London, UK

ARCHITECT: Ian Ritchie Architects

COMPLETED: 2018

AUDIENCE: 100

FORM: rectangular

The new Angela Burgess Recital Hall at the Royal Academy of Music was created as part of major refurbishments of the 1911 Royal Academy building. Due to the heritage restrictions of the Crown Estate, the hall (located directly above the opera theatre) could not be visible from surrounding public areas.

The overall room shape maximises the acoustic volume within the heritage building height constraints to create the rich reverberant sound. The angled roof sections also provide lateral sound reflections to increase the spaciousness of the room. Sound-diffusing surface finishes on the lower walls blend the early sound. Exposed roof beams within the hall maximise the available volume, acting to disrupt and blend the ceiling sound reflections. A flexible curtain system allows the acoustics of the hall to be adjusted to suit the performance. Structural isolation of the recital hall prevents noise transmission between the hall and the theatre below.

Ceiling detail – structure is internal to maximise available room acoustic volume.

View to the front of the hall from the stage, note sound-diffusing finishes. Note the angled upper walls and ceiling details.

National Sawdust

LOCATION: Brooklyn, New York, USA

ARCHITECT: Bureau V

COMPLETED: 2015

AUDIENCE: 200 seated, 350 standing

FORM: rectangular

Conceived by founder Kevin Dolan, this project was required to deliver the highest-quality chamber music experience, as well as hybrid forms of new music including amplified instruments and spatial audio.

National Sawdust was intended as a space where young artists could develop their work: to perform it for an audience, record live shows if desired, and use the venue as a recording studio. An initial concept was developed to fit these requirements by Bureau V, designed to fit on a standard lot in Williamsburg. The search for a site yielded a former sawdust factory. The exterior brick envelope was retained, and an isolated box-in-box recital space created to mitigate noise and vibration from the nearby subway. The resulting hall has received widespread critical acclaim for its acoustics and design, and the cutting-edge programming delivered.

An isolated masonry box forms the outer volume while inner sound-transparent metal skin is the architectural expression. In the cavity between these two layers, sound-absorbing curtains can be deployed to change the room acoustics. There is flexible flat floor space, with areas that can be raised to create a platform during side stage and end stage formats. There is a conventional house sound system as well as a full spatial audio system to allow new forms of electronic music, and to use as an active architecture system to vary the room reverberance.

View of the lobby to the hall. Seen to the right is a vertical sliding door that allows the hall to be coupled to the lobby for events, and also acts as a dramatic 'unveiling' of the room for arriving audience.

The view of the hall interior, from the upper balcony.

Milton Court, London

LOCATION: Barbican, London, UK

ARCHITECT: Aedas

COMPLETED: 2013

AUDIENCE: 625

FORM: shoebox with one balcony

Designed for use by the students of the Guildhall School of Music and Drama and for professional concerts promoted by the Barbican Centre, Milton Court is gaining widespread acclaim for its acoustics. It is the current residence of the Academy of Ancient Music, the Britten Sinfonia and the BBC Singers.

Tall narrow geometry with a top hat section provides a rich, warm reverberant sound with immediacy and vibrancy. A suspended reflector array provides support for the musicians on the platform, and delivers sound-diffusing early reflections to the audience, which especially aids string tone. The motorised system of sound-absorbing banners can be deployed to cover part, or all, of the wall surfaces above the balcony level to change reverberance and surface sound-reflecting performance. This allows the room to be used for both smaller-scale and amplified performances, and to subtly modify the response of the room for different genres of orchestral music. A variable-sized orchestral platform on hydraulic lifts provides flexibility in the size of the stage, allowing use of the hall for symphony orchestral rehearsal. In this condition all banners are deployed to control loudness. High-performance sound insulating and resiliently supported box-in-box concrete constructions control noise intrusion from the London Underground lines that run under the building.

View of the recital hall, looking towards the stage.

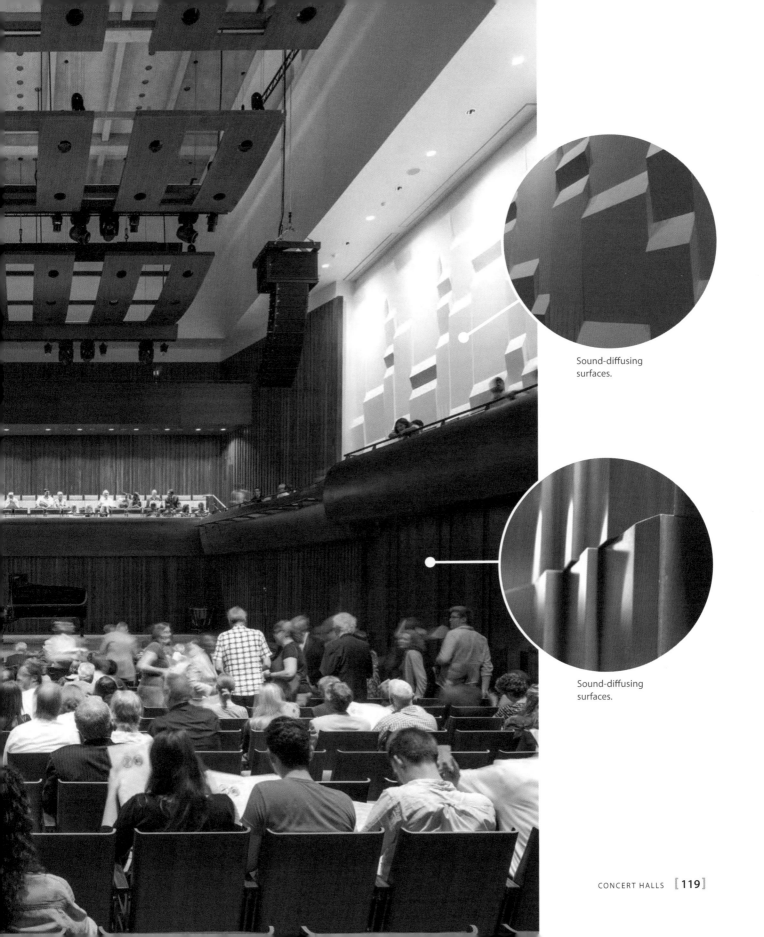

Sound-diffusing
surfaces.

Sound-diffusing
surfaces.

Isabel Bader Centre for the Performing Arts

LOCATION: Kingston, Ontario, Canada

ARCHITECT: Snøhetta and N45

COMPLETED: 2014

AUDIENCE: 550

FORM: shoebox with one balcony

Located at Queen's University, the centre includes a 550-seat performance hall, a large flat-floor music rehearsal room, black-box studio theatre, percussion practice rooms, film screening room, production studio, film edit suites, art gallery and teaching seminar rooms.

The university's goal for the main performance hall was to achieve a beautiful, inviting and intimate room for student and professional groups ranging in size from solo instruments to a 60-person orchestra.

The architectural inspiration of referencing geological patterns found in rock strata local to the Kingston area was integral to the design. This design concept was developed and refined to create a visually stunning timber wall finish that speaks to the rock strata architectural concept, and provides the optimum level of sound diffusion, surface texture and specular reflection. Operable elements allow the acoustics to be adjusted to fit varying performance types in the hall, from classical and choral ensembles through to percussion, samba and jazz.

An acoustical isolation joint structurally isolates the performance hall from the rest of the building, so activities occurring outside of the performance space do not disturb performances inside. The mechanical system was designed to provide supply air at very low velocity via an under-floor plenum to ensure background noise levels do not detract from the user experience. Surround loudspeakers embedded in the balcony front, designed as an integral part of the room acoustics, provide sound reinforcement for jazz, rock/pop and film.

View of stage and audience from balcony; note the modulation in timber finishes for sound diffusion, and the slots in the ceiling for lights and technical systems.

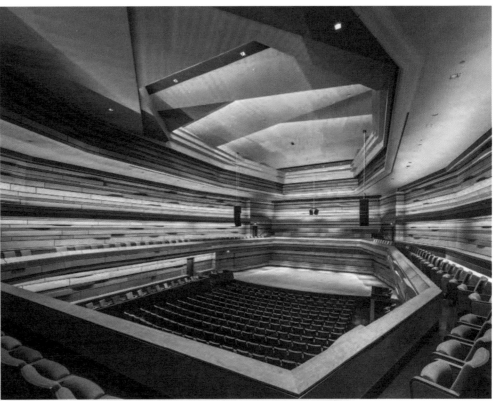

View of the stage from the first balcony; note the ceiling slots are no longer visible.

View from the stage to the audience.

Elisabeth Murdoch Hall

LOCATION: Melbourne, Australia

ARCHITECT: Ashton Raggatt McDougall

COMPLETED: 2009

AUDIENCE: 1,000

FORM: shoebox with one balcony

A modern re-imagining of the classic shoebox concert hall, taking inspiration from Vienna's classic Große Musikvereinssaal, the hall is used for chamber music and chamber orchestra performance.

Elisabeth Murdoch Hall, located within the Melbourne Recital Centre, has been acclaimed as the best chamber music hall in Australia since its opening. The narrow hall width, stepped side balconies and sound-reflecting side soffits provide strong lateral reflections to all seats. An unobstructed upper volume and minimal balcony overhangs mean that reverberant sound can reach the majority of seats.

A lowered ceiling section above the stage allows the musicians to better hear themselves and each other, which improves ensemble playing.

The walls and ceiling are decorated with modulated thick timber panels which reflect bass sound to provide a warm sound and diffuse treble; this creates a very rich, blended, spacious sound in the hall. Acoustic banners reduce the reverberation for amplified or spoken-word events. The background noise level is particularly quiet, which allows extremely delicate musical detail to be heard in all seats.

View to the rear of the hall from the stage.

Inset: Detail of wall sound-diffusing treatment.

Issue	Priority	Comments
Room acoustics	H	Speech is the highest priority in the theatre and impacts every aspect of the room acoustics design. Room volume and shape must be set correctly at the outset as errors can rarely be rectified later, resulting in poor acoustics.
		Type, distribution and acoustic performance of finishes is critical. In spaces where amplified sound is frequently used, additional consideration will be required.
Speech intelligibility	H	Speech needs to be clearly understood between the performers themselves and the audience, especially when actors are moving or turning their backs to the audience.
Audio systems design	H	Audio systems are generally used for three purposes: speech reinforcement, sound effects and music.
		There may be a high number of audio devices that need to be integrated into or visible within the architecture, impacting the room's design. Accommodating these behind architectural finishes will require those finishes to have a high level of acoustic transparency, and also allow for future technology upgrades where dimensional constraints can be limiting.
Sound insulation – external	H	Performance and other noise-sensitive spaces should be free of noise disturbance from outside the building. This usually requires a combination of mass-heavy building envelope materials, multiple layers of lightweight constructions separated by substantial airspaces and the separating of noise-sensitive spaces by noise-neutral (buffer) spaces.
		Smoke evacuation systems sometimes need venting directly to the outside, meaning that noise control must be included here too.
Sound insulation – internal	H	Performance and other noise-sensitive spaces should be free of noise disturbance from inside the building.
		If the placement of buffer spaces is not achievable, and/or any part of the noise-sensitive space is adjacent to the exterior or noise producing interior space, then mass-heavy or isolated constructions (e.g. box-in-box) may be unavoidable.
Speech privacy	M	Some spaces, such as dressing rooms, may require control of sound transmission to other spaces. The location of these spaces should be determined early.
Impact/vibration isolation	H	Impact sounds propagate vertically and horizontally, so adjacencies and potential impacts need to be understood in all directions. Impact and vibration must be very well controlled inside performance spaces otherwise concentration is easily broken.
Mechanical and electrical noise	H	In performance and rehearsal spaces, background noise is usually low (NR10–25) with a criterion set depending on use. Low noise is critical in ensuring voices can achieve their maximum dynamic range (the quietest and loudest sounds being easily heard and understood). Too quiet, and other noises from around the building will become more noticeable. Ducts need to be appropriately sized and shaped and main equipment quiet for low velocity and low noise. Terminal device selection is especially important to avoid airflow-generated noise.
		Incoming electrical supply is normally ground isolated. It enters the building with transformers provided to supply power to the necessary systems at the incoming location. Separate supply is provided for audio, lighting, theatre systems/rigging, etc. as needed to avoid cross-contamination noise from one system affecting the other.
Structure-borne noise	H	The most significant sources of structure-borne noise come from sources close to or outside the building envelope. If affected by these sources, the building may require whole construction vibration isolation, which will impact structure, building services system design and cost.
Environmental noise	M/H	Performance spaces are generally quite energy intensive. The mechanical and electrical systems may require equipment outside the building, which usually has the highest potential noise impact, while codes pertaining to environmental noise emission must be adhered to.

H – High   M – Medium   L – Low

Introduction

In the theatre, to ensure comprehension, understanding and emotional engagement between performers and audience, it is vitally important to achieve good speech intelligibility. This entails the right combination of room shape, form and volume, and the correct distribution and acoustic performance of the interior room finishes. In addition, it's critical that building services noise levels are low enough for a suitable dramatic dynamic range to aid speech intelligibility. Control of intrusive noise into the space is equally important so that performers and audience are not distracted by extraneous sounds.

Shape and form are the most critical early decisions to be made between client, architect, acoustician and theatre planner. There are a wide range of possible forms to start or develop from. These are the result of many years of theatre evolution across the world, each informed by cultural context, local tradition and variation in performance type. Examples include the rectilinear 'black box', fan, reverse fan, thrust stage and in-the-round. Each has unique acoustic challenges. The approach to acoustic design between the forms varies accordingly. The use of emerging immersive audio and visual technology will have a continuing impact upon the future development of the typology, as well as offering opportunities to supplement room acoustic design choices that may have otherwise led to speech intelligibility challenges.

As with many Western performing arts spaces, the evolution of the theatre form can be traced back to amphitheatres of classical antiquity, most famously the open-air theatre at Epidaurus (Greece) and in the first theatres with roofs and raised stages such as Aspendus (modern-day Turkey), and Agrippa (Greece). The latter is often cited as the first enclosed theatre, and notably features openings to the exterior, allowing sound to escape – this provided a sound-absorbing function as well as natural ventilation.

The artform developed and diverged through the flourishing of Elizabethan theatre in the UK (e.g. Shakespeare's Globe), the introduction of proscenium theatre (such as Teatro Olimpico in Venice with its curved rows set within an enclosed short box and a complex perspective stage) and across Europe and beyond (resulting in bell-shape, U-shape, horseshoe, ellipse and others). The horseshoe became the predominant form in Italian Baroque theatre. Theatres in the UK developed differently, as commercial theatre operations were established early and put more emphasis on better sightlines. This trend can also be seen in the post-18th-century development of theatre in North America. From the early 1950s onwards, further evolution occurred. Some examples emerged referencing early Greek theatre in their adoption of the thrust stage (e.g. The Guthrie Theater in Minneapolis), while new black-box theatres for smaller-scale intimate productions with increased use of technology also multiplied (themselves referencing smaller UK theatres such as the Georgian Theatre in Richmond, North Yorkshire).

Architectural style

Along with the evolution and variation in the typology outlined above comes a wide variety of approaches to the interior of the theatre. From an architectural standpoint, they begin quite simplistically, reaching a zenith of ornate flamboyance during the baroque era, before returning to sparser and/or technology-heavy spaces of the late-20th and early-21st centuries. Technology has always existed in the theatre. The use of perspective scenery, complex set and stage machinery and lighting experimentation can change the nature of the entire room, as can audio effects and sound experimentation.

Generally, in modern theatres the room as a whole is only seen during the period before the lights dim and the focus then shifts to the stage. The architect must think carefully about materials and style in conjunction with the client from the outset, to craft the intended audience experience. In the extreme of the black box, architectural character is not usually present beyond the 'technological' architecture that allows the space to operate.

Acoustic features

All aspects, including room form, key dimensions (length, width, height), materials and seating rake, should be optimised for direct sound propagation, and to maximise direct and early sound reflections from the stage to the audience members. Later sound reflections (beyond 50ms) should be minimised as far as is practical as this negatively impacts speech intelligibility. This usually requires:

- Minimising the room volume to avoid excessive reverberance – width should be optimised for seating layout and sightlines; height and length should only extend as much as is needed for audio, visual, lighting and theatrical equipment to function

- Surfaces onstage or very close to the stage should be treated to avoid sound reflections, which could distract the performers

- Wall areas at the front of the room (close to the stage) should direct sound reflections to the audience

- Side walls in the front 50% of the room should promote good sound reflections to the audience, without being too strident – this can require a combination of sound-reflecting and sound diffusing finishes

- Walls further from the stage and the rear wall usually require a combination of finishes crafted to the specifics of the room form as needed, to direct sound to the audience, be sound diffusing (scatter the sound to avoid strong reflections) and sound-absorbing (to take away as much reflection as needed)

Some theatres may require variable acoustics to accommodate a range of different shows, particularly when amplified sound or sound effects are used extensively.

The ceiling zone needs careful consideration:

- the visible 'architectural ceiling', which often serves the dual purpose of providing sound reflections back to the audience, as well as creating a visual screen for the technology above

- the catwalk access zone needed to allow technicians to be able to move around over the theatre during set-up and shows. This zone usually incorporates significant amounts of audio, lighting and visual technology (some of which requires enclosure to control the noise levels generated, and sometimes also dedicated cooling)

- the upper roof zone, usually the underside of the structural external envelope, which may be either sound diffusing or sound-absorbing depending on the room height – the higher the ceiling is, relative to the optimum height, the more likely it will need to be sound-absorbing to control late sound reflections in the space

Floors usually need to be as 'quiet' as possible in terms of both impact sounds (i.e. heels clicking on the floors) and to control sound reflections, and therefore are often carpeted. Other impact-resistant flooring such as linoleum or similar products are becoming more common, but using these materials requires careful consideration of the sound of shoes on the surface (especially generated by audiences shuffling around during performances).

Challenges

A key challenge in the theatre typology is to ensure good acoustics are maintained when the performer faces away from the audience. This is particularly true in larger proscenium and in-the-round theatres. Achieving the intended architectural aesthetic,

given the acoustic requirements for the finishes, requires close coordination and development from the very earliest stages of the project, as does the incorporation of audio and visual technology systems, control rooms and similar spaces connected to the main performance space. It is important to ensure that noise-creating areas or equipment are located away from the performance spaces, as far as is practical, in order to minimise the complexity and cost of sound insulating constructions or mechanical noise and vibration control.

Opportunities

Technology use is being deployed excitingly and creatively in theatre performance. Theatre spaces are likely to become much more technologically intensive as a result. The infrastructure supporting this must be designed in a way that allows for easy replacement over time. The ability to connect or employ new technology in or on the architecture easily will be a continued design challenge. Those creating dramatic productions will need as much flexibility as possible. Acoustics may also need to be adapted or to be made adaptable for future use.

The designer's challenge is how to give the space architectural character while also allowing the technological overlay to happen seamlessly. Some spaces do this by allowing the infrastructure to show the technological overlay as an explicit part of the design of the room. With the increasing use of recording and broadcast, either real-time or post-production, being able to recognise the room in its broadcast form may be important to some clients; therefore, architectural uniqueness will be an important factor in making spaces immediately identifiable.

Bord Gáis Energy Theatre.

Epidaurus

LOCATION: Epidaurus, Greece

ARCHITECT: Polykleitos the Younger

COMPLETED: 4th century B.C.

AUDIENCE: Up to 14,000

FORM: 290-degree amphitheatre

By far the most famous of the Greek theatres of classical antiquity, Epidaurus is particularly notable for its excellent acoustics.

While at the rear seats, the performers on stage may appear small, but they are clearly audible.

The site is rural, set into a hillside. The surrounding environment is very quiet, except for the sounds of birds and a light breeze audible through the trees, allowing good dynamic range from voices even in quiet passages. The steep bowl allows for excellent sightlines and is an important factor in the good transmission of direct sound from the performers to the very rear row of seats. The floor area surrounding the performers is sound-reflecting and crucial in directing early sound from the voices up to the audience. The curve of the step seating rake provides a 'whispering gallery' effect, so sounds travel around it, making voices clear even when the performer is facing away from the audience. In addition, the curvature of the upper part of the step creates a focused sound behind the listener – a natural, personalised surround-sound. It would have required great knowledge and skill to create such a sophisticated acoustic design; while there may have been some trial-and-error experimentation its form is certainly no accident.

Detail of the curvature of the stone steps, which results in a personal surround sound effect.

The view of the amphitheatre from the stage.

Hackney Empire

LOCATION: Hackney, London, UK

ARCHITECT: Frank Matcham (1901) and Tim Ronalds Architects (2001)

COMPLETED: 1901

AUDIENCE: 1,275

FORM: narrow fan

Designed originally as a music hall, the Hackney Empire has also been used as a traditional theatre, a studio space for TV productions, and a bingo hall. After a renovation, it reopened in 2001 with an expanded pit to allow a greater variety of touring shows, including touring opera.

The space is a hybrid, taking cues from the concert hall, opera house and theatre styles, with balconies that step back to minimise overhangs and expose much of the audience to the sound of the main room volume. Balcony seating is relatively steep to allow suitable sightlines to the stage.

The gilded style, popular at the time, is also very sound diffusing, which allows sounds to mix well in the space. Carpet on the floor and sound-absorbing treatment to the rear walls behind the balconies limit unwanted sound reflections back to the stage.

At the rear of the stalls level, the bar is able to serve the theatre directly during performances. By no means unique, it is much less common in modern auditoria and is an important aspect of how the character of the room works. Of course, there are noise-related issues to doing this, and it is not in operation for every performance, but it is an important consideration for future designs that may be looking to break away from the 'elitist' vibe theatre sometimes carries.

View to stage side and stage; the detailing on the surfaces helps sound diffusion.

View to the audience from the stage. Roller shutters to the rear of the stalls allow the bar to operate within the venue.

Bord Gáis Energy Theatre
(Grand Canal Theatre)

LOCATION: Dublin, Ireland

ARCHITECT: Daniel Libeskind, DDDA

COMPLETED: 2010

FORM: fixed seat

AUDIENCE: 2,111

Note the significant areas of sound-absorbing and diffusing wall finishes, steep rake and carpeted floors. The ceiling panels are perforated; some areas have a sound-reflecting backing, others are transparent with loudspeakers mounted behind and concealed, but these allow sound to pass through.

Kilden Performing Arts Centre

LOCATION: Kristiansand, Norway

ARCHITECT: ALA Architects and SMS Arkitekter

COMPLETED: 2012

FORM: rectilinear hall with curved seating rows

AUDIENCE: 1,185 seats (concert hall)

Note the extensive use of sound diffusing finishes on the walls (light grey modulated panels) and vertical slatted sound-transparent surfaces with sound-absorbing treatment or loudspeakers located behind. There are sound-absorbing curtains in the upper volume, and expanded metal mesh sound-absorbing panels in the flytower.

Richard Burton Theatre

LOCATION: Royal Welsh College of Music & Drama, Cardiff, UK

ARCHITECT: Flanagan Lawrence Architects

COMPLETED: 2011

FORM: horseshoe

AUDIENCE: 180 seats

An intimate 180-seat theatre optimised for speech intelligibility. Note the design of the balcony fronts, with the lower sections curved and sound diffusing, and the upper sections as open railings, transparent to sound.

Issue	Priority	Comments
Room acoustics	H	Positive audience and performer experiences are reliant on good acoustics, and are a key aspect of venue reputation.
		High-quality natural, un-amplified sound is the highest priority, but high-quality amplified sound, assisted by variable acoustic elements, is also important.
		Acoustic volume must be sufficient for reverberance, while good sightlines and controlled distance from audience to stage are critical for direct sound.
		Most surfaces other than seats must be sound-reflecting or diffusing and optimised geometrically to ensure all seat areas receive a good mix of reflected sound. Surfaces close to the proscenium arch are especially important. A degree of sound diffusing articulation to most surfaces is critical for tone quality.
		Singers must feel supported by the room, with tangible sound reflected back towards them and orchestral players by surfaces above and around the pit, which should be substantially open and spacious.
Speech intelligibility	H	Critical for opera, in which many passages are spoken, not sung, speech must be understood in the natural acoustic. Equally, it must be clearly understood when delivered in PAVA messages.
Audio systems design	H	It's essential to provide high-quality performance sound systems for some opera repertoire, but also for ballet and musical theatre productions. Spatial audio and electro-acoustic enhancement are likely to become increasingly important in the future. Audio systems overall present significant architectural integration challenges.
Sound insulation – external	H	External noise ingress must be prevented, as should noise emission from amplified shows in particular. Two layers of mass heavy constructions separated by a large cavity around the auditorium are to be expected.
		Ducts and other services penetrating sound insulating constructions need special attention.
Sound insulation – internal	H	No sound at all can be audible from other spaces, so a complete buffer zone is required, and building layout must be carefully planned to avoid sensitive adjacencies.
		All entrances must have lobbies/vestibules. Control rooms require high-performance, deep studio-type glazing.
		The auditorium may require full structural/acoustic box-in-box isolation on bearings, particularly if other performance spaces are housed within the same building.
Speech privacy	H	Essential, and aligned with sound insulation requirements above.
Impact/vibration isolation	H	Impact sound transfer from surrounding spaces must be eliminated by effective isolation of walking surfaces.
Mechanical and electrical noise	H	It is critical that background sound levels are very low (around NR10), close to the threshold of hearing.
		This means very low duct velocities, low-pressure-drop air systems, and generally a low-level distributed displacement supply into the auditorium. Space requirements are very significant.
		All building services and technical systems will require effective vibration isolation, to eliminate structure-borne components.
		Separate, isolated electrical feeds for performance audio, visual, lighting and theatre technical systems are required.
Structure-borne noise	H	Because of the very low background noise, the risk from external sources is elevated. Sources such as subways or trams will have the potential to transfer vibration through the ground into the structure, which will be heard within the auditorium. This must be assessed early in the design and the auditorium fully isolated if necessary, to avoid any sound transfer. If there are no existing sources, consider carefully the risk of changes in future.
Environmental noise	H	This must be assessed carefully, especially in relation to amplified performances and low-frequency sound emission, although the reciprocal requirement for control of noise ingress helps. In close proximity to neighbouring properties, low-frequency transfer is a very significant risk. Specific, onerous limits are likely to apply. The implications of non-compliance are very serious.

H – High   M – Medium   L – Low

Introduction

In an opera house, good acoustics are essential for audience and performers alike, enabling elevated performance levels and the magic of opera to be fully realised. Amplification is not generally used for productions of mainstream operatic repertoire, so the acoustics must support singers and orchestra naturally through good sightlines, appropriate form, room surface optimisation and materials. This requires detailed, iterative design development alongside theatre and acoustic specialists.

Significant space is required above, below and around the stage in the form of flytower, side and rear stages, and orchestra pit. In addition, the need to eliminate external noise intrusion means generous separation zones, and sometimes complete structural isolation of the auditorium itself. When the requirements for rehearsal, ancillary and administrative spaces are added, as well as large low-velocity air ducts for low noise levels, a large and complex building is demanded. Acoustic advice will be required at the earliest stage of planning.

Size, shape and form

The term opera encompasses a wide and diverse repertoire, spanning centuries. The earliest examples are noted in early 17th-century Venice, through Italian, English, German and French traditions in the 18th and 19th centuries, right up to a contemporary art form, still vibrant, relevant and evolving today. An engagement with opera's complex cultural, political and musical (as well as architectural) history is an invaluable aid to opera house design.

A consequence of this diverse history is a corresponding range of voices and singing styles, orchestral scoring and playing, and to some extent a correspondence between the size, form and features of historic opera houses and the repertoire that was fashionable when they were built. Contemporary opera buildings are generally intended to be suitable for a wide range of the repertoire, including the largest-scale (Wagner, Strauss)

works, whereas early opera is more suited to smaller theatres. The number of seats is a significant factor in determining how well a theatre will accommodate large-scale works, which is related to how loud the music will be (this will vary significantly by repertoire and within individual works) and is equally significant commercially. In spaces housing more than 1,800 seats it is challenging to achieve good sound levels in all audience areas, and in those with below 1,000 there is a significant risk that some pieces (and voices) will be loud or overpowering. Recently designed opera theatres tend toward 1,400–1,800 seats. Many historical houses have significantly higher capacities.

Fundamental design starting points are to ensure good sightlines, and to limit the distance from the audience to the stage. This usually results in a multi-tiered room, with shallow balconies or boxes to the sides, and deeper balconies to the rear. Here some audience areas will be overhung by the balcony above. The tension between the depth of overhang and the acoustic experience of the audience below will be a critical point of balance in the design. The aim is generally for a 'tight' and efficient seating plan to minimise audience distances.

Because of its large volume, the flytower can have a significant effect on the acoustics of the theatre itself. In smaller theatres the 'flytower effect' can be beneficially employed as a subtle source of reverberance, taking care to ensure it does not dominate. But in general, it is appropriate to employ some fixed absorbing materials into the flytower to ensure that its effect is minimal.

Some theatres must be compatible with symphonic concert performance, as part of a wider programme of uses. In this format the orchestra will be onstage, an enclosure formed around it, including a lid to seal off the upper volume of the flytower. The architectural challenge of creating a 'one room' effect in this format is considerable, but can be aided by incorporating the flexibility to expand or dissolve the proscenium opening completely.

Architectural style

While acoustic and theatrical considerations mean that architectural license becomes somewhat restricted by key volumetric parameters in opera spaces, a wide range of architectural styles can be accommodated without detriment to physical acoustics. This, however, should always be on the understanding that psychoacoustic factors (i.e. the context of the ear being led by the eye) are real and should always be considered to avoid jarring dissonances between sight and sound.

Many historical opera houses are known for having a high degree of ornamentation – ornate plasterwork and pilasters, an arched, grand proscenium opening between stage and theatre, tiers that wrap around and are divided for private boxes to the sides, solid balcony or box fronts, and a relatively high ceiling. All these features are very significant acoustically, and equivalent elements will be needed in a contemporary theatre. It is worth noting that the ornamentation serves the purpose of diffusing sound – especially at higher frequencies. This is necessary to some extent, to avoid over-brightness and glare, or a harsh tone quality. Contemporary architecture will therefore need to embrace a degree of surface texture and articulation. There is plenty of choice as to how this is achieved.

Acoustic features

A good design successfully blends theatrical and architectural elements with acoustic intent, so acoustic features need not necessarily be conspicuous.

The orchestra pit design is critical for orchestral sound production and balance with singers. Pits will normally incorporate two or more motorised lifts to enable different height settings, sizes and layouts of orchestra (these lifts will be raised to support front rows of audience seating when the pit is not in use). There is an increasing trend for generously sized and only partially overhung orchestra pits, to help reduce

players' sound level exposure. The result is generally louder, well-projected orchestral sound, which can overpower singers unless great care is taken.

A proscenium opening is generally preferred for theatrical reasons. Acoustically, the architectural elements just beyond the opening – within the auditorium – are critical because of their proximity to the singers and players. Singers' voices must be assisted by these surfaces, especially when the singer is not facing the room. A surface projection out into the room from the proscenium header is almost mandatory for helping orchestral players to hear each other as well as vocal projection.

Electroacoustic elements will also feature. For some operatic repertoire, ballet, and especially for musical theatre productions, an amplified sound system will be needed – employing loudspeakers mounted around the proscenium arch and stage front. Speakers can be covered by an acoustically transparent finish, and with some effort can often be 'integrated' architecturally. Especially for smaller theatres, where reverberance might be limited, an 'active architecture' system (a distributed series of loudspeakers embedded into walls) will be appropriate; sympathetically adding in late sound and (apparently) expanding the boundaries of the space.

Seats and their supports will strongly influence the sound and are normally designed as medium upholstered with sound-reflecting rear surfaces.

Variable acoustic elements – sound-absorbing elements in the form of heavy fabric drapes or banners – which can be brought in to cover wall surfaces, are an effective means of reducing reverberance to aid good amplified sound, as well as allowing acoustic adjustment within the operatic repertoire. The architectural impact of such elements is clearly significant although deployment to the rear of the theatre and at high level, where visual impact is generally less, can be acoustically effective.

Heavy room boundaries are necessary to support lower sound frequencies. Masonry, concrete and dense multi-layered build-ups are employed. This can be a challenge to amplified sound quality. Some lighter or variable elements to provide low-frequency sound-absorbing performance (usually panes) may be desirable.

Low-velocity, low-level air supply outlets for very low background noise levels are commonly incorporated into seat pedestals, or as under-seat floor grilles.

Shaping is a critical consideration and can be considered at three scales. Firstly, overall volume and distribution of volume. This will determine the amount and level of reverberance, its perceived locations, and colour. This is to some extent a question of choice, but it is reasonable to state that good sound is achieved when there is a mix of direct and/or early reflected sound from musician to listener, within a sense of reverberance which allows musical phrases to blend, breathe, and sustain a true *legato* effect. This requires sufficient overall room volume. An initial volume per seat allocation might be around 8m³, and this tends to push up ceiling heights. It can also be created by expanding the room boundaries at rear side walls out above the highest balcony level. A high ceiling makes integration of lighting bridges difficult, so a key design focus is the balance between ceiling height, lighting positions and their visibility within the room, and the overall volume.

Secondly, large-scale plan and sectional form. Key organisational features such as seating rake, parterre divisions, balconies, ceiling profile and proscenium zone, are all critical elements in shaping the overall balance of early to late sound. For any particular seating area, the combined effect of reflected sound from each of these elements must be considered in the context of both pit sources and singers. Ideally, direct sound will be accompanied by an ensemble of early reflected sound (within 100ms of the direct sound) which does not interfere strongly, but supports it sympathetically. Ideally, the furthest seats are not more than approximately 32m from the stage,

to keep this early sound at an appropriate level and to maintain the connection with the audience. Acoustic modelling and iteration are required to refine the plan and section, so that balance is maintained as far as possible across all seating areas.

Thirdly, smaller-scale surfaces such as balcony fronts and wall surface articulations strongly influence the character of early reflected sound. Detailing of these smaller-scale geometries and textures is acoustically subtle yet critical in determining final sound quality, and because of the visual impact requires close collaboration between architect and acoustician.

It is important to note that while not part of the fixed architecture, stage sets will have an acoustic effect, especially in relation to vocal projection and balance between singers and audience, an awareness of which is to be expected in production designs.

Challenges

Technical systems such as power flying, performance lighting, dimmers and associated control racks can generate noise which, if audible to the audience, can easily break the spell of performance. Careful selection to strict noise limits and reduced energy costs is essential.

Open pits ease sound exposure of musicians, but create challenges for balance with singers, and impact set and casting decisions. Development and adoption of personal hearing protection for singers is an industry priority.

The proscenium zone needs to be flexible and design is complicated. A single fire curtain to close off the opening is a standard requirement. An alternative approach would create more design opportunity.

Opportunities

Opera provides a rich opportunity to blend the old and new, or to distinctly celebrate one or the other. This will require spaces to be ever more flexible to accommodate technology change.

Semperoper

LOCATION: Dresden, Germany

ARCHITECT: Gottfried Semper (1841), Gottfried and Manfred Semper (1878), Wolfgang Hänsch (1985)

COMPLETED: 1841, 1878, 1985

AUDIENCE: 1,284 seated, 39 standing

FORM: horseshoe with narrow balcony

Originally destroyed by fire and rebuilt in 1878 in stone and marble, the building was again destroyed by Allied bombing in 1945. It was rebuilt to the 1878 specification, reopening in 1985. It is highly regarded for its acoustics, alongside Teatro Colon Buenos Aires and La Scala Milan.

While following the classic horseshoe opera house plan, the balconies are very narrow with limited or no overhangs, exposing all spectators to the main reverberant acoustic volume of the room. The sound diffusing surface treatments are similar to those seen in the famous shoebox concert halls of the same period. A notable acoustic feature around the room is the relatively deep columns and beams that support the perimeter walls and balconies. These surfaces help to capture direct reflections and focus them to the seats in front, creating a strong sense of envelopment in these seats (similar is found in Teatro Colon).

The orchestra pit is traditional for its time, with larger orchestras pushed below the stage and the pit height adjustable with lifts.

The columns and balcony support beams help to create focused early sound reflections in each bay, giving a heightened sense of envelopment.

View of the side balconies and proscenium arch, showing the sound-diffusing finish to surfaces. The perimeter walls are mainly flat and sound-reflecting, except at the very upper level.

Glyndebourne Opera House

LOCATION: Lewes, East Sussex, England

ARCHITECT: Michael Hopkins and Partners

COMPLETED: 1994

AUDIENCE: 1,243

FORM: circular with four balconies

Glyndeborne was the first of a series of new opera houses to be built over the next 25 years, all keeping to low seat counts to optimise acoustic performance.

The circular plan form allowed the distance of the furthest seat from the stage to be minimised, providing increased acoustic and visual intimacy. This presented design challenges of achieving optimum acoustics, and minimising sound focusing, with a modern material palette of concrete, brick and timber. Balcony fronts are carefully shaped and are different at each level, providing a mix of sound-reflecting, sound diffusing, and sound-transparent finish. On each subsequent level, the profile similarly changes from proscenium to centre line to best balance requirements for sound reflection and diffusion, minimising sound reflections back to the stage. Elsewhere wood of varying thicknesses is used, spaced from the walls on battens. In some locations it is convex, to help reduce focusing. Some minimal areas of sound-absorbing treatment are located behind slatted timber. Balcony soffits are precast concrete. Air is supplied from a plenum below the seats through seat pedestals.

View of the opera theatre, with varying balcony fronts and use of timber throughout, both to optimise acoustic performance.

Seat detail, showing pedestal air diffuser and slats under the seat, to ensure they have the same sound-absorbing performance in both the unoccupied and occupied condition.

Oslo Opera House

LOCATION: Oslo, Norway

ARCHITECT: Snøhetta

COMPLETED: 2008

AUDIENCE: 1,364

FORM: horseshoe

Scandinavian Opera tradition is for richer, longer reverberance. To achieve this the theatre has a traditional horseshoe form, but at the top balcony the plan steps out like an inverted top hat to increase the volume, which can be opened and closed using operable panels.

The challenge of the acoustic performance of the balcony fronts is solved using sculpted shaping. The balcony gives the appearance of being carved from a single piece of timber and the visible changes in sculpting can be seen at each level. The curvature of the walls behind each balcony level was developed to achieve a balance of sound reflection and sound diffusion. High sound levels are generated in orchestra pits, making hearing damage a cause for concern. As a result, pits in opera houses are being pushed forward into the house (rather than tucked under the stage) and it is a challenge to ensure balance between the orchestra and voices on the stage at each level of the house. The pit rail incorporates sound-absorbing components that can be used as needed.

The hall is also used for concert performance by deploying an orchestra shell on stage.

The rail on the right side of the orchestra pit incorporates sound-absorbing components that can be used as needed.

The balcony shaping is different at each level.

The wall shaping is sound-diffusing and reflecting.

The main foyer has significant sound-diffusing timber components on the exterior of the opera theatre wall, which help mix the sound and reduce the overall energy with only limited use of sound-absorbing materials.

Stavros Niarchos Foundation Cultural Center

LOCATION: Athens, Greece

ARCHITECT: Renzo Piano Building Workshop

COMPLETED: 2016

AUDIENCE: 1,400

FORM: horseshoe

One of the fundamental questions at the beginning of this project was to determine what the modern Greek opera house should sound like, and to conduct comprehensive measurements of spaces ancient and modern in and around Athens, to inform the design.

The room acoustics take the best features of classic opera theatres of Dresden and Buenos Aires (Teatro Colon) and blend them with modern design, to create a balanced sound for sung voices and music in the Mediterranean tradition. A key early design decision was to create a complete room, with special attention paid to the ceiling. As well as being a crucial acoustic surface to sustain reverberance, it was also designed to use modern techniques to simulate the sky around Athens using LED up-lighting and performance lighting (with spotlights and other technology integrated into ceiling niches, which are less visible from audience seated locations). The balcony fronts strike a balance between sound-reflecting and diffusing, changing profile along their length, with a different arrangement at each balcony level. The shaping of the walls at each level is optimised to balance sound diffusion while also providing focused sound reflections to the seats immediately in front of the walls. Deployable sound-absorbing curtains can cover 85% of the wall area for amplified concerts, conferences and similar events.

Most opera theatres have a secondary studio theatre. Here it is designed for an audience of 600 with a flat floor, retractable raked seating, a comprehensive set of variable sound-absorbing curtains, and audio-visual and theatre technology.

The chorus rehearsal room is designed to simulate the acoustics on the stage. It also incorporates variable sound-absorbing treatment on all walls to create a much more controlled acoustic for concentrated rehearsal that doesn't over-flatter the performers. A similar comprehensive approach is taken to the design of the orchestra rehearsal and recording room with fixed finishes on the walls (mainly sound diffusing, some sound-absorbing) designed to simulate the sound on the stage with the orchestra enclosure in place. In recording mode the room can be used live, and can also deploy variable sound-absorbing curtains as needed.

View of the opera theatre, with shaped balcony front and ceiling designs.

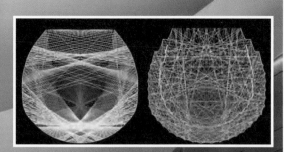

Left: Raytracing analysis, showing untreated smooth wall (left) and optimised shaping (right).

Right: Performance hall 2, shown in set-up mode; a temporary draped proscenium ready to be raised, variable sound-absorbing treatment (red curtains) on the sides and top, and other audio-visual and theatre technology.

The chorus rehearsal room, viewed from the rear, shows manual sound-absorbing curtains being deployed at the front, and sound-diffusing and absorbing panels on walls.

The orchestra rehearsal and recording room has fixed finishes on the walls (mainly sound-diffusing, some sound-absorbing), set up in recording mode with sound-absorbing curtains deployed in strategic locations.

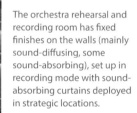

View of the theatre and flytower from the side.

Dance

Issue	Priority	Comments
Room acoustics	H	Requirements vary across the wide range of dance forms (e.g. classical ballet to contemporary), and dance styles from around the world. For example, classical ballet is often performed in traditional opera theatre settings and hybrid spaces with improved sightlines. A key question is how much of the dancers' physical movement needs to be audible to the audience. Some choreographers prefer to not hear any footfall or movement, conveying a grace and lightness of touch, while some like a range of emotion to be conveyed physically and audibly.
Speech intelligibility	H	Good speech intelligibility is crucial, especially when dance is accompanied by soundtrack, music, narrative or other material.
Audio systems design	H	Audio systems are generally used for three purposes; speech reinforcement, sound effects, and music. There may be a high number of audio devices that need to be integrated into, or visible within, the architecture thus impacting room design. Accommodating these behind architectural finishes will require those finishes to have a high level of acoustic transparency. These pose significant challenges for future technology upgrades, which will often have dimensional constraints.
Sound insulation – external	H	Performance and other noise sensitive spaces should be free of noise disturbance from outside the building. This usually requires a combination of mass heavy building envelope materials, multiple layers of lightweight constructions separated by substantial airspaces and the separating of noise sensitive spaces by noise-neutral (buffer) spaces.
Sound insulation – internal	H	Performance and other noise sensitive spaces should be free of noise disturbance from inside the building. If the placement of buffer spaces is not achievable, and/or any part of noise sensitive space is adjacent to the exterior or noise producing interior space, then mass heavy or isolated constructions (e.g. box-in-box) may be unavoidable. Since dance can have a high level of impact, it is important to consider spatial relationships between performance and rehearsal spaces. Stacking spaces vertically can be particularly challenging, very costly, and sometimes not achievable from an acoustic performance standpoint.
Speech privacy	M	Some spaces, such dressing rooms, will require control of sound transmission to other spaces. The location of these spaces should be determined early in the design process.
Impact/vibration isolation	H	Impact noises may come from diverse sources: people walking, doors slamming, building services, etc. Impact sounds propagate vertically and horizontally, so adjacencies and potential impacts need to be understood in all directions. Impact and vibration must be very well controlled inside performance spaces otherwise concentration is easily broken. Appropriate measures should be included in all systems wherever possible as they can be very difficult to retrofit later.
Mechanical and electrical noise	H	See guidance for opera and theatres.
Structure-borne noise	H	The most significant sources of structure-borne noise come from sources close to or outside the building envelope (e.g. transport infrastructure, underground parking, or service roads and tunnels). If affected by these sources, the building may require whole construction vibration isolation, which has space planning implications and will impact structure, building services system design and cost.
Environmental noise	M/H	Performance spaces are generally quite energy intensive. The mechanical and electrical systems may require equipment outside the building, which usually has the highest potential noise impact, while codes pertaining to environmental noise emission must be adhered to. Any equipment placed outdoors should be inherently quiet and/or incorporate noise and vibration control. The location of equipment will also have an impact – if it is on the roof, noise and vibration control to interior spaces will be required.

H – High   M – Medium   L – Low

Introduction

Buildings for dance tend to include spaces for both performance and rehearsal. Acoustics play an important part in conveying dancers' range of emotion in performance and warrant careful consideration. The user expectations for this should be defined at the design outset, and this often requires benchmarking visits with the client to define what is possible.

Acoustic requirements are variable depending on dance type. As such, broad guidance can be presented but the specifics of the dance styles to be accommodated must be properly understood. Some aspects of ballet are addressed in the opera section of this book.

In both rehearsal and performance spaces, the sound of the dancers – breath, physical movement, impact of feet (or other body parts) on the floor and/or other surfaces, physical interactions between dancers and/or objects – is often an important part of the performance.

Acoustic features

Sightlines to the stage in performance spaces are very important. Audience members should typically be able to see the dancers' feet at all positions on the stage. This is often achieved by a steep seating rake with a 'first row' sightline, so each audience member can see over the heads of those in front. This can result in early sound reflections from walls and ceilings being quickly absorbed by the seats or audience, resulting in a more 'direct' sound with low reverberance. In spaces that also have other natural acoustic uses, this requirement needs careful consideration.

Music commonly accompanies dance. Amplified music – especially contemporary bass-heavy amplified music – and spaces that use natural unamplified drums and other percussion, typically benefit from lower reverberance and higher clarity, achieved by incorporating sound-absorbing finishes. Conversely, spaces where the music is unamplified generally need supportive reverberance.

Dancing usually requires lifts and other vertical movements which (in rehearsal spaces especially) result in additional room height, naturally increasing reverberance, which usually necessitates increased areas of sound-absorbing finishes.

Teaching and instruction are important operational drivers – understanding where the instructor will typically be located, if microphones are used, where loudspeakers will be located, all need to be understood to optimise acoustics for that purpose. Where the dance instructor usually faces the mirror, the wall and ceiling above the mirror can be shaped to enhance the natural sound projection from their voice.

Understanding floor performance requirements is a crucial design aspect. A specific type of floor may be required with the right mobility for the dance type, and to reduce physical impact on the dancers. High levels of impact sound are created; isolating other spaces from these can be challenging. Good planning should aim to avoid locating dance spaces above noise sensitive spaces (vertically or horizontally). If this cannot be avoided, full box-in-box constructions will likely be needed to mitigate impact and airborne sound transfer.

Natural light is generally well liked (with the ability to black out), but typically as clerestory windows, avoiding direct external views of the dancers, so the dancers do not feel they are 'on display'. A mirror wall is usually essential, with the ability to cover it up using manually deployed panels or curtains in rehearsal spaces, automated versions in performance spaces.

Fixed and variable sound-absorbing treatment is common; the latter is usually manual movable curtains.

Historical context

Sadler's Wells Theatre

LOCATION: London, UK

ARCHITECT: RHWL

COMPLETED: 1998

AUDIENCE: 1,568

FORM: rectangular

Sadler's Wells is renowned as one of the world's leading dance venues; it also functions as a performance space for visiting companies, and a producing house.

Designed from scratch, this venue takes on a wide variety of features optimised for the theatre, based on user requirements developed over many years. The steep seating rake allows a second-row sightline – every person can see the feet of the dancers on the stage. The orchestra pit is designed to accommodate a wide variety of performance types with live music. As is common in modern orchestra pit design it is more open to the room, to ensure players are not exposed to overly loud conditions (long-term exposure to high sound levels is a common cause of hearing loss, especially in musicians). Seats are sound-absorbing to have the same acoustic performance unoccupied and occupied.

Expanded metal mesh on the side wall can be lit as needed architecturally, or for performance. Behind these are variable sound-absorbing panels on a concertina folding system, adjusted variably for performances, usually fully deployed for amplified content. For performances benefitting from natural acoustics they can be retracted. Expanded metal mesh panels to the sides of the proscenium and above the proscenium header allow loudspeakers to be located behind, and for sound to pass through them. A system of sound-absorbing panels, consisting primarily of black expanded metal mesh with 50mm black tissue faced mineral fibre of optimised densities, covers the remainder of the side and rear walls. This treatment is fixed, so in natural acoustic modes of room operation, the front section of the theatre is optimised to provide natural sound reflections, while the rear of the room is primarily sound-absorbing.

The underside of the catwalks feature perforated metal panels, lit to provide an architectural ceiling (rather than seeing a black void and/or technical equipment). This also allows loudspeakers to be mounted from the catwalks to cover rows of seating towards the rear of the theatre, behind this architectural feature.

View of the theatre from the stage, with steep seating rake.

View from the side; note the sound-transparent expanded metal mesh panels on balcony fronts and below ceiling catwalks and side walls. In the void between the side walls and panels, unseen variable sound-absorbing treatments are deployed.

Jerome Robbins Theater, Baryshnikov Arts Center

LOCATION: New York, USA

ARCHITECT: WASA, Studio A and Arup

COMPLETED: 2005

AUDIENCE: 238 seats

FORM: rectilinear

Designed for Mikhail Baryshnikov, the project was envisioned to serve as an intimate space for the performance of dance and music, with an additional emphasis on the developing role of technology in the performance environment.

One of the important early discussions was about how the sound of the dancers' feet and movement should be heard in the space. This was a driver for material selection around the stage; and shaping of the room. There is no raised stage, instead the main floor of the room serves as the stage. The seating is in a continuous block using benches rather than individual seats for intimacy. The seating block floats in the center of the space, with the front row level with the stage. The natural acoustics of the room occupy the whole space. Sound can energise the sides, rear and below the upper block of seating, creating an enveloping sensation for the audience.

Minimal sound-absorbing treatment is located strategically. Technology infrastructure is ubiquitous to allow deployment of lights, sound or projection surfaces over the entire perimeter of the room. The result is an intimate and engaging space to experience both dance and music.

View of the auditorium and the stage as one contiguous volume.

Detail of the sound-absorbing panels, located on the rear wall to provide some control of sound reflections returning to the stage.

Multi-use Halls

Issue	Priority	Comments
Room acoustics	H	The major challenge is to determine the range of acoustic uses, and then tailor every aspect of the room acoustics design to achieve those requirements. Usually one or two activity types will be the most important and will drive the selection of room shape, form, volume and range of variable acoustic features. Specific guidance is presented in the appropriate typology.
Speech intelligibility	H	A critical requirement in most multi-purpose halls.
Audio systems design	H	Audio systems are generally used for three purposes; speech reinforcement, sound effects and music. There may be a high number of audio devices that need to be integrated into or visible within the architecture, impacting on the room's design. Accommodating these behind architectural finishes will require those finishes to have a high level of acoustic transparency, and pose significant challenges for future technology upgrades (which will often have dimensional constraints).
Sound insulation – external	H	Performance and other noise sensitive spaces should be free of noise disturbance from outside the building. This usually requires a combination of mass heavy building envelope materials, multiple layers of lightweight constructions separated by substantial airspaces, and the separating of noise sensitive spaces by noise neutral (buffer) spaces. Smoke evacuation systems sometimes need venting directly to the outside, meaning that noise control must be included in systems and hatches where they exist.
Sound insulation – internal	H	Performance and other noise sensitive spaces should also be free of noise disturbance from inside the building. If the placement of buffer spaces is not achievable, and/or any noise sensitive space is adjacent to the exterior or noise producing interior space, then mass heavy or isolated constructions (e.g. box-in-box) may be unavoidable. This will impact space planning, building services systems, and structural design.
Speech privacy	M	Some spaces, such as dressing rooms, will require control of sound transmission to other spaces. The location of these spaces should be determined early in the design process.
Impact/vibration isolation	H	Impact noises may come from diverse sources: people walking, doors slamming, building services etc. External traffic may also be an issue (see structure-borne noise). Impact sounds propagate vertically and horizontally, so adjacencies and potential impacts need to be understood in all directions. Impact and vibration must be very well controlled inside performance spaces otherwise concentration is easily broken. Appropriate measures should be included in all systems wherever possible, as they can be very difficult to retrofit later.
Mechanical and electrical noise	H	See guidance in the most relevant primary use case study.
Structure-borne noise	H	The most significant sources of structure-borne noise come from sources close to or outside the building envelope (e.g transport infrastructure, underground parking, or service roads and tunnels). If affected by these sources, the building may require whole construction vibration isolation, which has space planning implications and will impact structure, building services system design and cost.
Environmental noise	M/H	Performance spaces are generally quite energy intensive. The mechanical and electrical systems may require equipment outside the building, which usually has the highest potential noise impact, while codes pertaining to environmental noise emission must be adhered to. Any equipment placed outdoors, should be inherently quiet and/or incorporate noise and vibration control. The location of equipment will also have an impact – if it is on the roof, noise and vibration control to interior spaces will be required.

H – High   M – Medium   L – Low

Introduction

Multi-purpose halls can be used for a variety of events, from amplified performances and spoken word, to natural acoustic concerts; they are a common design request. Understanding how the space will be used, and the corresponding range of acoustic requirements, is crucial to design success.

Architectural style

It is common for buildings to change use over time; performance spaces are no exception. In the great palaces of Europe, the ball court was commonly used for both ball sports and music performance. The Colosseum in Rome had the ability to change format based on event.

Civic auditoriums were built around the UK in the late 19th and early 20th centuries, often in town halls, to serve as spaces for debate, ceremony, local theatre, drama, music and other performances. In the interwar years, three particularly well-known examples included Watford Colosseum, Walthamstow Town Hall and Wembley (later Brent) Town Hall. Simultaneously, there was a boom in the construction of family-run variety theatres in the UK. Many of these have transformed across generations from variety to vaudeville, theatre, cinema, opera and ballet, sometimes hosting different events on and/or over multiple days per week.

Post-war, independent arts organisations began seeking homes outside the aforementioned spaces. Over the latter half of the 20th century, the result was a wide variety of hybrid multi-use venues catering to the specific requirements of the organisations hosted within them. Multi-purpose spaces were initially favoured as they were cheaper than building multiple separate buildings, and had greater revenue-generating potential. The disadvantage was that they generally had to compromise on multiple aspects of design that would otherwise be incorporated in single function spaces (e.g. lacking intimacy for theatre, reverberance for music, or clarity for opera). Over time, a better understanding of these limitations meant greater consideration was given to a room's primary use and ranking its secondary uses. This allowed the design to optimise a more limited range of performance and acoustic options (e.g. a concert hall that can be used for conferences, comedy or amplified music, but not theatre or opera). This is covered more comprehensively in the specific chapters on theatre, concert and recital halls and opera.

However, this did not necessarily reduce the need for multi-use spaces, especially for communities otherwise underserviced by the arts. Improvements in acoustic and theatrical technology allowed an increasing range of uses to be accommodated; orchestra shells and moving ceilings deployed in theatre stages and flytowers improve conditions for music, moving floors, stages and lifts vary seating configurations, and rakes change sightlines and acoustic conditions between concert and theatre modes. When planning a new building, it is fundamental to measure the cost of deployment of automated technologies to achieve the above, versus manual operations. Automation can be faster, allowing quicker and easier building changes between modes, at higher first day cost. Manual systems are initially cheaper, but typically take more time and people to make the changes.

Acoustic features

Multi-purpose halls of the 21st century can incorporate one or more of the following:

- The ability to make large-scale changes to room shape, form, volume and distribution of finishes, so that the space can change fully from the look and feel of a concert hall to a theatre. These changes are critical to change the sound reflection sequence, reverberance, clarity and loudness for the performance function.

- The option of introducing variable sound-absorbing treatment to the room to control the sound reflections from primary wall surfaces, which is especially important for amplified sound uses.

- The potential to introduce and tailor the sound system design for the performance type.

- Surround sound systems, for use as sound effects but also for cinema (with large movie screens complete with loudspeakers being deployed when needed, and stored in flytowers).

- 'Active architecture systems' that use arrays of microphones and loudspeakers to alter the acoustics of a space designed for speech or amplified purposes by adding sound reflections and reverberance to simulate the sound of a more reverberant space (e.g. concert hall). When originally developed and deployed in the 1960s these systems were criticised as the added acoustics sounded 'artificial'. Significant improvements in technology, coupled with better understanding of the acoustic, theatrical and architectural limitations of design and cost, are seeing these systems become ever more popular, not only for multi-purpose rooms, but also to give new opportunities to single purpose rooms.

Challenges

The main challenge remains ensuring that user expectations are properly determined and benchmarked in the early design stages, so that anticipated outcomes can be achieved.

Creating an architectural style that can maintain aesthetic continuity in different configurations should be an important design factor, and will require close collaboration between architect, acoustics and theatre consultant to achieve. These buildings still have an important place in communities. In some cases, they may be a community's only access to the performing arts. It is important they are designed diligently. They will continue to be an opportunity for experimentation in the arts, in ways that some mainstream arts spaces may not be able to achieve.

Prudential Hall, New Jersey Performing Arts Center

LOCATION: Newark, New Jersey, USA

ARCHITECT: Barton Myers

COMPLETED: 1997

AUDIENCE: 2,800

FORM: large shoebox

As well as providing the home of the New Jersey Symphony Orchestra, the hall offers a wide range of programming including conferences, comedy, musicals, opera and rock and pop concerts.

The form is a multi-tiered hybrid theatre, which takes a number of cues from New York's Carnegie Hall – an extended length and parallel side walls and balconies that step back and reduce overhangs to expose the audience to the reverberant main volume of the space. To accommodate the wide range of performance types, there is a full flytower, the orchestra plays on the stage with an orchestral shell around it (which couples to the main volume of the hall), and there is variable sound-absorbing treatment to cover the wall area for amplified performances.

The view of the auditorium from the stage.

Harpa

LOCATION: Reykjavík, Iceland

ARCHITECT: Henning Larsen

COMPLETED: 2011

AUDIENCE: 1,600–1,800

FORM: hybrid shoebox

The Harpa complex is exceptionally dynamic, containing the main concert hall, small auditorium, recital hall and large conference hall.

The main hall, Eldborg, is a world-class concert hall home to the Icelandic Symphony Orchestra. It was designed to accommodate natural acoustic performances for Iceland's own rich and broad musical traditions. It was also designed to present a wide range of performances, from classical music to concert opera, rock, pop, jazz, traditional music, conferences and other speech-based events.

To extend the reverberance and bass response of the room, the hall includes large reverberation chambers outside the main auditorium volume, with doors that allow the chambers to be opened. These are carefully adjusted to optimised settings via a computer-controlled system. For certain works, the chambers are also used to house performers, giving an ethereal, otherworldly sound.

A multi-piece canopy over the stage can act as single or multiple elements to change the sound for performers on stage.

Technical infrastructure for sound, light, projection, rigging and staging provides a wide range of flexibility. Variable sound-absorbing curtains can cover approximately 75% of the wall area. This allows the space to be used for speech and amplified music, as well as hybrid performances and concert opera.

The view of the rear from the stage.

View of the stage, with the doors to the reverberation chambers open on the top right.

Storesal Stormen Culture Center

Location: Bodø, Norway

Architect: DRDH Architects

Completed: 2012

Audience: 950 seat main, 300 seat flexible

Form: rectilinear hall

Situated above the Arctic Circle in the Norwegian city of Bodø, Stormen is a cultural centre housing a waterfront library and four performing arts venues.

The hall in concert mode.

The centrepiece is the Store Sal – a 944-seat space that converts from concert to theatre mode using an innovative approach designed to be truly dual-purpose without compromising quality. As a theatre, its large stage, full-height flytower and variable-sized orchestra pit allow it to host complex theatrical and televised shows. When transformed to a traditional shoebox concert hall, it can deliver world-class symphonic performances. Conversion between the two modes takes just over 60 minutes.

Instead of a conventional orchestral shell, which would require significant onstage storage space, the orchestra is enclosed by 14m high wall panels. These move easily (by one person) on an overhead track system and store against a side stage wall. Acoustic reflectors and motorised ceiling panels can be flown or folded into place above the stage, and, together with the wall panels, dramatically change the acoustics and aesthetics of the space. In theatre-mode, a pair of panels hinge around to form the sides of the proscenium arch, and the top is completed with a folding header panel.

The side and rear walls of the auditorium conceal a series of sliding panels that vary the acoustic character of the room. There is a moving lighting bridge which provides access to lighting positions and strong points set in the auditorium ceiling, accessed from a high-level technical gallery and a forestage rigging grid. The flytower houses a full set of motorised flying bars for scenery and lighting.

The hall in the process of converting between modes.

Tempe Center for the Arts

LOCATION: Tempe, Arizona, USA

ARCHITECT: Barton Myers Associates & Architekton

COMPLETED: 2007

AUDIENCE: 600

FORM: proscenium theatre

A vital community resource, with repertoire spanning from symphonic concerts to theatre and spoken word.

The challenge of this project was to provide a multi-use hall at low cost, on a site with low-flying jet aircraft fly-bys every 90 seconds. The latter required a very high level of sound insulation from exterior to interior. The site and budget would not allow for a large enough volume for a concert hall, so an alternative approach was taken. The space is designed with optimum natural acoustics for theatre. It features a demountable orchestra shell to couple the full flytower to the theatre volume and provide a surface around the orchestra for early sound reflections. An active architecture system, with loudspeakers discreet integrated into the form, is used to electronically create symphonic concert hall conditions. Systems like this require many loudspeakers, most of which need to be hidden or integrated into the architecture; this project has 114. There are 12 loudspeakers over the stage (in two groups mounted on line sets in the flytower), two over the audience, two at the front of the room and two at the first catwalk. Over the upper balcony there are six at the rear catwalk. Additionally there are 14 in mezzanine balcony fronts for lateral reflections, as well as 38 under each balcony.

The stage in concert mode, with orchestral shell in place. Loudspeakers can be seen on the balcony fronts that form part of the active architecture system.

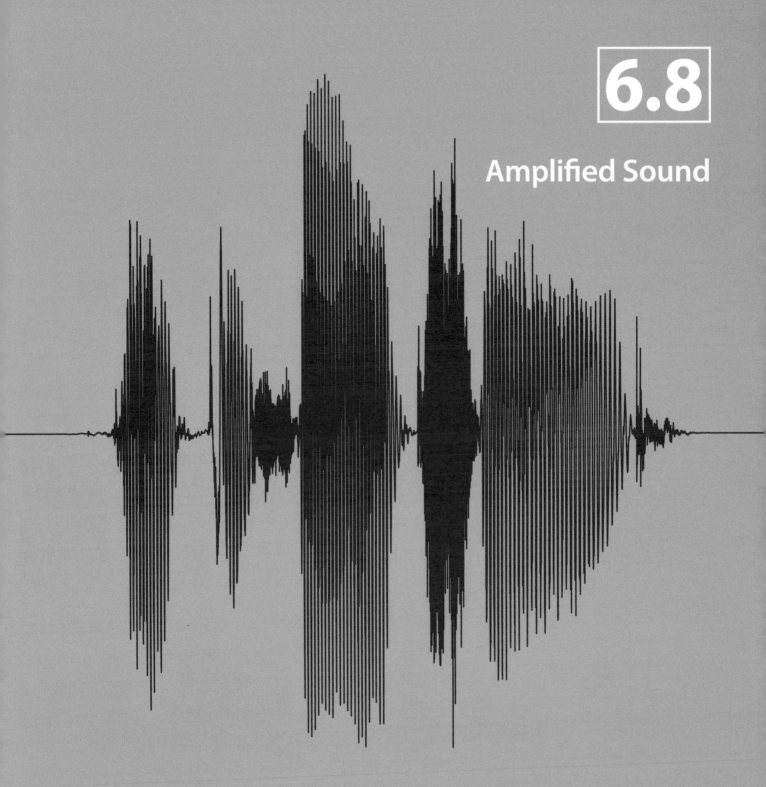

6.8

Amplified Sound

Issue	Priority	Comments
Room acoustics	H	Emphasis is placed on having a high quality of amplified sound achieved through good room acoustics control. Expect extensive areas of sound-absorbing finishes on all ceilings and walls. Where control of low-frequency sound is required, the depth of the wall finishes can be 150–500mm thick. It is important to understand the required range of performance type, to determine room acoustic design parameters. For some live venues, a balance to ensure that crowd excitement is maintained may require careful thinking on the extent of sound-absorbing treatment.
Speech intelligibility	H	Good speech intelligibility is important in some spaces, but it is usually attained in the course of achieving the high level of musical acoustics that is required.
Audio systems design	H	Equipment selection is usually a very specialist process and a specific consultant may be bought on board to advise solely on this. Fit-out is usually done by the facility operator or their specialist consultant according to their specific requirements.
Sound insulation – external	H	Noise emission to neighbours is a key design driver. The noise environment around the building must be measured, with the sound insulation of the building envelope designed to ensure that noise emission can meet required targets. This is usually as important in new build projects as it is in refurbishment or adaptive reuse of existing buildings.
Sound insulation – internal	H	Some separation between critical back-of-house spaces and high sound levels in front-of-house spaces should be expected (to specialist control rooms, green rooms, dressing rooms, etc.).
Speech privacy	L	Not usually an important consideration.
Impact/vibration isolation	H	This may be a consideration in some venues where spaces are stacked vertically, with different simultaneous events as part of the program.
Mechanical and electrical noise	H	Audiophile listening spaces may require low-noise environments, like recording or broadcast studio level criteria. For rock and pop venues and clubs, this tends to be less critical, although background noise levels in excess of NR35–40 are unlikely to be acceptable.
Structure-borne noise	H	Audiophile spaces often have requirements similar to broadcast and recording. Others may be less sensitive.
Environmental noise	H	See sound insulation – external.

H – High   M – Medium   L – Low

Introduction

In spaces where audience experience is reliant on amplified sound, optimised design of both room acoustics and sound systems are especially important for a positive outcome. If sound levels are very high, special attention to space planning and building envelope design can also be important factors in managing environmental impact of venues on their surroundings.

Architectural style

Amplified sound is common in many building types. Relevant chapters in this book address audio systems commonly encountered in these spaces, and the room acoustic considerations to ensure that amplified sound can be delivered at the appropriate quality. This section briefly addresses issues not covered elsewhere, namely for venues where amplified sound is the primary design requirement. These could be broadly described as falling into three categories:

- Rock, pop and similar amplified music venues
- Venues for DJ performance, nightclubs, dancing
- Audiophile listening environments, for both live performance and listening to vinyl

Acoustic features

These spaces can vary widely in design approach, but they share some general common acoustic requirements. Room acoustics generally need to be as well-controlled as possible, although in some venues there also needs to be a balance so there is feedback from crowd participation.

Extensive areas of sound-absorbing treatment are typically required, particularly on walls and ceilings. The depth of treatment can vary from 50–500mm depending on the specific acoustic requirements (achieving better low-frequency 'bass' sound-absorbing performance usually requires more depth). These may require a protective, acoustically transparent facing, especially when located close to the audience (to avoid damage). Note that these treatments are important for both sound quality and loudness control. Good sound insulation to adjacent spaces or the outside is important, especially if environmental noise emission is an issue.

In some critical listening environments, low-noise M+E systems may be required, otherwise in louder rock and pop venues, higher noise levels can be tolerated (usually in the range NR35–NR40).

Challenges

The quantity of sound-absorbing treatment required to achieve appropriate acoustic conditions can be extensive, and potentially costly. Simple industrial grade solutions are common, using standard mineral fibre, fibreglass, or cotton/denim/polyester equivalent, either black or with a black tissue facing, behind expanded metal mesh or similar finish.

In higher-quality listening environments, sound-absorbing, diffusing and reflecting finishes may be required. Some of these are commercially available. Others will be bespoke, sometimes made by a specialist fabricator, sometimes designed by the client, acoustic consultant and architect in collaboration. Understanding this will be a crucial aspect of the design process.

Loudspeakers are frequently visible, exposed and even a design feature. It is important for the designer to embrace this to successfully integrate them into the scheme.

For venues with very high interior sound levels, emission of noise to the environment, especially to residences or noise-sensitive spaces outside the venue itself, are an important consideration. Limiting interior sound levels may be a necessary operational requirement. Community engagement is often a critical aspect of being a good neighbour and ensuring venues can operate successfully.

Ministry of Sound

LOCATION: Southwark, London, UK

ARCHITECT: Casper Mueller Kneer Ltd

COMPLETED: 1991

AUDIENCE: 400 (The Courtyard), 600 (The Box)

The brainchild of Justin Berkmann, Ministry of Sound opened in September 1991. It is a conversion of a disused bus garage that took its inspiration from New York's Paradise Garage to create London's first club devoted to American house music.

The original vision was a space that considered sound first and foremost, with the initial investments in a high-quality sound system and improvements to the sound insulation, to mitigate noise to neighbours. Spaces were latterly upgraded to include significant sound-absorbing treatment to the upper walls and ceilings. As of 2016, the main room, The Box, has a Dolby Atmos spatial sound system of 22 channels with 64 loudspeakers, which allow the DJs to manipulate the sound in 3D within the room, while playing live.

The 103 is the main connector space between venues, with a capacity of 500 people.

The Box; the world-renowned main space at The MoS.

Brooklyn Steel

LOCATION: Williamsburg, New York, USA

ARCHITECT: HLW Architects

COMPLETED: 2017

AUDIENCE: 1,800

A former steelworks with a brick exterior envelope and lightweight steel deck roof.

The challenge of the building conversion was to control noise emission from the building to the adjacent public housing project to meet the stringent New York City Noise Code. The solution, since the existing steel deck could not take any more weight, was to build a green roof structure with a new steelwork frame supported from the brick perimeter, optimised for the required sound insulation performance. Simple industrial materials of metal wire mesh and 100mm black tissue-faced mineral fibre distributed over the walls and ceiling provided the main acoustic control strategy. In some areas, thickness of material was increased to 200–400mm to deal with high levels of low-frequency sound. Elsewhere, a strategy was developed to create buffer zones between the venue and exterior doors to serve as noise-control vestibules.

View of the venue, with wire mesh sound-absorbing treatment visible on side walls.

Inset: The green roof increases sound-insulation performance. Note the dense housing development surrounding the venue; this was a key driver for the roof sound-insulation strategy.

Public Records

LOCATION: Brooklyn, NY, USA

ARCHITECT: Public Records

COMPLETED: 2019

Located in the post-industrial Gowanus
neighbourhood of Brooklyn, Public Records describes
itself as 'a multi-faceted music driven social space'.

The building features four main areas; a hi-fi record
bar showcasing rare record collections, a performance
space featuring both live acts and vinyl-leaning DJs
with a fully bespoke sound system, an all-day vegan
cafe and magazine shop, and an exterior courtyard,
equipped with a sound system to allow broadcast
of events from the interior. Public Records is an
example of a new breed of publicly accessible curated
audiophile space. It is designed for the playing of live
music, or vinyl records, in surroundings optimised for
the purpose.

As it was adjacent to both residential and commercial
premises, ensuring appropriate sound insulation of the
building envelope was a key design driver, not only to
limit sound emission to neighbours, but also external
sound coming into the building.

The performance space is an isolated box-in-box
construction built in gypsum board, with bespoke
designed sound-absorbing material to provide a
highly controlled reverberance across the audible
frequency spectrum. This is achieved using plywood
of varying thickness, perforation type, spacing from
the wall, and thickness of acoustic batt material
(made of black recycled denim cotton) behind the
panels. The result is a room finely tuned to allow the
sound system to deliver the sound of recorded vinyl
in studio-like conditions, and with a focus on live
instruments without any significant room acoustic
effects. The visual character of the room is varied using
a colour-changing LED system that can be adjusted
independently for the ceiling and for each wall.

Elsewhere in the building, a lean palette of materials is
used creatively. In the hi-fi record bar, sound-absorbing
acoustic batt (in light grey fabric wrap) cover the wall
areas above the booths and across the ceiling.

The hi-fi record bar.

The sound room;
mixer location.

Immersive Spaces

Issue	Priority	Comments
Room acoustics	H	Requirements vary depending on the use of the immersive space. Any use of spatial audio will generally require a well-controlled room acoustic, with sound-absorbing finishes to all ceilings and walls. To ensure appropriate control of low-frequency sound within these spaces, the depth of the wall finishes can be between 50 and 500mm thick.
Speech intelligibility	H	Good speech intelligibility is a critical performance requirement for AV systems, and between users in the space.
Audio systems design	H	Technical fit-out is a complex process generally requiring specialist design. Equipment is usually selected by the designer or the facility operator according to their specific requirements. Equipment can be located at the perimeter room boundary and/or in the room. Understanding the usable floor space for the immersive experience is a critical early planning factor. Equipment configuration can take several forms; visual displays often vary widely, impacting plan and section dimensions, and locations of loudspeakers if the screen is not acoustically transparent. Many spaces require deep cavities for infrastructure in the walls, floors and ceilings to run cabling as needed. Adjacent spaces may be required for locating main equipment racks to keep noise out of the immersive space itself.
Sound insulation – external	H	Spaces are usually located internal to the building plan and not directly adjacent to the external façades. Many immersive environments are sensitive to external noise intrusion so sound insulation of the building envelope must be designed to ensure that it does not affect the space. Not all noise sources will be visible; some may be regular, others intermittent. Future noise sources, from transport or construction, should also be considered.
Sound insulation – internal	H	Critical listening spaces require significant sound insulation to and from adjacent spaces, to avoid sound disturbance within the space. This often requires independent drywall or masonry walls, floating floors and independent lids. Lobbied sets of heavy acoustic doors are usually required.
Speech privacy	L	This is not usually an important consideration.
Impact/vibration isolation	H	Acoustically critical spaces are often built as box-in-box constructions, with concrete floating floors on resilient bearings with independent inner walls and 'lids' of either concrete/masonry or plasterboard. This type of construction can provide excellent control of impact sound in surrounding spaces.
Mechanical and electrical noise	H	A low noise level from building systems is essential to ensure that the quality of the audio reproduction is not degraded, or that high dynamic range of sound can be achieved. Delivering large volumes of conditioned air quietly often requires large duct sizes with sufficient length to incorporate attenuation.
Structure-borne noise	H	Concrete floating floors on resilient bearings are often used in these spaces, which to a certain extent can be tuned to attenuate sources of ground-borne noise such as underground trains, trams, road traffic or nearby construction noise. If vibration sources are significant, whole or partial building isolation may be required.
Environmental noise	H	Building systems equipment located on the roof or venting to the exterior are usually the main source of environmental noise. This issue is particularly relevant for facilities located close to residential buildings. Some spaces may also produce high sound levels in operation, and environmental impact should be considered.

H – High   M – Medium   L – Low

Introduction

Immersive venues and environments are an emerging typology usually designed for the delivery of more than one sensory experience. They generally require a controlled or neutral baseline for this to be achieved successfully. Good acoustics are a critical factor.

Acoustic features

Immersive and experiential spaces exist in a range of different disciplines, from teaching and learning, to healthcare, architecture and design, entertainment and the arts. The terminology means different things in each, so understanding what is expected by the client is crucial. This section focuses primarily on venue-type spaces.

These spaces generally offer opportunities for interaction in 'full surround'. This incorporates any combination of auditory, visual (light/visuals), touch (haptic), vibration/movement and smell, which can encompass both physical and digital experiences. Environments can be deployed for a variety of uses including (but not limited to) design, cross-disciplinary research and development, experimentation, installation experiences, digital collaboration and live performance. Furthermore, such activities may be predetermined or can happen in real-time. Increasingly these spaces make use of multiple technologies layered together to facilitate the intended experience, for example the layering of spatial audio with immersive visuals, augmented reality, and/or virtual reality.

Common requirements to assist with the successful delivery of the aforementioned include controlled room acoustics to deliver specific audio experience, high-performing sound and vibration insulation from internal and external sources (to enable experiences to be delivered accurately), low background noise, controllable lighting, and good technical infrastructure for AV, IT, data and communications. Immersive spaces share and combine many of the acoustic needs found in performing arts, cinema, broadcast and recording environments.

The type of technologies deployed can vary widely, especially those used for visualisation (including individual or combined projections, LED/LCD screens, head-mounted displays, tablets and mobile phones). It is important to understand the anticipated technologies and the expected acoustic criteria from the client early in the design process. This can have significant impact on space planning and design.

Challenges

Design approach varies widely from industry to industry. In some, such as cinema, the standardisation of typology usually happens quickly, to enable content transfer and presentation in multiple spaces at scale.

In other industries it may take significantly longer for standards to develop, if they standardise at all. Rapid technology development will mean that architecture must incorporate acoustic needs and allow for fast turnover and/or replacement of technology systems.

Opportunities

The delivery of accurate spatial audio to recreate genuine 360-degree spherical sound experiences and sound movement will continue to develop alongside the computing and processing power required to achieve this, especially in real-time. As techniques become more sophisticated, loudspeaker types, quantities, densities and locations will develop and future-proofing physical design to accommodate the range of anticipated change will be important.

Similarly, vibration and movement devices are becoming more sophisticated. They are able to accurately recreate subtle physical effects (e.g. movement from vibration on a train, the floor plates in a tall building, or a crowd of people on a stadium terrace). Incorporation of floors that can move vertically and horizontally within the sound-insulating envelope of the room, and with sufficient noise control, will be an important design factor.

Arup Facilities

LOCATION: various, worldwide

ARCHITECT: Arup

COMPLETED: 1998–present

Arup has pioneered immersive experience environments for use in design and research.

In 1998 Arup created an ambisonic listening room. For the first time outside of a research institution, people were able to listen to buildings before they were built using this technology.

The room has evolved and developed considerably since then. The most recent lab has a full 360-degree projection capability, an ambisonic sound system, wave field synthesis (WFS) and a calibrated motion platform that can simulate vibration and structural dynamics. These allow one to hear, feel and see potential environments, allowing subjective decision making in the design process.

These tools are also a vital part of engaging the public in design dialogue and have been used extensively in consultation for major infrastructure projects around the world including Heathrow Airport's third runway, Perth Airport, and Texas High Speed Rail.

In addition, these environments may also be used with virtual and augmented reality, with the advantage that a full spatial audio system allows the user in VR to hear audio matched to the scene.

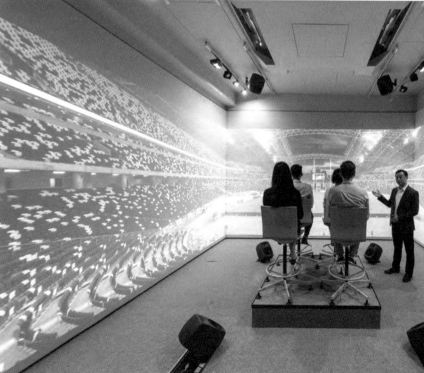

Arup Immersion Lab Singapore has immersive screens on four sides of the room (transparent to let sound through).

Arup iLab London was designed for 1:1 scale visual immersion, also with immersive sound.

Above: Arup SoundLab New York, with ambisonics and wave field synthesis.

Right: Arup m|Lab was designed to be mobile; as with all lab environments, this is one of the only ways to create real-time sync between visuals and sound for VR immersive experiences.

The Cube,
Moss Arts Center

LOCATION: Moss Arts Center, Virginia Tech, USA

ARCHITECT: Snøhetta and STV Incorporated

COMPLETED: 2013

The Cube was conceived by identifying an opportunity for cross-disciplinary collaboration between programmes available at Virginia Tech, if the right design and research space was made available.

The Cube measures 127cm w x 102cm l x 81cm h and is column free. It is able to control the acoustics using sound-absorbing curtains, deployable in sets at each of the four levels of the facility. A spatial audio system can immerse the listener in sound. There are many deployable projection options. Unlike traditional virtual spaces, this collaborative research environment for augmented team exploration (CREATE) enables multi-person (social) collaboration with data. It offers a dedicated high-bandwidth digital audio-visual network to support research, broadcasting/streaming, and real-time interaction with remote artists, schools and researchers. The space is intended to create the framework for new explorations in data mining visualisation, and sonification.

Horizontal cube
visualisation mode.

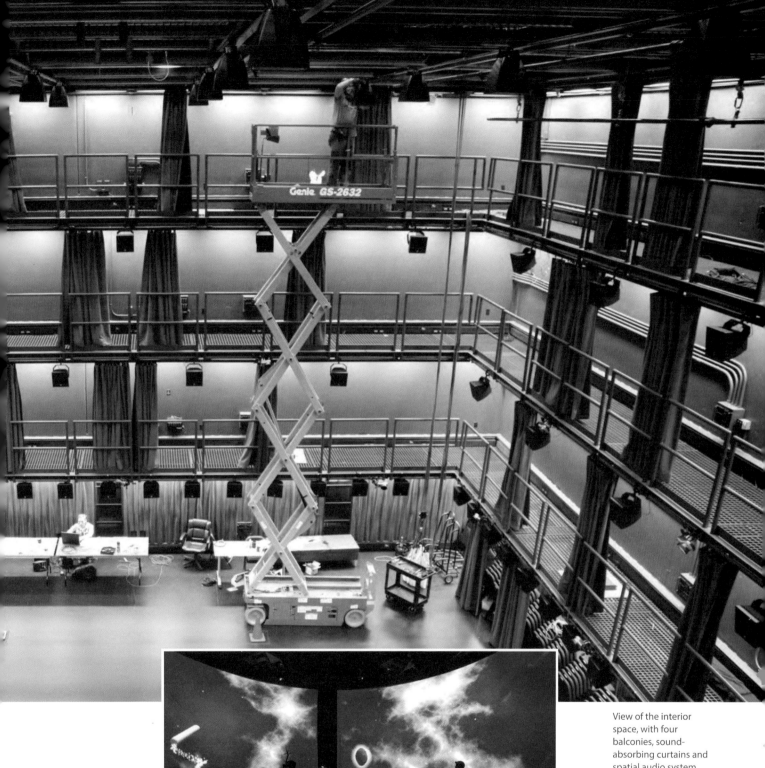

Multi-user screen, VR and spatial audio mode.

View of the interior space, with four balconies, sound-absorbing curtains and spatial audio system loudspeakers.

Health and Wellness

Issue	Priority	Comments
Room acoustics	H	The importance of good acoustics (and reduction of noise) in the recovery process is becoming increasingly appreciated by healthcare professionals, resulting in positive impacts on building design. For hygiene and maintenance reasons, sound-absorbing treatment is normally restricted to ceilings and upper wall areas, and specialist products suitable for healthcare environments need to be used.
		The relationship between private and common areas (wards or corridors) requires careful planning to create barriers for controlling sound propagation (e.g. staggered or sawtooth plan geometry).
		Soft/porous furnishings help to offset the inherent lack of sound-absorbing surfaces in hospitals. Furniture layouts can also be used to break sound propagation paths and absorb sound.
		Wellness facilities may place a greater emphasis on creating specific sound environments based on activity and have less onerous requirements for acoustic materials and locations.
Speech intelligibility	H	This is critical in many spaces to ensure that important information (e.g. concerning diagnoses and treatment) can be easily conveyed and clearly understood.
Audio systems design	H	PAVA systems require careful planning, given relatively reverberant conditions. Routine use of PA for general announcements is usually in very selective locations to avoid disturbing patients or staff (other options such as mobile device apps are also used for this purpose).
		Sound masking and soundscape systems are becoming increasingly recognised as useful for creating 'positive sound' environments.
Sound insulation – external	M	Internal background noise needs to be sufficiently low to promote sleep and rest. It is important to ensure that the façade sound insulation performance reduces incoming noise appropriately. This is particularly important for hospitals located in busy locations, close to noisy equipment (e.g. MEP), and/or when rooftops are used for helicopters.
Sound insulation – internal	M–H	Good sound insulation is typically important for rooms where speech privacy or noise sensitivity is important (e.g. patient consultation rooms), spaces that generate high noise levels (e.g. MRIs, plant rooms), and those with high sensitivity to noise ingress (e.g. patient rooms).
Speech privacy	H	This is an important requirement for areas where practitioner-to-practitioner or practitioner-to-patient confidentiality is required. Where mass heavy constructions are not possible, sound-masking systems may be necessary to achieve requirements.
Impact/vibration isolation	H	Wherever practical, soft or resilient floor finishes should be provided in wards to reduce impact from footfall noise and equipment being moved between spaces. Doors are opened and closed with high frequency and acoustic mitigation should be considered.
Mechanical and electrical noise	H	Set a target range and achieve it, understanding that high noise levels negatively impact rest, communication and concentration. Low noise levels can cause irritation both inside and outside the space.
Structure-borne noise	H	Consider transport noise and vibration sources that could require vibration isolation for part or all of the building. Medical equipment may be especially sensitive to vibration, or it might generate high noise levels, requiring specialised structural design approaches, localised equipment isolation mounting, and perhaps even structural isolation of the floor, wall partitions and/or ceiling.
Environmental noise		Building systems equipment or venting located to the exterior are usually the main source of environmental noise. This issue is particularly relevant when close to residential buildings.

H – High   M – Medium   L – Low

Introduction

Good acoustics play a significant role in promoting human health and wellness, while noise can be seriously detrimental to it. Supported by a growing body of research, control of noise and introduction of pleasing sounds (as a natural part of the architecture of specially designed features), are playing an increasingly important role in these buildings.

Architectural style

The earliest examples of dedicated healthcare environments date back to the ancient civilisations of Egypt, Greece, India, the Incas and the Aztecs. Modern hospital design developed in the UK during the Victorian era. In 1872, when St Thomas' hospital in London relocated to new premises, Florence Nightingale's writings helped guide its design, pioneering the use of separate buildings that were interconnected to form one larger complex, paying close attention to the importance of good light and air. The ability to easily clean and sanitise was – and remains – crucial. This informed the first healthcare facility design standards introduced in the 1940s, leading to a predominance of hard materials that are generally sound-reflecting.

An ever-increasing body of research has documented the detrimental effects of noise on health; whether exposure is short, medium or long-term. These can include sleep disturbance, reduced focus, impaired cognitive and task performance, poor memory retention, hypertension, stress, high blood pressure and cardiac function impacts, as well as a range of other physiological and psychological conditions. As a result, standards for noise in hospitals continue to develop.

Increasing global recognition of the impact of health and wellness in all building types has seen requirements encapsulated in rating systems such as WELL, LEED, BREEAM and Green Star. This has been accompanied by movement toward a greater diversity of spaces that provide autonomy and choices for occupants based on the activity being undertaken by staff, or the treatments being received by patients.

As the public becomes concerned about noise impact on their quality of life, expectation for high-quality sound environments is increasing. Cities are noisy (and getting noisier) due to population growth and increased strain on urban spatial planning. Rural areas are faced with other challenges (e.g. noise from wind power or transport infrastructure) with residents being more susceptible to effects of noise due to the quieter outdoor environment. The broader design conversation is moving away from simplistic mitigation of negative noise impacts, to a more comprehensive view of positive sound experience; better outcomes are achieved by curating the entire 'soundscape' through good design and the introduction of the right sounds.

Acoustic features

Acoustics need to support patient recovery and the functional needs of healthcare providers. Good speech intelligibility is important in medical emergencies for spoken communication to be clearly understood. At the same time, speech privacy is important in certain spaces to protect patient confidentiality. The right sound in a space may also be critical for precision work.

Activity noise is an unavoidable by-product of hospital operations, particularly during busy periods of the day. A wide range of complex activities, with plan adjacencies that are not always ideal acoustically, are necessary (in some cases) for the right treatment sequence. In hospital wards, it is necessary to monitor patients via nurses' stations, using monitors and alarms. These sounds must be discernible above general background noise. From a planning perspective, for intensive care units and accident/ emergency departments, fast and easy access is crucial. In these spaces the low sound insulation, and easy sound and noise propagation that results from such design, is not beneficial for patients.

Strategies for balancing these conflicting noise objectives include:

- Strategic planning of room adjacencies, e.g. locating consultation spaces away from high noise-generating or frequently occupied spaces

- Operational measures, e.g. designated daily 'quiet times' in hospital wards, when noise is intentionally minimised

- Use of materials with high sound-absorbing performance – these are limited to ceilings for hygiene purposes, and to avoid compromising other requirements (there are numerous specialist products for this purpose)

Challenges

Control of building systems noise is a challenge as many hospital facilities will not allow internal fibrous acoustical lining of ducts. Control must be provided by dedicated pack-less or hospital-grade sound attenuators. Some operating rooms may require stainless-steel cleanable ducts, and some spaces with NMR or MRI machines may require iron-free building products within a defined proximity.

Opportunities

Holistic healing environments have become increasingly popular. Sound and light were first introduced as background elements. More recently they have become integral to healing activities themselves. The commercial wellness industry continues to grow rapidly. As it progresses, it is experimenting with immersive sound systems, visuals and lighting including circadian lighting, to create experiences that form the basis of treatments. These are often delivered in spaces with well-defined, bespoke acoustic environments. As research continues, some of these are likely to be introduced into more traditional healthcare facilities.

Audio-visual systems are increasingly popular in traditional healthcare settings. The opportunities and possibilities for the sonification of medical data may also lead to the development of specialist listening environments to undertake data capture and analysis. The use of VR and AR in professional healthcare are being investigated for potential benefits and are showing promise. These can be especially useful for patients during extended recovery and for those with limited mobility and in hospice care. This will likely result in the need for specialist spaces with controlled sound and light environments, incorporating spatial sound and immersive video systems (see the immersive spaces chapter for additional information).

As 'personal' health technology increases in prevalence, it is likely that personal monitoring and remote data collection may change how hospital equipment is spatially arranged, reducing the in-patient population in hospitals and requiring new means of remote communication between practitioners and patients, all of which may result in a shift in acoustic design approaches.

Immersive Spaces

PROJECT: Woom Center

LOCATION: New York, USA

ARCHITECT: Asa Barak

COMPLETED: 2016

A yoga studio, with sessions accompanied by sound, vibration and scent.

PROJECT: Inscape Meditation Studio

LOCATION: New York, USA

ARCHITECT: Archi-Tectonics

COMPLETED: 2017

A holistic meditation and mindfulness space, with audio-guided sessions.

These two projects give an indication of the kinds of alternative health and wellness environments we might see migrate into the traditional hospital setting over time. Both take a holistic approach to the entire building design considering acoustics, sound, lighting, smell and food/taste as integral to the visitor experience.

The studio spaces are designed to be immersive sound and light experiences. Sound-absorbing treatment is well-integrated into the architecture and designed to support spatial audio systems to surround and envelop visitors in sound, with specific content designed for the various activities taking place. They both have a high level of sound insulation so that their main studio spaces are free of disturbance from other areas within the building and outside noise. Noise from HVAC systems is strictly controlled to between NR25 and NR30.

They take contrasting approaches to light, with Inscape using muted coloured lighting to create a feeling of warmth and comfort. Woom Center uses projection on all four wall surfaces, which can be static, colour-changing or include dynamic content.

The Woom yoga
studio, with students.

The Inscape dome
meditation room.

Kaiser Permanente San Diego Medical Center, San Diego

LOCATION: San Diego, USA

ARCHITECT: CO Architects

COMPLETED: 2017

Kaiser Permanente San Diego (KPSD) is a new hospital serving the city and surrounding areas. Kaiser invested in improving the acoustic environment to benefit patients' comfort and overall health outcomes.

This facility features 61,600m² hospital with a central plant and an ambulatory care building.

The hospital site is located approximately five kilometres south of the Marine Corps Air Station Miramar, where fighter jet operations are a source of extremely high levels of noise. The design of the façade reduces noise ingress to minimise its impact on the healing environment. Auralisation demonstrations allowed the client to make an informed decision based on subjective understanding of the flight impacts.

A new patient room and nurse station layout was developed, aimed at reducing noise impact on patients. Traditionally the layout of a centralised nurse station means a high degree of foot traffic and noise, disrupting numerous patient and treatment rooms. De-centralised nurse stations reduce this by requiring a smaller number of staff to move shorter distances.

Typically medical equipment and user interface technology are placed outboard of patient demising walls, which takes up valuable floor space. The demising wall between patient rooms at this facility includes recessed head and foot walls to more easily accommodate this equipment. The sound insulation detailing of the recess was achieved using drywall, maintaining performance while not adding additional labour or material costs.

Patient room showing detail of recessed wall above bed used here for improved lighting conditions.

Sound-absorbing treatment locations are usually limited to ceilings for maintenance and durability. Note here nurse stations are distributed, one per two patient rooms, to minimise traffic and associated noise in the hallways.

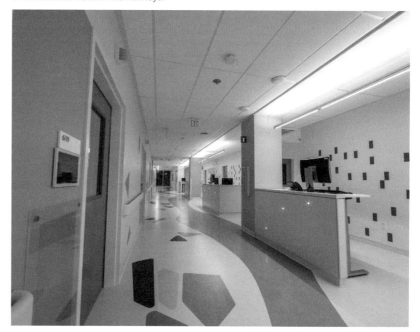

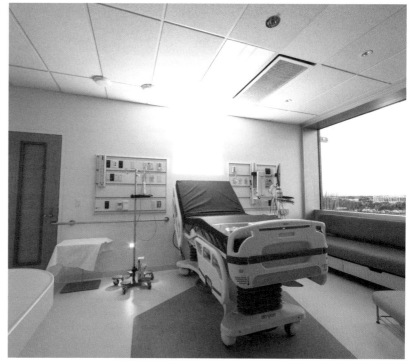

Issue	Priority	Comments
Room acoustics	H	The acoustic criteria and design approach for each workspace should be specifically developed to best suit the intended function. In offices, meeting rooms and other areas where person-to-person communication, AV or VC use is critical. Room acoustics must be optimised accordingly. The placement of materials that provide good early sound reflections and reduce reverberance is essential. In large open-plan offices, sound-absorbing or diffusing materials should be deployed to mitigate general occupational noise levels and early sound reflection paths that transfer sound from one end to another of the space via walls and ceilings. Furniture layout and incorporation of sound-absorbing treatment into desk partitions is an effective strategy for local acoustic mitigation.
Speech intelligibility	H	Where high-quality person-to-person communication is required, good speech intelligibility is essential.
Audio systems design	H	PAVA systems are commonly used throughout large office buildings while AV systems are common in individual rooms and should be optimised for these particular spaces. Phone and video conferencing are now ubiquitous. The sound quality of calls necessitates excellent acoustics to ensure that signal transfer is free of reverberance and noise. Appropriate levels of continuous background noise are essential in work environments. If these are not provided by the HVAC, a separate sound-masking system may be necessary. It will likely require higher-density loudspeaker layouts than PAVA and will need to be operated continuously.
Sound insulation – external	H	The noise environment around the building must be quantified to optimise the façade performance. Not all noise sources will be visible; some may be regular, others intermittent. This is especially important if the building is to be fully or partially naturally ventilated, as sound-attenuating air paths may be needed.
Sound insulation – internal	M–H	Pay close attention to noise propagation from circulation spaces, common spaces, open plan working areas and building equipment rooms to private or other noise sensitive spaces.
Speech privacy	M	Requirements should be identified early so that the plan can situate noise-producing areas away from private spaces where possible.
Impact/vibration isolation	H	Footfall impact noise (both airborne and structure-borne) within and between spaces, vertically and horizontally must be considered. Impact isolation above, below or within the final floor finish should incorporated as required.
Mechanical and electrical noise	M–H	A target range must be set and adhered to. High noise levels negatively impact concentration and communication and increase stress. Low noise levels emphasise noise from colleagues and/or from outside. This needs to be considered in conjunction with the facade design to produce optimum results.
Structure-borne noise	H	Sources can include underground car parks or transport systems. It is important to determine if existing (or future) transport systems are located at street level or below the building. Mitigation may require vibration isolation for either all or part of the structure.
Environmental noise	M	Building systems equipment located in or venting to the exterior are usually the main source of environmental noise. This issue is particularly pertinent for workplaces located close to residential buildings.

H – High   M – Medium   L – Low

Introduction

From enclosed private offices and meeting rooms to large areas with partitioned cubicles or completely open spaces, contemporary workplaces and their associated acoustics are increasingly being refined to suit changing working approaches.

Architectural style

The workplace typology has changed greatly since the Industrial Revolution, when process dictated building form. Machinery was tightly packed into spaces for maximum production output with minimal mitigation of heat, dirt and dust. Poor air quality and high noise levels (with associated noise-induced hearing loss) were an everyday hazard.

During the North American office building boom of the late 19th and early 20th centuries, companies replicated earlier factory models by placing rows of desks in large, open-plan office spaces, creating what is now considered the 'standard' workplace arrangement.

Acoustic features

Early examples of offices tended to utilise predominantly sound-reflecting materials. The noise generated was found to be detrimental to productivity and wellbeing. To address this, sound-absorbing treatment was retrofitted to existing buildings and incorporated into the design of newer ones. It was soon found that too much sound-absorbing material also decreased productivity, as quiet spaces draw attention to other noises, both internal and external.

The introduction of sealed building façades over the course of the 20th century raised new issues. These façades helped control incoming noise but did not reduce sound levels equally at all frequencies. Some sounds were now more intrusive, especially if intermittent (e.g. aircraft). In addition, HVAC systems were introduced to condition the air, requiring noise standards to be developed to ensure that the noise produced was neither too loud nor too quiet. If designed well, background noise from HVAC can help to 'mask' some internal and external sounds. To be successful in this regard they must operate continuously, as changing sound levels can also have a detrimental impact upon concentration.

Challenges

Some studies have concluded that sealed buildings give rise to a variety of health issues. Others have indicated that the open-plan office environment is not optimal for collaboration, concentration or wellbeing. Sustainable approaches to building design are encouraging a return to natural ventilation and the challenge of attenuating the resulting incoming noise is fuelling the development of new acoustic technologies to tackle the problem.

Opportunities

Since the invention of the Sony Walkman in the early 1980s, users have taken to controlling their own sonic environments via headphones. In the future, localised environmental control could expand to encompass the addition of soundscapes that enhance wellbeing, learning competency and specific task performance.

As AR and VR become more prevalent, they will likely have an impact on both working practices and the spaces needed to accommodate them. For example, large-scale projections or VR collaborative rooms for multiple participants will require improved acoustics, and potentially 3D spatial sound systems. As a result, some workspaces might require much higher quality acoustics.

It is also likely that advances in sensor technology will be paired with active architecture and mechanical and audio-visual systems, to vary the acoustics of spaces based on their use or occupancy.

Historical context

E-ON HQ

LOCATION: Coventry, UK

ARCHITECT: Bennetts Associates

COMPLETED: 1994

A new headquarters building with a highly efficient working environment for its core staff, commensurate with its need to focus on operational costs and integration of a previously dispersed organisation.

This ambitious design sought to incorporate a ceiling of appropriate thermal mass for passive cooling in the summer. This also necessitated a minimum surface area to be effective, requiring the use of some curvature to increase the area over a regular flat ceiling. Another major challenge was to minimise use of materials. The design team worked together to develop a solution for the ceiling that addressed the integral requirements for structural, thermal, light and acoustic performance within the ceiling element.

The basic concept was a coffered precast concrete ceiling with a hung element, incorporating lighting (downward facing and reflecting from the coffer) with a sound-absorbing 'wing' at each side. The challenge was to optimise the coffer shape for the best lighting conditions and to make the best use of sound-absorbing properties of the wing, via sound incidence from below reflected back down from the coffer. A generative computer modelling process was used to assess performance using ray tracing. The result is an elegant solution that achieves the design goals.

Control of noise from the atrium is achieved using sound-absorbing ceiling elements on the underside of the leading edge of the floor slab, to capture sound before it can penetrate the floorplates.

Floor plates from the atrium show concrete coffers on multiple levels, and leading edge sound-absorbing treatment to control sound coming up from the floor of the central atrium.

Detailed view of optimised coffer design, with integrated lighting and acoustics.

LightHouse for the Blind and Visually Impaired

LOCATION: San Francisco, California, USA

ARCHITECT: Mark Cavagnero Associates Architects

COMPLETED: 2016

Designed for the blind, by the blind, the new LightHouse for the Blind headquarters uses innovative lighting, technology and architectural design features to set a new standard of universal design for people with all levels of sight.

Acoustics was a fundamental driver in the design of every aspect of the project, given the importance of hearing and listening to people who are visually impaired.

The entry to the lobby, stairwells, corridors and all public spaces are based on the key premise that sound is information for blind users of the space. The concrete floor allows for the cadence of a cane tapping to be heard around the corner, and lower background noise levels ease listening.

Auralisation was key to the process; blind stakeholders for the LightHouse determined where to place sound-absorbing panels to provide a sense of comfort and intelligibility within the sensibility of beautiful, well-crafted architecture.

The LightHouse also developed new ways to provide accessible corporate, educational and creative technologies without presuming the privilege of sight. Remarkably, this included the development of a tactile control panel used to operate the sophisticated technologies of a corporate boardroom. Through extensive physical mock-up and custom programming, the physical user interface was made to address the needs of the blind and visually impaired while being intuitive for sighted users. While this design technique is becoming more rare in architecture, it is still used extensively by product and industrial designers, the automotive industry and others, where the sound and tactility of use is key to the experience of quality, and knowing that an action is completed as it sounds and feels right.

The meeting room; note that the distribution of sound-absorbing treatment is slightly different to that of a conventional meeting room, and the controls for the room are manual and tactile rather than digital.

In the lobby, the slatted timber areas incorporate sound-absorbing treatment. The quantity of treatment was determined through auralisation, so that blind users could best navigate the space.

R/GA HQ

LOCATION: New York, USA

ARCHITECT: Foster + Partners

COMPLETED: 2017

This project consolidated several of the R/GA offices into a single location. An existing 15,300 square-metre warehouse has been completely refurbished to foster collaboration, with each floor being larger than a football field.

A combined vision of Foster + Partners and R/GA CEO Bob Greenberg, the project impetus was to create a completely 'connected' office, seamlessly merging the digital and analogue worlds, and to act as a template that could be deployed in their other offices globally. Key components of the acoustic design were to create exemplar spaces with acoustics and speech intelligibility to allow high-quality multi-office design meetings and collaboration, a sense of a lively office environment, enclosed offices that were easy to change (e.g. demount and move location, increase in plan area, adjust function), integrate all necessary acoustics and AV requirements, and not break the visual continuity of space.

The offices were all created using Unistrut, a modular metal-channel framing system with simple bolt fixing, with only enough mass added to the walls as needed for optimum sound insulation. They have writing and projection surfaces on one or more sides, and integrated AV technology.

Sound-absorbing treatment is judiciously located in the coffers of the ceiling to provide varying zones with different levels of acoustic control. Projection and audio technology are used in the social spaces to create large-scale digital experiences for the visitors and staff.

The social and collaborative spaces are the heart of the plan, arranged around a dining area and coffee bar. A town-hall style staircase connects two floors, encouraging chance meetings and extending the social space for large meetings. The overall aesthetic is simple and utilitarian.

View of interconnecting stair. Floor finish materials were carefully chosen to reduce footfall impact.

View of open floor plate with modular enclosed meeting room on the left. Framing system, doors and interior finishes are also modular, allowing reconfiguration and reuse of all components.

Issue	Priority	Comments
Room acoustics	H	Studies have shown significant benefits from suitably controlled classroom acoustics. For teachers, these include better voice support (reducing voice strain), reduced stress, increased wellbeing and satisfaction. For students, improvements in behaviour, comprehension for both hearing and hearing-impaired pupils, and overall improved academic performance.
		Making sure teaching spaces have the right shape and form, surfaces that promote good early sound reflections between teacher and students, and acoustic treatments to control reverberance and late reflections is crucial.
		Special teaching areas (e.g. music, speech, occupational therapies) may have specific room acoustic needs.
Speech intelligibility	H	Very good speech intelligibility is essential for communication and comprehension. Achieving requirements is very closely linked to good room acoustic design.
Audio systems design	H	Traditionally smaller classrooms do not have audio systems, although this is changing in some schools to support those with hearing or visual impairments.
		In larger lecture theatres, speech reinforcement systems are typically necessary to achieve appropriate sound levels and intelligibility. Any systems must be integrated with the aids and technologies used by hearing-impaired students.
		In many schools and universities, it has become standard practice to record audio and video of classes for archiving or online learning. Room acoustics can require studio-like conditions for clear microphone pick-up and recording. Thoughtful placement of loudspeakers, microphones and video cameras is required.
Sound insulation – external	H	Limiting noise coming into the building from external sources is crucial to maintain good learning conditions. Traffic noise sources tend to be most significant, with intermittent sources such as aircraft particularly problematic. If natural ventilation is considered, this requires significant attention.
Sound insulation – internal	H	This is particularly important to ensure noise between teaching spaces, or between teaching and other functions (circulation, gyms, etc.) is appropriately controlled. Full-height (slab-to-slab) partitions are generally required. Moveable walls often perform poorly and should be used with caution, particularly in spaces where a range of different teaching activities – with different acoustic requirements – are taking place.
Speech privacy	M	Some areas will require high levels of privacy for private conversations (e.g. between heads of school departments).
Impact/vibration isolation	H	During planning, it is important to ensure that high traffic areas or rooms with high floor impacts, such as dance studios or gyms, are located sufficiently far from noise sensitive spaces.
		Impact sound insulation provided by a carpet or an impact sound insulating vinyl is often essential for controlling the transmission of footfall or 'chair scrape' noise to rooms below.
Mechanical and electrical noise	M–H	It is important to ensure that background noise levels in teaching spaces are appropriately low so that speech can be clearly heard and understood.
Structure-borne noise	M	Special consideration should be given to spaces such as workshops, sports facilities, music practice and plant rooms. Unless there is a significant rail or traffic source outside or below the building, whole building isolation is unlikely to be necessary.
Environmental noise	M	Understanding prevailing and possible future noise conditions around the site is essential.
		Some schools generate additional income via the rental of their larger spaces – noise impacts to the environs should be considered.

H – High   M – Medium   L – Low

Introduction

In any learning environment, well-controlled acoustic conditions that support good speech intelligibility and undistracted learning are critical. The acoustic environment becomes even more vital in spaces used by students learning in a foreign language and for the hearing impaired. Many studies have linked good acoustics with better academic results, improved class behaviour, lower classroom noise levels and a reduction in teachers' voice strain and work-related stress.

Architectural style

Education buildings have changed and developed significantly over time. In 1848 Henry Barnard (secretary of the boards of education in Connecticut and Rhode Island) described early school buildings as 'almost universally, badly located, exposed to the noise, dust and danger of the highway, unattractive, if not positively repulsive in their external and internal experience'.

In the post-war period, there was a dedicated effort to replace old Edwardian and Victorian era schools with buildings that reflected changes in curricula, pedagogy and technology. In England and Wales, school-building accelerated between 1950 and 1970. By the 1970s, the building systems of the Consortium of Local Authorities Special Programme (CLASP), the Metropolitan Architectural Consortium for Education (MACE) and the Second Consortium of Local Authorities (SCOLA) dominated school design. These systems included the integration of acoustic control into schools, typically in the form of sound-absorbing lay-in-grid ceilings.

In 1981, the Department for Education published 'Building Note 17', which provided guidance for acoustic conditions in schools and was referenced from 'The Education (School Premises) Regulations' as the standard for environmental design. This was revised in 1997 as 'Building Bulletin 87', which was advisory only. In 2003, 'Building Bulletin 93' (BB93) was published and provided a comprehensive set of acoustic standards for schools. At the same time, the document was referenced in the 'Building Regulations Approved Document E' – thus making minimum acoustic standards mandatory in new school buildings in England and Wales. BB93 was updated in 2014 to provide only design criteria. Design guidance in England and Wales is now provided in 'Acoustic design of schools: performance standards' – jointly published by the Institute of Acoustics (IOA) and Association of Noise Consultants (ANC).

In recent years, there has been a resurgence of interest in flexible school layouts. Specific guidance has been included for open plan layouts in the latest versions of BB93 although in general terms, open plan layouts are not considered appropriate from an acoustic standpoint. While the educational concepts behind innovative and flexible layouts have many supporters, in an open plan design with more than one class activity in the same room, volume needs very careful consideration. In open plan teaching areas, a large floor area to provide distance between class groups and large areas of sound-absorbing finishes is essential to reduce detrimental disturbing and distracting noise between teaching activities.

Acoustic features

Recent studies have explored the relationship between room reverberation and objective and subjective evidence. Very strong correlations were reported between reverberation time and perceived quality of the teaching environment for both speech and listening. Changes to the room acoustics also resulted in a significant reduction in noise levels. Improved acoustic control has also been linked to significant improvements in behaviour.

Historical context

This evidence is informing current good practice for teaching spaces and encouraging designers to provide optimum teaching conditions, rather than the minimum standards given in BB93.

In education buildings this means:

■ In classrooms for flexible teaching methods with 40 students, a room volume of between 160m^3 and 210m^3 and reverberation times between 0.5 and 0.6 seconds

■ In large lecture rooms, optimising useful early sound reflections from ceilings and side walls, and locating sound-absorbing finishes on wall and ceiling surfaces towards the rear of the room

■ Early acoustic input into the design of flexible or non-standard learning spaces

■ Sound-absorbing finishes in corridors and carefully detailed ventilation pathways to limit noise transfer between classrooms and corridors

■ Well-designed separating walls between classroom spaces and provision of well-sealed doors to corridors

■ Assessment of façades to adequately attenuate noise from external sources. Natural ventilation of classrooms in many city-centre sites is only possible if sound-attenuating vents are provided

■ Inclusion of impact noise control finishes in floor build-ups for multi-storey buildings

Challenges

All buildings need to be increasingly energy efficient. This can mean exposing the concrete frame and slabs to provide thermal mass. This requires contemporary design solutions for room acoustic control. Timber-framed buildings reduce the construction carbon footprint but bring new challenges for maintaining sound insulation between spaces because of the relatively low density of cross-laminated timber (CLT) and its poor impact noise properties.

Opportunities

Modern classrooms must accommodate flexible layouts for small-group and individual work. In higher education, visually and physically connected spaces are encouraged to foster collaboration across departments. The growing demand to update skills across a person's working life is requiring education facilities to cater to older students, some of whom may have impaired hearing. Excellent acoustic control is needed throughout this variety of large spaces to provide flexibility and optimal learning conditions. Many universities now film classes for online learning or to live stream to other locations, often requiring much more controlled 'studio-like' conditions, which in turn require voice amplification to deal with the controlled acoustics.

Design is also required to adapt for future flexibility, to allow for teaching of new emerging technologies and subjects. Such changes are already dramatically impacting pedagogy, with the majority of learning materials now delivered digitally. There is also an emphasis on collaboration and teaching in small groups. As in many modern workspaces, this is likely to result in a growing need for small semi-enclosed spaces that allow small teams to collaborate without disturbing others, or 'concentration pods' for tasks that require more focused attention.

Evelyn Grace Academy

LOCATION: Brixton, London, UK

ARCHITECT: Zaha Hadid Architects

COMPLETED: 2010

Academy schools are required to meet the stringent UK schools design standards, which at the time of design and construction was BB93.

The school is located between two main residential roads and near a train line. Computer noise modelling was used to predict façade noise levels and their effect on the background noise in the building, which informed the ventilation strategy that allowed natural ventilation where possible.[1]

The façade construction uses stick curtain wall components, which have special detailing to ensure flanking sound insulation meets the requirements. This includes specialist solid and rubber fill elements to the mullions at walls and expanding foam at mullions passing each floor slab.

In addition, music and drama studios, fitness studios, changing rooms, common halls and the kitchen each had additional sound insulating features incorporated into the design to improve their acoustic performance to meet or exceed the BB93 requirements. Acoustic finishes were incorporated to ensure a suitable internal acoustic environment, but fewer of these finishes were needed due to the advantageous architectural shaping of several rooms with angled walls, that were used to direct sound onto minimal areas of sound-absorbing treatment for maximum performance.

Communal working rooms have extensive areas of sound-absorbing ceiling and carpet floors. Bookshelves provide additional sound-absorbing and sound-diffusing components.

Slab-to-slab partitions ensure that sound insulation standards are achieved between classroom and circulation spaces.

Kroon Hall

LOCATION: Yale University, Connecticut, USA

ARCHITECT: Hopkins Architects and Centerbrook Architects and Planners

COMPLETED: 2010

Kroon Hall, home for the Yale School of Forestry and Environmental Studies (FES) needed to make an unmistakable statement about the commitment of both the FES and Yale to sustainability and environmental stewardship.

The aim was to deliver a building that would bring light, openness and a connection to the natural world, and change the way the university built buildings – hopefully inspiring and challenging other institutions as well. Assisted natural ventilation was a key part of the strategy. The building has a long, narrow rectangular plan, with main teaching and office spaces on the perimeter and common areas and an interior stair and atrium along the centre, connecting the floors together. Yale has especially high sound insulation standards (for privacy purposes) that need to be maintained between private offices and common areas. To achieve this with minimal pressure drop from the exterior spaces to the central atrium, the aircube®, designed by Arup's Chris Field, was used in the walls above each office door.

Working closely with the architects, a modular scheme for the building finishes was developed, incorporating solid and slatted panels, allowing sound-absorbing and diffusing finishes to be located strategically as needed for optimised performance. This was particularly useful for the large lecture spaces located at the ends of the building. Sound-absorbing material is bonded recycled denim throughout.

View of lounge. Perforated panels incorporate sound-absorbing material behind. Windows are operable for natural ventilation.

Perforated panels above
the doors conceal the
acoustic airflow product
that helps maintain sound
insulation and attenuates
noise transfer while
allowing airflow with
minimum pressure drop.

Issue	Priority	Comments
Room acoustics	H	Spaces within this typology range from public to private, necessitating a tailored room acoustic design approach to reflect the different requirements concerning confidentiality and intelligibility.
		In court rooms, hearing rooms, town halls, offices, meeting rooms and other areas where person-to-person communication, AV or VC use is critical, room acoustics must be optimised.
Speech intelligibility	H	High-quality person-to-person communication is generally crucial, therefore good (AV-assisted) speech intelligibility is imperative.
Audio systems design	H	AV systems use is widespread in courthouses, primarily as these mainly assist speech intelligibility. They also facilitate recordings and occasionally broadcasting. Room acoustics and AV systems must be developed to work together.
		PAVA systems are commonly used across internal offices. More public parts of the building and areas for detainees require bespoke (often non-auditory) alarm systems.
		Future digitisation of processes will introduce more tele- and video conferencing, necessitating acoustics that promote signal transfer that is as free of reflections and noise as possible.
		Appropriate levels of continuous background noise are essential in offices and interview rooms. If not provided by the HVAC, sound-masking systems may be necessary.
Sound insulation – external	M–H	The noise environment around the building must be quantified to optimise the façade performance. Not all noise sources will be visible; some may be regular, others intermittent. Consider current and future noise sources. This is especially important if the building is to be fully or partially naturally ventilated, as sound attenuating air paths may be needed.
Sound insulation – internal	H	Pay close attention to sound isolation of adjacent spaces for privacy reasons and noise propagation (from circulation spaces and building equipment rooms) to noise sensitive spaces.
		Given the close proximity of rooms with opposing or sensitive functions, good planning, and use of vestibules, will be useful in reducing costly and space-intensive high-performance partitions.
Speech privacy	H	Strict separation is required between some spaces (e.g. courthouse areas for prosecution, defence and judiciary) or confidential hearings, making this an essential requirement in many spaces.
Impact/vibration isolation	H	Footfall impact noise (both airborne and structure-borne) within and between spaces, vertically and horizontally must be considered, with impact isolation installed below or as the final floor finish as needed.
Mechanical and electrical noise	M–H	Set a target range and achieve it, understanding that high noise levels negatively impact concentration and communication and increase stress. Low noise levels increase annoyance from outside and impact privacy/confidentiality. Consider this carefully in conjunction with the façade design to produce optimum results. Good planning of service paths and sealing of penetrations is essential.
Structure-borne noise	H	Sources might include, for example, transport systems or underground car parks. Determine where existing or future transport systems are located. Mitigation may require vibration isolation for either part of or the entire building.
Environmental noise	M	Building systems equipment located in or venting to the exterior is usually the main source of environmental noise. This issue is particularly relevant when located close to residential buildings.

H – High   M – Medium   L – Low

Introduction

With spaces ranging from formal yet inviting public areas, to highly confidential chambers, to typical office environments, these buildings host a broad range of activities – each with their own acoustic requirements. What they generally have in common is a need for a combination of privacy, confidentiality and good speech intelligibility that is crucial for day-to-day operations.

Architectural style

Purpose-built law courts have been extant for centuries. The transition from an oral system to physical written documents in the 17th century required dedicated, enclosed spaces for practising law.

The first courthouses and town halls were traditionally monumental buildings with large public spaces to reflect stature. Professionalisation, particularly in legal and operational aspects, as well as security requirements, later required a stricter spatial separation of activities and personas (e.g. the accused, defence, prosecution, jury, judges and public). This led to internalising many functions and reducing transparency.

Even today the formal legal procedure retains a component of ritual and theatre. Courtroom layout remains bound to tradition, with judges positioned physically higher than the rest of the room to reflect their autonomy and stature. Moreover, modern democratic society expects unambiguous judicial systems, which is reflected in modern civic building design. They increasingly offer physical transparency and opportunities for the public to view – and hear – the official proceedings in action. It also reflects a growing appreciation for better daylight for working purposes in interior spaces.

Acoustic features

Spaces often feature stone, marble and wood – finished to be primarily sound-reflecting, in relatively large volumes – resulting in long reverberance and poor speech intelligibility. There have historically been cases where the judge declared a mistrial because the jury couldn't hear the witnesses due to poor speech intelligibility. Today these materials are being used more creatively for better acoustic outcomes. As a result, modern spaces are expected to be designed to stricter acoustic standards, good speech intelligibility being paramount. It is important to note that some standards require certain dimensions which are larger than ideal acoustically. Including acoustic treatments to meet room acoustics and speech intelligibility requirements is a necessity.

In order to assist speech intelligibility and for recording or broadcasting of proceedings, some spaces can be AV-intensive. This requires further consideration of room dimensions, sound-absorbing finishes, furniture and equipment in the acoustic design.

While intelligibility is the governing auditory parameter, confidentiality is the next most important thing to consider for most spaces. High sound insulation is critical for achieving this. A careful balance between room layout, sound insulation, sound-absorbing treatment and the appropriate level of background noise from HVAC is of paramount importance.

Challenges

With careful acoustic design, modern rooms generally have a good speech intelligibility – but this does not necessarily mean the conditions are conducive for reliable recordings or broadcast. Improving the quality of recordings can be achieved by either upgrading or augmenting room acoustics and/or by fine-tuning the AV-equipment set-up, especially microphone placement.

Opportunities

In terms of technology, many authorities remain relatively conservative due to the strict formalities involved in proceedings. However, 'new' technologies are slowly being embraced, and the implementation of video technology combined with audio is providing more remote access, thus impacting day-to-day operations – potentially even changing the need for as many large, physical spaces in the future.

GLA Building, London City Hall

LOCATION: London, UK

ARCHITECT: Foster + Partners

COMPLETED: 2002

The building serves as headquarters for the Mayor of London and the London Assembly.

Working closely with the architects from the earliest phases of the project, the primary acoustic challenge was the design of the main debating chamber. The centrepiece of the winning competition, this was originally envisaged as a smooth glass curved flute extending from the base to the apex of the building. However, that presented significant acoustic complications, as it provided no ability to control sound within the chamber and meet the required speech intelligibility criteria.

To solve the issue, initial hand sketches were developed looking at ways to capture sound as it travelled vertically upwards, and to optimise the chamber design at low level to enhance early reflections. These sketches quickly moved into 3D. A combination of proprietary and bespoke tools was used to create 3D visualisations of the sound showing real-time propagation of the sound reflections in the space. That process allowed significant improvement in the understanding of the problem between the stakeholders. Through an iterative process, the design goals were achieved in the final form of the internal ramp that rises up the building, incorporation of sound-absorbing treatment within it, and how this is rationalised and connected to the floor plates throughout the building.

The main debating chamber.

View looking vertically at the spiral ramp; this achieves the ideal internal acoustic conditions, enables transparency to be maintained and has the minimum possible quantity of sound-absorbing material.

Senedd, National Assembly

LOCATION: Cardiff, UK

ARCHITECT: Rogers Stirk Harbour + Partners
(as Richard Rogers Partnership)

COMPLETED: 2006

The building houses the National Assembly of Wales, the democratically elected body that represents the interests of Wales and its people, makes laws, agrees taxes and holds the Welsh government to account.

This image highlights one of the key challenges of civic building design. To befit the building's status, the expectation is for a large room volume – in this case light-filled and momentous in scale. This is much larger than acoustically ideal for the number of people and the activity occurring within. Issues in this case were exacerbated by the curved walls of the chamber and the conical roof. This is deftly mitigated with extensive use of sound-absorbing treatment integrated behind the timber finishes, and an audio system to amplify voices as needed. As a result, a fine internal acoustic is achieved.

View of chamber; the timber finishes have sound-absorbing treatment integrated.

United States Courthouse for the District of Utah

LOCATION: Salt Lake City, Utah, USA

ARCHITECT: Thomas Phifer and Partners

COMPLETED: 2014

Designed to the 2007 US Courts Design Guide, which advocates for good daylight and optimum acoustics in the courtrooms, this project took an integrated approach to acoustic design from the outset.

As part of the design process, US federal judges took part in reviewing the designs of their new courthouses, usually by means of visiting a 1:1 scale mock-up created in plywood, that is often modified several times during the design process. In this case, the mock-ups were all created virtually. A 3D visualisation model was paired with auralisations to allow the judges to experience the courthouse acoustics for themselves, from their own standard location, but also as jurors, counsel, and observers.

The design incorporates a curved precast concrete ceiling which is optimised in shape and form to propagate sound across and along the room. Sound-absorbing treatments are strategically located behind slatted timber panels. Carpet is used throughout.

The main courtroom, with curved concrete ceiling.

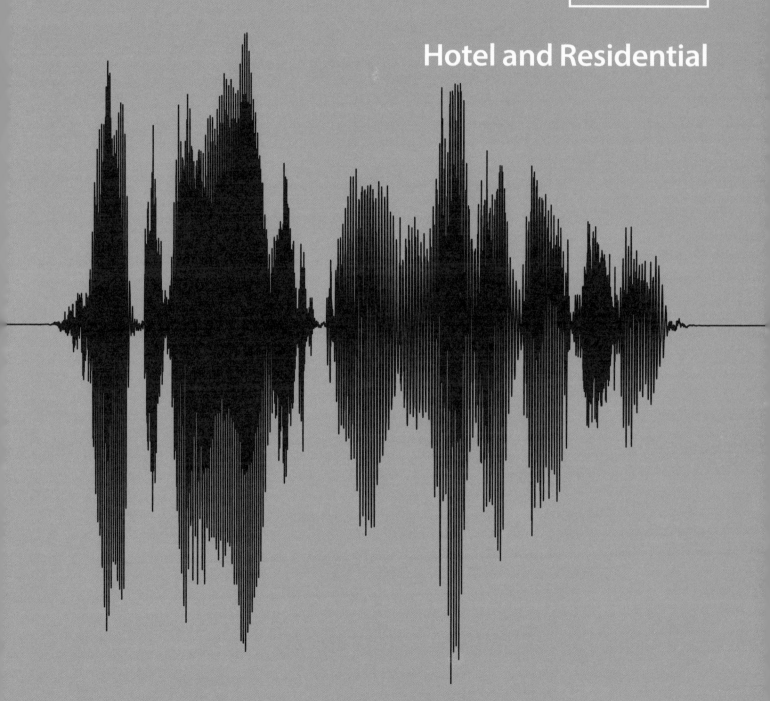

Issue	Priority	Comments
Room acoustics	M–H	Room acoustics are usually managed by selection of the finishes and furniture, which is dictated by individual taste (residential) or brand (hotels).
		UK building regulations set parameters for acoustic control in corridors and circulation spaces to mitigate impacts to dwellings.
		Many hotels also include conferencing and meeting facilities, with speaking a primary use. Appropriate room acoustics are needed to achieve speech intelligibility targets, usually requiring the inclusion of sound-absorbing finishes on walls, floors and ceilings.
Speech intelligibility	H	Good speech intelligibility is essential where high quality person-to-person and person-to-group communication is required, as in conference settings.
Audio systems design	H	PAVA is often used throughout large hotel and residential buildings, with AV systems being the norm in communal spaces and meeting rooms.
		Spaces such as spas, gyms, lounges, relaxation areas, etc. may have particular requirements for audio system design and performance based on the type of activity.
Sound insulation – external	M–H	Sound insulation requirements will vary dependent on location. Sleeping, rest and relaxation areas are usually most critical.
		Hotels located within or near airports or railway stations require specialist advice – see below regarding structure-borne noise.
Sound insulation – internal	H	Internal sound insulation between bedrooms is critical, and is governed by building regulations.
		Hotels may include entertainment facilities that generate high internal noise levels, and therefore require significant sound insulation performance. Determining insulation for gyms and swimming pools requires specialist advice.
Speech privacy	M	Hotels often use operable walls to subdivide spaces to increase utility or function. The sound insulation performance of single operable walls is limited and should be properly understood. This approach should only be used if the types of simultaneous activity occurring are suited to this deployment. Detailing of operable walls is critical for sound insulation standards to be achieved in practice. Regular maintenance is also essential to ensure ongoing acoustic performance is achieved.
Impact/vibration isolation	H	Specific building regulations usually apply to impact noise insulation affecting bedrooms.
		Spaces such as gyms, kitchens and loading docks are particularly notable sources of impact noise. Planning to avoid proximity of impact sources to bedrooms is strongly advisable, as is incorporating impact isolation below or in the final floor finish as needed.
Mechanical and electrical noise	M–H	Appropriate target ranges for noise based on room function are essential. High noise levels will negatively impact sleep, rest and relaxation. If noise is too low, it will draw more attention to activity in adjacent rooms or from outside.
		The above is equally important to other sensitive activities, such as conferences and meetings.
Structure-borne noise	H	Gyms located in the basements of hotels or residential complexes can be a prominent source of vibration, which will require mitigation.
		Appropriate consideration must be given to transport systems or underground car parks, which, if in close proximity, may require vibration isolation for part of or the entire building.
Environmental noise	M–H	Building systems equipment (e.g. air-conditioning or kitchens) or venting located to the exterior can produce environmental noise.
		Entertainment noise emission from hotels may need addressing, depending on location.

H – High   M – Medium   L – Low

Introduction

Residential and hotel developments range from small, stand-alone, single person or family dwellings, to very large multi-use developments. In a complex mix of noise-generating and noise-sensitive spaces, delivering conditions conducive to rest and relaxation is usually a primary design concern, for which acoustics are a guiding requirement.

Architectural style

Design approaches for these buildings have changed greatly over the last century. There is an increasing trend towards multi-dwelling buildings and high-rise developments in urban centres. These are often 'mixed use', e.g. commercial, retail, entertainment and residential in a single development.

Acoustic features

Achieving appropriate conditions for sleep, rest and relaxation are essential; this requires good interior room acoustics, the right background sounds, and measures to minimise disturbance from other sources of noise or vibration. These acoustic concerns affect every aspect of the building design approach, including fundamental spatial planning and adjacencies (horizonal and vertical).

The World Health Organization has provided guidance on noise limits in sleeping areas of residences which have subsequently been incorporated into national guidelines across the world.

UK building regulations have statutory guidance for sound insulation between domestic units or sleep areas, and impose pre-completion testing on developers to demonstrate compliance. To assist this process, a set of standard 'robust details' which are known to achieve acoustic requirements can be used by developers to achieve the right outcomes.

Exterior environmental noise requires increasing consideration in early design phases. It does not allow for reproduction of one façade design solution in multiple locations with different surrounding noise conditions. Increasing recognition is being given to the importance of vibrant day and night activity in cities. Noise is one component of this and can come from entertainment, retail, transport infrastructure, etc. Standards now require developers and architects to incorporate necessary sound insulation into the design of their buildings to mitigate existing sources – a major shift in design responsibilities.

Challenges

Regulations should be considered a minimum standard, and there is a good case for improving on these. Some countries have significantly more onerous standards for sound insulation and impact isolation, as do some hotel operators. This has space implications (for deeper partitions) and associated costs.

All noise and vibration transfer paths between spaces must be carefully considered. Walls and floors are most obvious, but other paths are equally problematic (e.g. curtain walls, ducts, ceiling and floor voids, and penetrations for building services). Some spaces will require special attention for improved acoustics to aid the activities they host, such as spas or leisure spaces. Others will need specific noise and vibration mitigation, such as heavily equipped gyms.

Modular construction and dense 'micro housing' exacerbate the potential issues and each require careful attention to acoustics issues.

Although many hotel residents increasingly expect fully air-conditioned rooms as standard, this is not ubiquitous in residential buildings in the UK and Europe, which often rely on natural ventilation. This approach can be problematic when external noise levels are high. While new technologies are being developed to provide improved air flow and noise attenuation, good planning – orientation of building sensitive spaces away from external noise, and use of buffer spaces between sensitive rooms and external noise sources – is and will remain good design practice.

Television Centre

LOCATION: London, UK

ARCHITECT: AHMM

COMPLETED: 2017

The task was converting a large broadcasting complex into a mix of uses, including residential, boutique hotel, leisure, state-of-the-art office facilities, food and beverage, and retaining some existing studios.

Existing constructions in the Grade II listed building were upgraded to achieve exacting sound insulation standards for high-quality residential apartments. With operational studios, it was important to both meet the BBC performance standards inside the studios, and to protect residential apartments from noise and vibration created within them. The environment around the site is dominated by nearby railway noise, which was a specific imperative for the design of the new high-performance building façade.

Auralisation enabled the client to listen to a wide variety of design options and make a fully informed decision on the subjective performance for final decision making.

View of the converted, mixed-use complex.

Bosco Verticale

LOCATION: Milan, Italy

ARCHITECT: Studio Boeri

COMPLETED: 2015

Close to Milano Centre, the complex was developed on two plots in the Isola district. It is a mixed-use complex development comprising two residential towers, a low-rise residential building, one office block with three basement levels for parking, and a green area.

The balconies of the apartments, duplexes and penthouses extend outwards by approximately three and a half metres to host an abundance of trees, shrubs and plants, creating the overall effect of a huge hanging garden. In total, 900 trees, measuring between three and six metres, together with 5,000 shrubs and 11,000 floral plants, have been planted on terraces up to the 27th floor. The greenery on the building will create oxygen and humidity while absorbing CO_2 and dust particles. The design also includes photovoltaic systems to provide renewable energy. The greenery creates pleasant masking noise when it sways in the wind, and encourages additional sounds from birds and insects, mitigating environmental noise from traffic sources.

The towers sit on top of an array of vibration isolation springs. The site is directly above two underground train tunnels, and mitigation of vibration was an essential component of the design.

Vibration isolation springs on a base slab.

An exterior view of the complex.

Pacific Place

Location: Hong Kong

Architect: Ng Chun Man

Completed: 2011

A mixed-use development with three Grade-A office towers, a quartet of renowned five-star hotels (The Upper House, Conrad, Island Shangri-La and JW Marriott), plus a 270-suite apartment residence.

The Pacific Place development features a sound insulating ceiling (multi-layer plasterboard on vibration isolation hangers) in its ballroom to control noise transfer to sensitive spaces above. High standards of sound insulation required special details to upgrade the curtain wall between the individual units. Impact-absorbing finish in the loading dock controls impact noise affecting the hotel accommodation. Special sound insulating constructions control noise from the cinema complex, which could also have impacted the hotel. Inclusion of acoustic finishes on the walls in meeting rooms is used to improve room acoustics and a high-quality fixed PA system in the main retail atrium allows for shows and events.

External view of the Pacific Place mixed-use development.

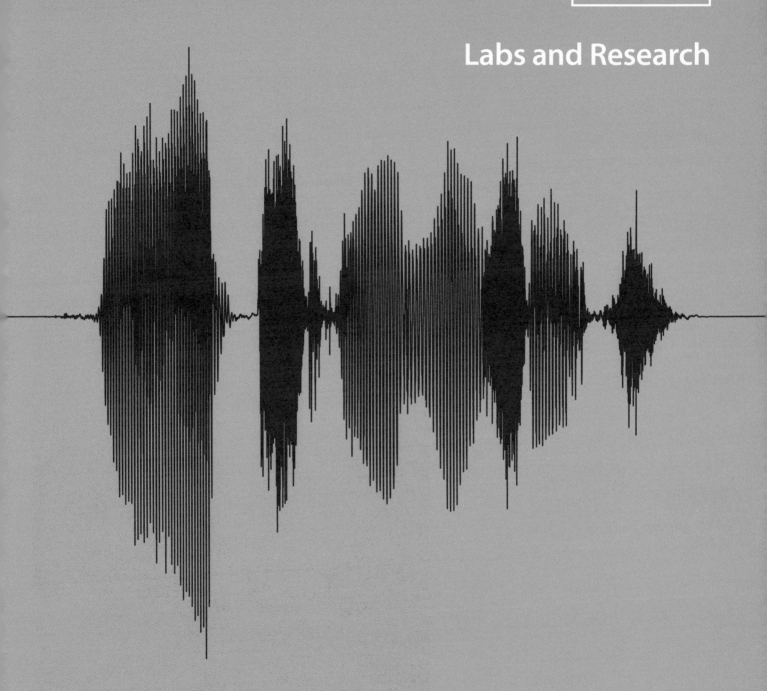

Issue	Priority	Comments
Room acoustics	M	Requirements vary widely based on type of space, ranging from minimal standards to critically important (e.g. anechoic chambers). Sound-absorbing finishes may be required to control noise produced by laboratory equipment, especially if labs are occupied regularly and/or used for teaching and instruction.
		The suitability of fibrous sound-absorbing materials, including the ability to clean them in a laboratory setting, should be considered when designing the space. Specialist materials are available for this purpose.
Speech intelligibility	M	Good speech intelligibility is usually critical for teaching and where precision work requires person-to-person communication.
Audio systems design	L	Requirements for audio systems depend on the type of research being conducted. PAVA systems may be required for clear, intelligible announcements for both information and safety purposes.
Sound insulation – external	H	Impacts from and mitigation of external vibration sources such as road and rail activity must be assessed. Vibration-sensitive buildings sometimes require whole or partial building vibration isolation to effectively mitigate these sources. This can have a big impact on planning, architecture and building systems design.
Sound insulation – internal	H	Noise and vibration from internal sources need to be controlled to ensure vibration limits for laboratory spaces or equipment in those spaces can be met. This impacts floor slab design, as well as the placement of vibration-sensitive spaces.
Speech privacy	L/H	Typically not a major consideration for laboratories, unless the research is confidential in nature, this is more important for office and classroom spaces.
Impact/vibration isolation	H	Footfall vibration induced in the building structure needs to be at or below specified vibration limits. The structural engineer should analyse the predicted floor slab response to ensure it meets building vibration criteria (this is usually shared and iterated with the acoustic consultant and architect).
Mechanical and electrical noise	M–H	Noise from fume hoods and other lab equipment requires special attention to provide appropriate background noise levels for research and teaching.
Structure-borne noise	H	Structure-borne noise and vibration from internal sources (human activity, building systems, escalators, elevators etc.) require mitigation through vibration isolation, as well as good planning to locate vibration sources away from sensitive areas where possible.
Environmental noise	M–H	Rooftop exhaust fans, often found in laboratory spaces, can be very loud and tonal – their acoustic impact upon surrounding buildings needs to be considered.

H – High   M – Medium   L – Low

Introduction

Laboratories and research spaces often require highly controlled or optimised environmental conditions. Acoustics, noise and vibration criteria are frequently critical for performance requirements.

Architectural style

These research spaces can be found in a range of settings, from schools and universities to medical, industrial, commercial, etc. They may be used for a single function or have multiple uses. Over time these have traced divergent evolutionary arcs. A significant influence has been the development of technical equipment, which will continue to dictate space planning and building criteria, including acoustics, noise and vibration, in the future. Working practices within the spaces is the other major design driver.

Acoustic features

Design criteria vary depending on use. Some spaces and equipment are highly sensitive to noise and vibration. Some cases require very optimised acoustics (e.g. anechoic or semi-anechoic chambers). Specialist instrumentation – such as nanofabrication, high-precision lasers, high-resolution optical and electron microscopy, MRI, or high-energy particle systems (e.g. linear accelerators, synchrotrons) – is often highly sensitive to vibration.

Manufacturers of laboratory equipment typically provide specifications for structural vibration specific to their product. This often informs the building design targets. Conducting baseline measurements in existing spaces is also beneficial in establishing criteria, as existing real-life conditions are often different to manufacturer 'recommended' criteria.

Sensitive equipment should generally be located on at-grade slabs and/or near building columns where the floor slabs are often stiffer. It should also be located away from local vibration sources. Dynamic response of the building structure, the floor slabs especially, should be designed to ensure human activity and building operations do not exceed the vibration limits. Floor footfall response requires special attention. In some cases, it may be possible to mount equipment on passive or active vibration isolation systems. Bio-resource facilities in particular are sensitive to both noise and vibration. Such needs may therefore require spaces that are physically isolated, with high sound insulation requirements.

Challenges

General workplace environment trends are starting to affect this building type, with a move away from enclosed offices to more open-plan, collaborative environments. This presents adjustment challenges for occupants. Benchmarking existing spaces and communicating acoustic impacts to end users in advance helps smooth this process.

Spaces used for education often require more stringent control of background noise to enable appropriate speech intelligibility. Material selection in these kinds of spaces often requires specialist knowledge. Sound-absorbing finishes in laboratory spaces often need to be non-fibrous and easy to clean, sterilise and maintain. The location of these materials usually needs to be away from surfaces that require regular maintenance. Reduction of mechanical noise using fibreglass ducts and silencers is often not possible; instead other non-fibrous means are needed. Equipment that uses magnetic resonance may require an absence of ferrous material within a specific radius.

Opportunities

Audio-visual equipment is increasingly used in these lab and research contexts for displaying results. Specialist immersive environments are also emerging as a way to visualise and sonify data to provide new insights (see Immersive Spaces), which will bring new acoustic standards and requirements.

Frick Chemistry Laboratory

LOCATION: Princeton University, New Jersey, USA

ARCHITECT: Hopkins Architects and Payette Associates

COMPLETED: 2010

Designed to be part of one of the most environmentally sustainable areas of the university campus, providing space for faculty research and teaching, office spaces and a large auditorium. The laboratories accommodate a wide range of testing equipment, making good space use and planning critical to functionality.

The spaces in this building are used extensively for teaching and research; many are densely packed with equipment. Mechanical services are exposed and plentiful. Understanding noise control requirements for these is crucial, as well as understanding vibration limits for equipment to determine if the structure needs to be vibration isolated, or if equipment can be isolated at source. The main atrium serves as a communal and collaborative space. Sound-absorbing treatment is integrated behind perforated timber panels and to the undersides of stairs and landings, helping to limit noise transfer vertically through the building and create a pleasant ambience in the space. It also serves as respite from more intensive working areas – the atrium is also used to hold large events.

A nuclear magnetic resonance (NMR) facility is located on the ground and basement levels. These machines require a level of vibration as close as possible to zero, so sit on two three-metre thick concrete blocks anchored to reinforcement embedded in the Princeton bedrock, two and a half metres below ground level. The NMR pit, which is

The atrium provides respite from cramped working spaces. Acoustic treatments are integrated under ceilings and behind vertical slotted panels to maintain a light, airy feel, but provide reverberance control.

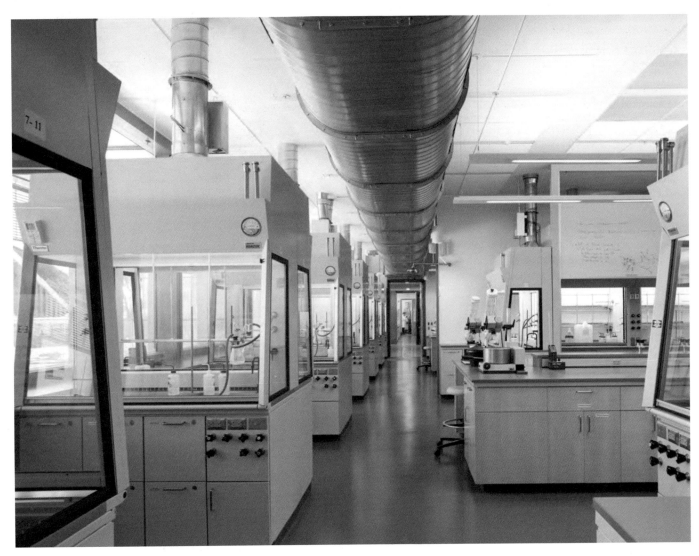

below the water table, is isolated from the rest of the building by perimeter joints to minimise vibration. It is enclosed by waterproofing that discreetly bridges the isolation joint. The systems supplying the NMR were also designed to be low vibration, using vibration isolation for rotating equipment, and interconnected piping and ductwork.

The entire laboratory also had a requirement for all building materials to be non-ferrous. Nothing in a six-metre radius zone of influence was to be made of iron, including reinforcing steel; all metal had to be stainless steel, aluminium a non-ferrous metal or a non-metallic substitute. Miscellaneous structures (e.g. catwalks, ladders, and railings) and ductwork are of stainless steel. All other piping in the area is copper, including the sprinkler system. All metal studs were replaced with wood. Close collaboration between the acoustic, structural and mechanical engineers was imperative to meet the design requirements.

Lab spaces are often tightly packed with equipment, leaving the ceiling as the main area for sound-absorbing treatment. The significant duct sizes require good noise control and sound insulation.

World Conservation and Exhibitions Centre

LOCATION: The British Museum, London, UK

ARCHITECT: Rogers Stirk Harbour + Partners (RSHP)

COMPLETED: 2014

One of the largest redevelopment projects in the British Museum's 260-year history, this nine-storey addition provides a new major exhibition gallery, state-of-the-art laboratories and studios, and world-class storage for the collection, as well as important facilities to support its extensive UK and international loan programme.

Spaces for conservation of artefacts come in a wide range of forms. Many museums require large spaces to work on restoration of substantially sized works. It is important to benchmark existing facilities and talk to user groups about acoustic expectations, as this can have a direct impact on the ability to concentrate on delicate tasks.

When spaces require controlled daylight from the side and top, accommodation of sound-absorbing treatments can be challenging, and the ceiling may be the only option. In some environments solar shades may be the only source of sound absorption (the performance of which is only useful at very high frequency).

A variety of air or dust control and extraction systems and equipment can be required, sometimes mobile and on flexible ducts, making the location of the noise source in the spaces variable. It is important to understand how much noise the equipment can make, and whether any specific noise and vibration control is required.

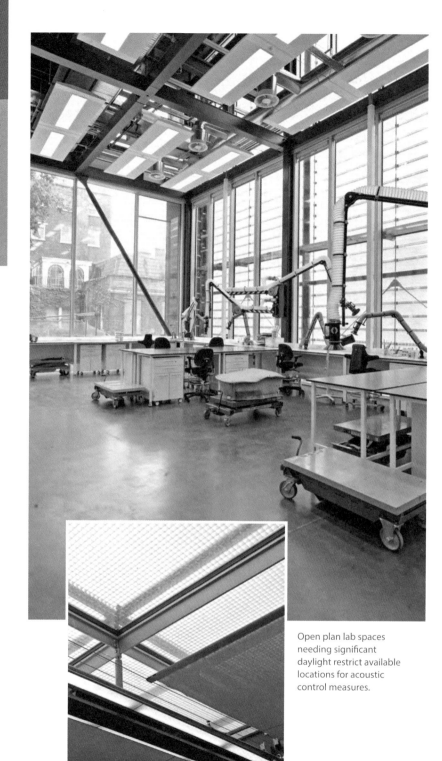

Open plan lab spaces needing significant daylight restrict available locations for acoustic control measures.

Shades for daylight control provide minimal acoustic benefit.

Issue	Priority	Comments
Room acoustics	H	Libraries have many spaces that are interconnected, without doors, full-height partitions or other barriers. Controlling sound propagation between spaces, and occupational noise, is crucial for enabling intended functions to take place without distraction. In large open-volume areas, the 'calm' environment usually desirous for reading and private study doesn't mean one free of noise, but one with the right balance of occupational noise, early sound reflections, reverberance and soundscape. To achieve this, a combination of careful consideration of the floor plan (using buffer or neutral spaces between noise producing or sound critical space) and the strategic placement of the correct quantities of sound-absorbing treatment, is needed. Future use and adaptability should be taken into account.
Speech intelligibility	H	Room acoustics must be optimised to promote good speech intelligibility in meeting rooms, storytelling spaces and other areas where person-to-person communication, AV or VC use is critical.
Audio systems design	H	AV systems are common, and should be optimised for function. Increasingly they are used for data visualisation and sonification in environments that otherwise need to be quiet, and must be designed in a way that is not intrusive or distracting. Areas used for public programming (such as open atria or common spaces) may have fixed or temporary systems; these should be optimised for the acoustic design.
Sound insulation – external	H	The noise environment around the building must be quantified, considering sources of transport infrastructure noise. The façade's acoustic performance must be optimised, especially where natural ventilation strategies are being used, as sound attenuating elements within air paths may be required.
Sound insulation – internal	M–H	Sound propagation from noise generating spaces, such as cafés, crèches, children's library areas, teaching spaces, entryways and open working areas, to private reading/study rooms or other noise sensitive spaces, requires careful attention.
Speech privacy	M	This is a necessity for meeting rooms, presentation spaces and children's storytelling areas. These needs should be identified early in the planning process so the areas can be situated accordingly.
Impact/vibration isolation	H	Footfall impact noise (both airborne and structure-borne) is usually a major issue in high traffic areas (from staff or the public). Incorporate impact isolation below or in the final floor finish as needed.
Mechanical and electrical noise	M–H	High noise levels negatively impact concentration and communication, and increase stress, but low background noise levels increase annoyance as the sounds of people nearby and outside are more noticeable, due to lack of a 'masking' effect (usually provided by building services systems). A target range must be set and achieved.
Structure-borne noise	H	Structure-borne noise sources specific to this building type might include, for example, book retrieval systems that run throughout the building and can generate noise and vibration in quiet environments. Large public and national libraries often include specialist areas (such as sound and music archives) that require special design (see appropriate typology chapter).
Environmental noise	M	Externally located equipment (air handling units, cooling towers, etc.) or venting to the exterior are usually the main source of environmental noise. This issue is particularly relevant for libraries located close to residential buildings where stringent noise limits apply.

H – High   M – Medium   L – Low

Introduction

Libraries are reinventing themselves in the 21st century, re-establishing their place at the heart of the communities they serve. To ensure long-term sustainability, these spaces are diversifying to service a broad cross-section of people with different needs.

Architectural style

As a building typology intertwined with the evolution of recorded information, libraries were originally sites for the preservation of knowledge – traditionally static physical documents. As they became more widespread during the classical era, buildings predominantly used masonry constructions to create grand spaces, along with timber, and materials were generally finished in a sound-reflecting manner, resulting in spaces both rich and reverberant when occupied. Since this made sound or noise very obvious, user behaviour responded to the architecture and use of space, and the library became a place of hushed reverence and scholarly activity.

Libraries evolved to become gathering and learning spaces, and the building typology changed to accommodate more functions, resulting in a diversification of acoustics responding to the different uses.

This evolution seems set to continue as visitor numbers are increasing and libraries are adapting to remain relevant. New library buildings are increasingly scaled to urban context, where new acoustic challenges emerge.

Acoustic features

To accommodate a wide range of uses, the acoustics within libraries must be tailored to the use of individual spaces. There are specific, and sometimes conflicting, requirements for separate areas within a library. At the same time libraries are becoming more transparent, open and connected, meaning fewer physical barriers for acoustic separation.

Acoustic design was historically reliant upon the sound-absorbing properties of the books themselves, and, in some areas, carpeted surfaces, tapestries, wall hangings and similar. Since books are no longer always stored in open stacks and information is accessed differently, successful acoustic design is reliant upon good space planning plus strategic use of sound-absorbing and/or diffusing treatment to control early sound reflections, and reduce noise from occupational activities. Thinking through how the building will be used, where areas of high occupancy or noise producing activity will occur, and how to control noise propagation is key. Allowing areas of different acoustic character to suit different users and their varying expectations for study is also important. All of this should be tackled on a space-by-space basis.

Challenges

Control of external noise intrusion is crucial for any learning environment, requiring a façade design that responds to this need. Increasingly, sustainable design principles promote natural ventilation; this makes the challenge of noise mitigation more complex.

The storage of information in libraries is increasingly reliant on audio and visual materials. This requires space for the storage, retrieval and playback of these media, increasing the building's acoustic complexity. In the case of some larger regional and national libraries, comprehensive recording and digitisation studios may require recording studio quality acoustics.

Opportunities

New technologies continue to impact knowledge transfer in the digital age. The growing use of AR and VR, smart devices and surfaces that allow interaction with information easily, means that physical and digital space will overlap further, allowing a more seamless experience. Audio is becoming an increasingly prevalent aspect of these systems and therefore must be an important design consideration.

Historical context

The British Library, St Pancras

LOCATION: London, UK

ARCHITECT: Colin St John and
Long & Kentish Architects

COMPLETED: 1997, 2014

The largest national library in the world, the British Library had a long and complicated project history and has received its fair share of criticism and praise since opening.

The building and plaza are surrounded by a wall that screens the street-level areas of the building from both road and rail traffic noise, which allows the public plaza to be a pleasant respite from the King's Cross neighbourhood during all times of day.

The main atrium and surrounding spaces were designed with the expectation that it would become a 'living room' for London, attracting tourists, scholars, and students from the surrounding universities, as well as supporting a vibrant public programme of events. Use of digital technology was changing at the time, and a flexible infrastructure was accommodated. The area connecting all levels of the building is at the front closest to the entrance, and incorporates sound-absorbing treatment strategically. As you move up the stairs and through the landings, discrete areas for open working, with sound-absorbing treatments integrated into walls, floors and ceilings, are inherent in the architecture throughout. The conservation centre continues these themes, in a lighter palette with sound-absorbing treatment behind perforated gypsum board. It also contains acoustically optimised spaces for specific activities like the sound archive.

Aerial site image shows surrounding wall screening the plaza and building from traffic noise.

Perforated gypsum board (seen here in the conservation centre upper wall areas) mitigates reverberant sound and occupational noise, while maintaining a light and airy feel.

The building also contains specialist areas such as the sound and music archive and conservation space, full box-in-box isolated constructions, with interior acoustic optimised for critical listening.

dlr LexIcon

LOCATION: Dún Laoghaire, Ireland

ARCHITECT: Carr Cotter & Naessens

COMPLETED: 2014

The building re-interprets the traditional idea of a library by delivering a cultural, modern building that encourages social and community interaction as rigorously as it facilitates enquiry and learning.

Sitting between the historic harbour and the town, the Dún Laoghaire library is organised into two distinct forms. Along one edge is a regular sequence of intimate scaled rooms, workshops, meeting spaces and reading rooms, with windows that address the street. The other provides voluminous space in the lounge and the principal open plan space above it, each with long windows framing views to the park. The tapering roof, cut with large precast beams, rises up gradually to form the tall slender portico looking out to sea.

Sound-absorbing treatment behind slatted timber panels is architecturally integrated into the ceiling, walls and bookshelves, creating a unified aesthetic. There is a large enclosed auditorium used for performances and presentations. A series of interlocking voids and double volumes allow different parts of the building to connect whilst minimising noise transfer between spaces. There is careful integration of sound-absorbing treatment into the large open plan spaces to control their occupational noise levels, provide maximum user comfort, and integrate with daylight and electric lighting design approaches. Sound-absorbing treatment is also integrated into lighting rafts suspended above reading areas and quiet zones.

High-performance sound insulating constructions control noise from the basement auditorium and enable maximum flexibility in the use of this space and its adjacent open plan library and study areas. Integration of variable acoustic treatment into the design of the basement auditorium enables acoustics to be optimised for a diverse range of events.

The building is located in close proximity to a railway, and structure-borne noise was an issue on some parts of the site. To eliminate the need for vibration isolation of the structure, the plan layout of the building was developed to locate noise sensitive spaces at distances far enough away to eliminate the issue.

Above: Sound-absorbing treatment is integrated throughout.

In areas with predominantly concrete ceilings, sound-absorbing treatment is provided more extensively on mid and upper wall areas.

Left: Sound-absorbing treatment and building services are integrated behind transparent timber slats.

Seattle Central Library

LOCATION: Seattle, Washington, USA

ARCHITECT: OMA and LMN

COMPLETED: 2004

The architecture for this library has been praised and reappraised over the years since it opened, with a variety of viewpoints. From an acoustic standpoint the building is quite successful, although a visual inspection of photographs might not necessarily lead to that conclusion.

The interior of the building façade, with its structural detailing penetrating into the space, results in a powerful sound diffusing effect which tempers the strong reflections of reverberance one might expect. The areas below the significant angled glass spaces are carpeted, which means any sound reflections are quickly absorbed. The result is that the main floor area of the building is acoustically quite welcoming, and successful for rental events where the building sound system delivers good speech intelligibility.

Sound-absorbing treatments through the building are black-tissue faced mineral fibre behind expanded metal. Their colour is not concealed; it is a prominent visual component of the architecture. Throughout the building the angular nature is maximised for acoustic effect, to direct sound reflections from these surfaces onto sound-absorbing ones, thereby minimising the total area of sound-absorbing treatment. While the acoustic design may have capitalised on these aesthetic choices, they were not a key driver.

Another notable aspect is the auditorium at the rear of the seating rake, which then descends to the basement level. It has no enclosing rear wall and is open to the main atrium. While this requires some management, it is generally acoustically successful as noise propagation into the atrium is minimised through crowd control.

The depth profile of the façade is sound-diffusing, and angles help to direct sound energy onto sound-absorbing surfaces that are coloured black throughout.

View of the auditorium; behind the back row of seats it is generally kept open to the main foyer, with no enclosing rear wall.

Issue	Priority	Comments
Room acoustics	H	In cinemas, well-controlled room acoustics are required to achieve clear reproduction of sound.
		Ceilings usually need to provide efficient, high sound-absorbing performance (from low to high frequency) and be dark in colour so they do not appear bright from the light of the projector – they are often composed of high-performing black lay-in sound-absorbing ceiling tiles).
		Walls are usually lined with sound-absorbing fabric-faced panels, approximately 30–50mm thick.
		Most commercial cinema operators employ a specialist contractor for the final interior fit-out, which includes room acoustic finishes.
Speech intelligibility	H	Clear speech intelligibility is a critical part of the design in order to support both film dialogue and any live events, such as talks or Q&As.
Audio systems design	H	At minimum, most cinemas will have three large loudspeaker stacks and sub-bass units situated behind an acoustically transparent screen, with surround loudspeakers mounted along the three remaining walls. New emerging spatial audio systems sometimes include additional loudspeakers suspended from the ceiling, and/or below the floor (and sometimes the seats too).
		Most commercial cinema operators design and install their own audio systems.
Sound insulation – external	H	The noise environment around the building must be measured. The sound insulation of the building envelope should then be designed accordingly to ensure that external noise ingress does not exceed the limits set by the operator. Consideration should be given to current and future noise sources, including changes in road, rail or aviation paths as well as potential construction sites.
Sound insulation – internal	H	The positioning of auditoria directly next to each other should be avoided, especially on the screen elevation; they should be placed side by side, or on top of each other in the same plan configuration, not in opposing configuration i.e. with the screen wall sharing the rear of an adjacent audience area.
		Each auditorium of a commercial cinema typically has its own concrete floating floor, twin stud drywall constructions between auditoria that are around 550mm thick (excluding finishes) and a resiliently hung drywall ceiling.
		It is essential to have a sound and light lock lobby as part of each auditorium entrance.
Speech privacy	L	Given the cinema screen's core function, this is not usually an important consideration.
Impact/vibration isolation	H	Concrete floating floors on resilient bearings with independent inner walls (that sit on the floating floor) and drywall 'lids' help provide excellent control of impact sound from surrounding spaces.
Mechanical and electrical noise	H	Mechanical and electrical noise is typically limited to NR25–30, which is quiet, requiring low air velocities.
		Each auditorium must be served by a separate ventilation system. The running of ducts should not cross between auditoria; each should have supply and extract branches from main ducts located in another noise neutral space.
Structure-borne noise	H	The concrete floating floors mentioned above can, to a certain extent, be tuned to attenuate sources of ground-borne noise, such as underground trains, trams, road traffic or nearby construction noise. If the source noise or vibration is very high, complex mitigation approaches and coordination may be required.
Environmental noise	H	Two key considerations are noise emissions from the building's services equipment, and those emanating from the cinema's audio systems. These require attenuation/screening and careful roof design respectively. The local planning authority will usually provide requirements for both.

H – High   M – Medium   L – Low

Introduction

From small boutique venues to large-scale multiplex and IMAX, the cinema is a place for immersing oneself in the magic of film's sound and visuals, and experiencing them collectively. While interior and exterior design approaches vary widely, the core need for high-quality room acoustics and good sound insulation is a constant when it comes to excellent cinematic experiences.

Architectural style

The 1895 screening of ten short films by the Lumière brothers, in Paris, marked the starting point of the development of modern cinema. Initially presented in storefront settings or as part of travelling shows, short films soon migrated into vaudeville theatres. By 1905, the first dedicated single screen cinemas had opened, and by the 1920s the picture palaces of the art deco era had arrived.

Over time, new developments in film technology – particularly the integration of sound with moving images in the early 1930s – as well as a growing audience demand for cinema shaped the architecture of spaces where film is presented, and with it the associated acoustic requirements. As television increasingly became a competitor, audience expectation of the cinematic experience also developed. In the 1960s, multiplexes became the norm. One of the key challenges of their modern design is the provision of appropriate sound insulation between internal spaces and the external environment. Audio systems have become significantly more elaborate and powerful over time, developing from mono to stereo, and on to surround sound formats. A careful balance of room acoustics and sound system design is crucial for facilitating outstanding cinematic experiences.

Acoustic features

Key standards that influence the design and performance of cinema spaces are provided by SMPTE, Dolby, THX and IMAX. Becoming an accredited or branded cinema that is recognised as being in adherence of these standards requires verification tests. In addition, most commercial cinema operators have their own specific acoustic design requirements which may apply to both core-and-shell and the interior's fit-out. These are primarily related to sound and impact insulation and structure-borne noise. Typically, the design responsibilities of the architect will be limited to the isolated acoustic shells of the cinema. The fit-out of wall, floor and ceiling finishes, seats, building services and AV equipment will be undertaken separately from this. The requirements for soundtrack noise emission to the external environment are usually driven by the standards set by the local planning authority and may require higher standards than the commercial operator requires. This can pose a challenge if operations run late into the night (which they often do).

Independent cinemas usually require a design for the entire space, often following a similar acoustic brief as the larger commercial operators. It should be noted that current incarnations of independent cinemas include 'luxury' and more spacious environments, where food and drink may be served during a showing, necessitating a full understanding of the client's expectations for design.

Room acoustics are usually well controlled. Sound-absorbing treatments to walls, floors and ceilings are the norm; they can take a variety of aesthetic forms from the very basic to the highly ornate. Seats are usually sound-absorbing.

Good sound insulation between spaces is crucial. Careful space planning from an early stage is an essential part of the design process for keeping cinema auditoria as far away as possible from noise sensitive and noise generating spaces. The use of buffer spaces, such as escape corridors, can be particularly effective here. The screen wall of one auditorium (which the main soundtrack loudspeakers are directly located behind) should not back directly onto another auditorium. Traditionally, multiplex cinemas have the auditoria all facing the same way to allow a single projection room that backs onto the rear of all spaces. The rise of digital projectors within each auditorium has led to more flexibility in this respect. Furthermore, in many multiplex cinemas spaces are stacked vertically, increasing the attention that needs to be paid to both horizontal and vertical airborne and impact sound insulation requirements.

Inside the screening spaces themselves, each auditorium usually has a concrete floating floor on resilient bearings to avoid flanking sound though a common slab, and to provide control of ground-borne noise. This can either be a flat slab with a timber rake built on top, or a floating concrete rake on a steel frame, depending on how the space below is to be used. Auditorium walls are typically composed of multiple layers of acoustic grade plasterboard to each side of twin independent studs, one on the floating floor and one on the base slab. Often a layer of plywood is incorporated into the build-up of the inner wall to enable items such as sound-absorbing panels and surround loudspeakers to be directly fixed to the walls.

A plasterboard 'lid' on resilient hangers is often installed to control flanking sound transmission through the common slab or roof construction above. Separate resilient suspended hangers, penetrating the lid, are often provided for the suspension of a sound-absorbing ceiling, projectors, lighting and loudspeakers. Walls also require a zone for the mounting of surround audio devices and incorporation of sufficient sound-absorbing treatment to meet stringent design standards. This zone is typically 200–500mm deep.

Challenges and opportunities

Cinema continues to evolve as a medium, and with it the technology and spaces that present it. For example, immersive film format (using three screens at the front and expanding to both side walls) was introduced in 2015. While it has been adopted in some new-build cinemas it has not resulted in significant retrofit of older projects – yet.

While cinema sound systems are unlikely to increase in loudness, what is likely to grow are the number of loudspeakers required for immersive and spatial sound, as their artistic use continues to evolve. The integration of additional immersive and experiential features should also be anticipated – for example, vibration motion capabilities (from seats and/or floor) and airflow for effects, or even smells, will introduce further complexities into the design, all requiring close collaboration between architect, acoustic consultant and structural engineer.

Use of archive film formats (e.g. celluloid, 70mm, 35mm, 16mm projectors) have very specialist requirements, especially in the projection room design. It is crucial to understand if these are required at project inception.

Sky Cinema

Location: Sky Central, London, UK

Architect: PLP Architecture

Completed: 2016

Located at the media headquarters at Sky Central, the flagship building of the broadcaster's West London campus is situated directly below an open plan office area and in close proximity to the news studio. Containing high levels of sound from the Dolby Atmos audio systems was a key priority.

While the inner designs of cinemas can take many forms, the fundamental aspects of the interior acoustic designs remain relatively uniform; predominantly sound-absorbing finishes to walls, floors, ceilings and seats throughout. Loudspeakers for the surround sound system are often clearly visible on the room perimeter. The front-centre, left and right loudspeaker channels, and sub-bass units, are usually located behind the projection screen, and rear surround loudspeakers are typically visible in the room.

A box-in-box construction is usually required in multiplex cinemas, or where noise ingress from adjacent spaces could be problematic. A floating floor usually supports the inner walls, and an upper isolated structure allows an independent ceiling to be hung from it. It is important to ensure no bridging of the isolation joint between the two structures, as noise and vibration will find its way through the path of least resistance.

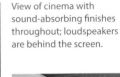

View of cinema with sound-absorbing finishes throughout; loudspeakers are behind the screen.

White beams support the secondary structure for the box-in-box isolation, supported on isolating neoprene bearing.

View of inner gypsum board framing and construction of inner isolated box.

Preparations for laying sound-isolated floor on perimeter neoprene bearings and fibreglass between the floors.

Issue	Priority	Comments
Room acoustics	H	Museums and galleries can vary widely in acoustic response. Historic buildings with sound-reflecting finishes tend toward a reverberant sound – eliciting a hushed and reverent response from visitors. For these, incorporation of materials to control acoustics was generally not considered, and retrofit can be a challenge. In newer buildings, acoustics receive increasing attention, especially where art or exhibits are likely to feature amplified sound. Large openings with no doors connect spaces, and sound propagation between them is an issue. High visitor numbers require occupational noise control. External rental of spaces intended for revenue generation usually requires amplified sound, and corresponding good acoustics. Some institutions vary acoustic design between spaces to better accommodate different exhibit types (e.g. audio-visual intensive, special and temporary exhibitions that are fitted out specifically, and where acoustic treatments are added as part of the exhibit). Fixed sound-absorbing treatment is usually limited to ceiling and certain upper wall areas to maximise presentation space.
Speech intelligibility	H	Clear speech intelligibility is usually important for rental spaces, lecture theatres, conference rooms, etc. It is also important where PAVA is needed for routing paging and emergency purposes.
Audio systems design	M–H	Building-wide PAVA and fixed or temporary sound systems for rental spaces are commonplace. Both require consideration of device numbers and locations for design integration.
Sound insulation – external	M	Specific areas may be sensitive to noise (e.g. audio art, conservation or study areas) and good early planning can locate them away from noise producing spaces to limit costly sound insulating constructions. In urban environments, external noise can be an issue. Understand the conditions early and develop the façade design to meet desired limits – this can be particularly challenging when there is a significant amount of glazing.
Sound insulation – internal	H	Modern buildings tend to be both open and transparent. Sound propagation between spaces without doors requires special consideration to ensure operational requirements for exhibitions can be achieved. Noise sensitive spaces should ideally be located away from these areas.
Speech privacy	L–M	This is not usually an important consideration except in office and administration areas, and spaces for more sensitive working (conservation, study, etc.).
Impact/vibration isolation	M	Large areas of hard, sound-reflecting floors can be expected. To limit footfall noise, impact isolation is usually incorporated below the finished floor. The airborne sound of footfall on the floor should also be carefully considered when large visitor numbers are expected.
Mechanical and electrical noise	M–H	Interior mechanical noise levels should be benchmarked where appropriate to determine the right design levels. NR30–40 is usually acceptable for most spaces; the upper range usually for large gallery and exhibit areas, public foyers, atria and similar.
Structure-borne noise	M	Apart from the usual considerations of urban transport sources, loading docks, freight elevators and café and restaurant kitchens are other primary sources for consideration in planning to minimise impact to front- and back-of-house spaces.
Environmental noise	H	The main source of external noise emission is generally MEP equipment exhaust to outside. This must be carefully considered close to residential areas, or remote museums in very quiet environments. Institutions are increasingly incorporating after-hours and weekend programming, including live events which are often amplified – noise emission to residents should be considered.

H – High   M – Medium   L – Low

Introduction

The purpose of the modern museum or gallery can vary widely by institution. It might include display of collections, education, research, conservation and other functions. Acoustics are an important part of the museum experience and a key factor in how people behave in these spaces. Good acoustics can be essential to how work is experienced, and how alternative uses of those spaces can be realised.

Architectural style

The first museums and displays of art were primarily found in the private collections of royalty, and in the homes of the wealthy. These were generally domestic spaces where soft furnishings were the principal sound-absorbing materials, though later on books and other printed materials also contributed.

The first 'public' institutions founded during the classical era tended to have corresponding grand architecture, comprised of large acoustic volumes and predominantly hard, sound-reflecting materials. At the time these were somewhat tempered by soft furnishings, such as tapestries, curtains or wall hangings. These have largely disappeared, except in spaces where they are the artefacts themselves. With grand works on display in spaces that could become noisy or distracting in high-occupancy conditions, the behavioural etiquette that developed was hushed and reverential.

From the mid-19th century, emerging art was first displayed in salons, representing a return to a space with more domestic acoustics. By the mid-20th century, the shift towards utilising warehouses and industrial buildings as spaces for showing modern art brought with it a different acoustic character.

Acoustic features

The need to preserve artefacts in controlled environmental conditions during the 20th century led to more sealed buildings, with constant HVAC and controlled humidity (with the resulting constant background noise) and controlled light levels. Some spaces from this era use sound-absorbing ceilings as the primary means to control occupational noise, especially in spaces expecting high numbers of visitors, school group tours, etc.

In the late 20th century, the introduction of daylight back into many museums in a controlled manner (that met preservation standards) became common. In many cases, spaces are top-lit, with all or part of the ceiling developed for lighting control, in turn compromising a zone once primarily used for sound-absorbing treatment.

The result today is a wide range of different acoustic conditions, from the hushed and reverential to the acoustically controlled. In the refurbishment of existing spaces, or the design of new buildings, it is important to understand any specific acoustic design criteria which are usually driven by how spaces will be used. The main aspects to consider are:

- The overall sound and character of background noise from HVAC systems, which need to be controlled appropriately based on function and use of the spaces

- Expected occupancy levels and desired behaviour will impact room acoustics – higher occupancy, large and frequent numbers of education or school groups, or regular guided tours with commentary will require more attention. Sometimes only a limited quantity of sound-absorbing and sound-diffusing treatment can significantly change the room acoustics of a space

- Spaces with a more educational function, or interactive elements, can require significantly

Historical context

more audio and video infrastructure than other spaces, with associated acoustic conditions to be considered

- Permanent exhibition and collection galleries may be treated very differently than temporary spaces that have more frequent changeovers or accommodate touring shows. In the latter, it is important to determine if the base conditions need to have acoustics to accommodate a wide range of exhibit types, or if they are recalibrated for each new exhibit – an approach that can be costly in terms of material purchase, and carries a sustainability consideration in terms of what happens to those materials when they are no longer needed

- For institutions showing work where sound is a primary component, curators will need to decide if this can be shown in all spaces, or whether specific galleries are selected for this, where acoustics are more controlled than in others

- Sound propagation from space to space is often an important consideration, especially in museums with fewer physical barriers between different areas. This requires careful consideration in the display areas themselves, but also between spaces; specifically designed transition zones may be required (a decision often driven by considerations other than acoustic)

- For funding purposes, many institutions rely on rental revenue. To get maximum use from specific rooms, or to have multiple spaces in use for events simultaneously, requires careful consideration of both room acoustics and sound propagation, as well as the design of appropriate and sufficiently adaptable sound systems

Challenges

While it may be harder to incorporate sound-absorbing treatment in top-lit gallery spaces, it is possible. Creating good sound diffusing surfaces is also highly beneficial and should be incorporated within the design as early as possible. In many modern museum and gallery spaces, extensive areas of seamless white walls are preferred. Acoustic plaster products that achieve this look are available, but careful thought should be given to their use. Maintenance and upgrades to those surfaces, while maintaining acoustic performance, can be a challenge.

Opportunities

The increasing use of sound in art will continue to challenge design approaches for spaces as specialist sound – art areas are developed further. Some artists may want to use space acoustics very specifically within their practice. Certain works require highly controlled acoustics for accurate delivery, as intended by the artist (e.g. Doug Wheeler's 'Synthetic Desert IV'), while others may use acoustic challenge as a means of creating art that emphasises it (e.g. Alvin Lucier's 'I am sitting in a room').

Performance and other cross-disciplinary art must increasingly be integrated into new buildings, resulting in new space typologies. In the arts, 'white space' is often referred to as the space between objects, sounds, movements, etc. 'White box theatres' provide transformable environments that can work as traditional spaces, as well as for experimental work and hybrid performances. AR could also begin to rely more on personal audio delivered over headphones (replacing existing audio guides), and potentially change the way people behave acoustically. Immersive environments for replaying 3D video and audio recordings of major works (perhaps with VR or AR) to recreate specific experiences for archive and future study are already on the horizon, and may become permanent fixtures in the future.

Los Angeles County Museum of Art (LACMA)

LOCATION: California, USA

ARCHITECT: Renzo Piano Building Workshop Architects

COMPLETED: 2008

The following three examples show different approaches for dealing with sound-absorbing materials in museum spaces.

At LACMA a more industrial approach was taken, very similar to that in manufacturing spaces found throughout the USA and beyond. The outer sawtooth profile lets light in as desired. Sound-absorbing panels are hung vertically and coloured white to reflect as much light as possible. A light-diffusing, sound-transparent scrim is located on the underside of the truss.

LACMA, Los Angeles, USA; top-lit galleries with hanging sound-absorbing baffles.

New Museum of Contemporary Art

LOCATION: New York, USA

ARCHITECT: Kazuyo Sejima & Ryue Nishizawa (SANAA)

COMPLETED: 2007

An industrial approach was also taken at the New Museum. The underside of the ceiling is expanded metal mesh coloured white. Sound-absorbing treatment is fixed to the underside of the profiled metal deck where needed.

New Museum, New York, USA; an industrial approach.

High Museum of Art

LOCATION: Woodruff Arts Center, Atlanta, Georgia, USA

ARCHITECT: Renzo Piano Building Workshop Architects

COMPLETED: 2005

At the High Museum, the upper gallery design was driven by the need for diffused daylight. Acoustics were not a primary requirement, although the museum was keen to avoid harsh acoustics to ensure a pleasant environment for art viewing, mindful of large numbers of people are in the space (especially school groups). The shape of the lighting scoops had a significant sound diffusing effect. Consideration was given to hanging a sound-absorbing element within the conical profile, but through a combination of auralisation studies, it was agreed to rely on the sound diffusing alone to temper the sound in the space.

Atlanta High Museum of Art, Georgia, USA; top-lit gallery.

Met Breuer

LOCATION: New York, USA

ARCHITECT: Marcel Breuer and Beyer Blinder Belle

COMPLETED: 1966, 2016

The Breuer is an iconic New York building. Originally built as the home for the Whitney Museum of American Art, it was renovated and expanded in a series of phases. In 2015 The Breuer was restored by Beyer Blinder Belle.

This building represents a rare, rich and well-balanced approach to architecture for the senses, a likely result of the great multi-disciplinary design heritage of the Bauhaus, where Breuer was a member.

There is little in the way of sound-absorbing treatment in the building, apart from the fireproof spray coating to the steel beams in the ceilings of each floor. The ceiling voids carry most of the mechanical and electrical services, lighting and data infrastructure. Below the ceiling on most of the gallery floors is a concrete coffer grid that forms the main visual impression of the ceiling, hiding most of the ceiling void. Theses coffers, the void and the services combined provide a significant amount of sound diffusing and absorbing performance.

The remainder of the materials are generally sound-reflecting in nature; concrete, timber, steel and bluestone floors. Throughout the building rough textures are prevalent (particularly in the concrete), which act as more sound diffusing. The result is a well-balanced sounding space that is also particularly welcoming to touch. Add to that how visually striking the building is, both on the inside and outside, and from the inside looking out; the building is a rare treat.

The sound-reflecting bluestone floors create balance with the sound-diffusing rough textures elsewhere.

The mixture of materials and resulting acoustics in the stairwells creates contrast with the galleries, as you traverse between them, without the use of any sound-absorbing treatment.

View of the museum lobby; note the various textures in the concrete.

View of the gallery, with concrete coffer ceiling.

St Louis Art Museum Expansion

LOCATION: St Louis, Missouri, USA

ARCHITECT: David Chipperfield Architects

COMPLETED: 2013

In the design of the 20,000 square-metre extension to an existing 1902 Cass Gilbert building, acoustics and audio-visual systems design were principal considerations from the start.

Extensive discussion regarding the impact of the acoustics, audio systems and technical infrastructure were conducted with the building staff. Measurements were made in existing spaces for benchmarking, as well as establishing an understanding of other aspirational benchmark buildings. Controlling sound transfer from audio-intensive exhibits to other areas of the museum, achieving good acoustics, and high speech intelligibility in the rental spaces were key requirements.

The building design features a ceiling of regular concrete coffers that allow angled roof lights to let daylight into the building. One of the design requirements was to both redirect and diffuse this light to create even daylighting conditions in the space, supplemented by electric lighting. The design team developed a hybrid element to achieve this effect using a 150mm frame with an electrical supply, incorporating the light control element to the upper surface, and a light diffusing, micro-perforated membrane (Barisol®) beneath. The cavity depth was optimised so that the assembly produced the best sound-absorbing performance possible. Lights, loudspeakers, cameras, and other devices are attached to and receive power from the frame.

In some spaces, where the daylighting requirement was less critical, a more conventional sound-absorbing tile replaces the surface on the underside of the assembly. For temporary exhibits, the width of the coffer downstands was optimised to accommodate art walls, as well as to allow for the width of higher sound-insulating walls if needed. These temporary floors can be installed from the finished floor, or down to the concrete floor slab below if needed, depending on the acoustic performance requirements. Air is supplied through grilles under the floor, and the cavity also provides routing for audio, visual and digital infrastructure to support exhibits.

In the restaurant the hybrid element is simplified, with a regular perforated metal sound-absorbing underside.

One of the main gallery spaces, showing the coffers and hybrid elements between them, which include sound-absorbing and audio requirements. The underfloor air supply and technical routes are visible, in perforated black metal.

SFMOMA

LOCATION: San Francisco, California, USA

ARCHITECT: Mario Botta (original) and Snøhetta (extension and refurbishment)

COMPLETED: 1995, 2016

A modern art museum and nonprofit organisation, SFMOMA holds an internationally acclaimed collection of modern and contemporary art, and was the first museum on the West Coast of the United States devoted solely to 20th-century art.

The top-lit gallery with sculpted, sound-absorbing ceiling panels.

Because some of the museum's exhibits feature sound and video, it was necessary to create the right environment for these and mitigate sound transmission between adjacent exhibition areas.

The acoustics, tailored for audio reproduction and sound isolation, include 100mm-thick sound-absorbing ceiling panels that reduce reverberance, improving audio fidelity especially in the lower/bass frequencies. Sound-isolating floors, ceilings and walls were designed to contain sound and avoid disturbing neighbouring spaces. Low-noise heating, ventilation and air-conditioning (HVAC) systems improve the detail and dynamic range of audio content.

The long 'City Stair' connects the galleries at each level in the building. They are designed to create a natural 'flutter echo' giving each stair a unique acoustic signature, which is activated by the sounds made by visitors, for example, footsteps and whispers. Each sound creates a unique sonic artwork. This acoustic signature can be specifically activated by artists, should they choose. Usual rules of acoustic design suggest adding sound-absorbing material to neutralise these artefacts. The team decided to retain them to create additional engagement, and tell a story around design and multi-sensory experience of spaces.

The acoustic design for the public areas creates peaceful spaces for quiet contemplation. Galleries incorporate sculpted glass fibre-reinforced gypsum (GFRG) panels that scatter light and sound. In the high-density entry area, strategically located sound-absorbing finishes control the build-up of noise from visitors, helping to keep the ticketing experience calm and pleasant. The amount of sound-absorbing treatment required was determined using proprietary acoustic models based on the architecture and anticipated occupancy. In the large column-free gallery spaces, the museum can vary configurations using temporary walls.

The Wattis Theatre at SFMOMA, the well-known cinema within the original Botta building, was completely renovated as part of the expansion project. The design includes architecturally integrated acoustic features that both recreate the acoustics of the original theatre and support an active architecture system that can electronically alter the acoustics of the room for different performance types. The ability to vary the room acoustics at the push of a button enables the museum to present a wide range of events.

The long City Stair creates a flutter echo from the footsteps and conversation of visitors.

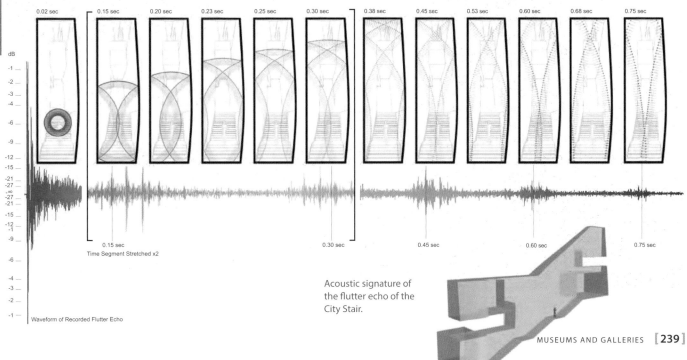

| 0.02 sec | 0.15 sec | 0.20 sec | 0.23 sec | 0.25 sec | 0.30 sec | 0.38 sec | 0.45 sec | 0.53 sec | 0.60 sec | 0.68 sec | 0.75 sec |

dB
-1
-2
-3
-4
-6
-9
-12
-15
-21
-27
-∞
-27
-21
-15
-12
-1
-9

-6
-4
-3
-2
-1

0.15 sec
Time Segment Stretched x2

0.30 sec

0.45 sec

0.60 sec

0.75 sec

Waveform of Recorded Flutter Echo

Acoustic signature of the flutter echo of the City Stair.

The White Box Theatre is an entirely new space for live performance, accommodating theatre-in-the-round configurations, multi-screen projections and special installations. It means that for the first time SFMOMA has the full range of flexibility and infrastructure necessary for performance-based work, allowing artists to explore movement and film in new ways. The design of this space provides support for performances that are suited neither to the separation of a proscenium stage, nor to a gallery with acoustic bleed, that may contain art with particular conservation needs. This space fosters works that call for continuous action over long periods of time, or live pieces rooted in intimate audience – performer exchange, and group dynamics. The fixed technical grid, control room, and audio-visual and theatrical infrastructure support a wide variety of performances, installations, board meetings and artworks.

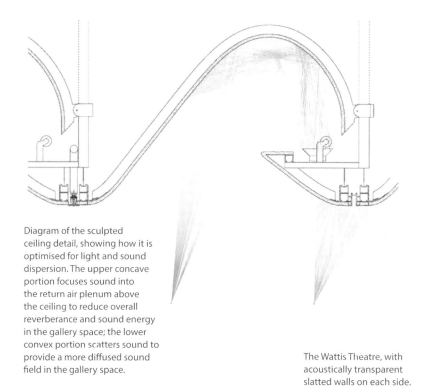

Diagram of the sculpted ceiling detail, showing how it is optimised for light and sound dispersion. The upper concave portion focuses sound into the return air plenum above the ceiling to reduce overall reverberance and sound energy in the gallery space; the lower convex portion scatters sound to provide a more diffused sound field in the gallery space.

The Wattis Theatre, with acoustically transparent slatted walls on each side.

Acoustic design features of the media arts galleries.

A continuous multi-layer gypsum ceiling creates a robust and cost-effective sound barrier to the occupied spaces above the Media Arts

Continous gypsum wallboard down-stands allow temporary walls to be acoustically sealed for maximum sound isolation between galleries

A unistrut ceiling grid provides a flexible mounting solution without comprimising the abillity to seal temporary partitions

An acoustically-isolated floor system mitigates sound transfer to the occupied spaces below Media Arts

Modular sound-absorbing ceiling panels absorb the full spectrum of sound to improve the audio reproduction quality of sound art pieces

White Box Gallery.

Recording and Broadcast

Issue	Priority	Comments
Room acoustics	H	Most studios for TV, radio and amplified music require highly controlled room acoustics with sound-absorbing finishes on all ceilings and walls. To ensure appropriate control of low-frequency sound within these spaces, the depth of the wall finishes can be between 150 and 500mm thick.
		Spaces for recording orchestral music require a natural reverberance, and appropriately directed early sound reflections to aid orchestral ensemble; this is often achieved using special arrays of sound reflectors.
Speech intelligibility	H	Good speech intelligibility is a critical part of the design of live microphone spaces such as drama studios, voice-over booths or radio studios.
Audio systems design	H	Technical fit-out is a highly complex process requiring specialist design. Equipment selection for studios and playback/editing equipment in post-production spaces is usually done by the facility operator according to their specific requirements.
		Many large broadcast spaces require deep cavity, raised access floors to provide sufficient space for the cabling infrastructure.
Sound insulation – external	H	The noise environment around the building must be measured. The sound insulation of the building envelope must be designed to ensure that external noise does not affect the production process. Not all noise sources will be visible; some may be constant others intermittent. Both current and future noise sources including travel infrastructure and construction works should be considered.
Sound insulation – internal	H	Live microphone and critical listening spaces require significant sound insulation to and from adjacent spaces to avoid sound disturbance during the production process. This often requires independent plasterboard or masonry walls, floating floors and independent lids, and lobbied sets of heavy acoustic doors. TV studios usually require tall and heavy sliding acoustic get-in doors, around 3–4m high.
Speech privacy	L	This is not usually an important consideration as the emphasis is upon clear speech being captured by microphones.
Impact/vibration isolation	H	Acoustically critical spaces are often built as box-in-box constructions with concrete floating floors on resilient bearings with independent inner walls and 'lids' of either concrete/masonry or plasterboard. This approach provides opportunity for excellent control of impact sound from surrounding spaces.
Mechanical and electrical noise	H	A low noise level from building systems is essential in live microphone spaces such as studios or voiceover booths to ensure that the quality of the audio recording or broadcast is not diminished.
		In post-production spaces (dubbing suites, etc.) the background noise level must be low to enable critical listening by the engineer.
		Delivering large volumes of conditioned air quietly often requires large duct sizes with sufficient length to incorporate attenuation.
Structure-borne noise	H	The concrete floating floors on resilient bearings often used in studio spaces can be tuned to attenuate sources of ground-borne noise, such as underground trains, trams, road traffic or nearby construction noise.
Environmental noise	H	Building systems equipment located on the roof or venting to the exterior is usually the main source of environmental noise. This issue is particularly relevant for facilities adjacent to residential buildings.

H – High   M – Medium   L – Low

Introduction

Traditionally, the acoustically critical spaces in recording or broadcast facilities fall into two main categories: live microphone spaces (studios) and production/post-production spaces (control rooms, editing suites, dubbing rooms, etc.). For studios, the key acoustic priorities are to provide a space with excellent conditions for recorded sound, and an environment where presenters and performers can hear themselves and others appropriately. For production or post-production spaces, the emphasis is on enabling the users to concentrate on a specific task. A range of acoustic standards is typically required, driven by the function of the room. Critical listening spaces such as sound control rooms and dubbing suites have much more stringent acoustic requirements than, for example, video editing suites.

Architectural style

The mid-to-late 19th century saw the simultaneous development of a range of technologies that enabled radio broadcast, television broadcast, and the recording of speech and music to be realised. Prior to the invention of electrical recording, analogue acoustic recordings (such as Thomas Edison's 1887 phonograph) were made by allowing a sound to vibrate in a simple diaphragm and then imprinting the vibration onto a rotating cylinder (initially covered in tin foil, later commonly made of wax). Given the sensitivity of the equipment, it was easy to pick up noise. The first studios were simple rooms as isolated from their external environments as possible.

Microphones, amplifiers and loudspeakers essential to electrical recording saw rapid development in the late 19th and early 20th centuries. By the early 1930s acoustic recording was obsolete. Due to limitations of the technology – the inherent susceptibility of microphones to surrounding noise, and the need for a significant amount of equipment to capture and broadcast sound – the first purpose-built studios

separated core functions from each other, but as it was often not possible to achieve high sound insulation performance, most made-do with the best they could achieve pragmatically. These 'core' functions consisted of the recording 'studio' itself, control rooms, equipment rooms and broadcast equipment spaces. Spaces for the broadcast of high-quality speech started to incorporate significant amounts of sound-absorbing materials to ensure that the signal received by the microphone was as free from room disturbance (early sound reflections and reverberance) as possible.

Technology continued to develop and improve over the 20th century, but not to the extent that necessitated major changes to building form and design approach. This is also because the requirements for live or pre-recorded radio and television broadcast generally still required separation between spaces for operational purposes, and to be free of significant disturbance from exterior noises while allowing recording activity to continue undisturbed. Certain activities, such as broadcast news, have changed format from completely enclosed studio spaces to more open plan layouts, with a working newsroom, or the outside environment being visible. This brings with it some operational management issues which need to be understood in order to design appropriately. Digital technology democratised the recording process. Now anyone can broadcast video, or make music, from a laptop. Note, the use of any analogue source still requires an absence of noise and the control of room acoustics to get the best signal.

It is worth mentioning that the acoustic quality of some spaces can be an important part of a recording or broadcast, and this is actively used in some cases to give the recorded medium character. That might mean placing microphones in a particular place in a concert hall to pick up certain sound reflections, and mix them into the recording, or music recording studios that sometimes have 'live rooms' or chambers coveted for their natural 'reverberance'. Understanding the acoustic design needs at the outset of a project is paramount for achieving the right outcome for the client.

Acoustic features

Recording and broadcast facilities usually incorporate a wide variety of spaces, some of which are highly noise sensitive and some of which generate high levels of sound. Careful space planning at the beginning of a project can help minimise the use of heavy, structurally challenging constructions that occupy more floor area. In some areas there will inevitably be the need for floating box-in-box constructions and deep cavity wall/floor build-ups.

Television studios are typically rectangular spaces with a wide range of floor areas from around 100m^2 to 800m^2, with internal ceiling heights of (often) up to ten metres or more. Larger studios frequently incorporate multiple sets, or provision for a live audience. Low background noise levels are required, typically NR25, for both broadcast audio quality and to aid the concentration of the presenters/performers. Low-velocity supply and return air infrastructure is typically located at ceiling level to keep the walls and floors clear for flexibility of set design. Microphone technique varies from the use of lapel mics (for news readers or other presenters) to boom microphones (out of shot) for drama.

Isolated box-in-box constructions (masonry or drywall) on resilient bearings are very often required to control noise and vibration entering the space, and to contain high levels of sound such as amplified bands from surrounding spaces. Entrances usually have lobbies lined in sound-absorbing material with good quality sound-isolating doors. Large, heavy,

sliding 'get-in' doors (often four by four metres) are required for bringing in sets, and to access TV studios, which are usually located on the ground floor (level with the loading dock). Studio floors are typically a super flat epoxy surface, screeded for smooth tracking of cameras.

The room acoustic environment needs to be as free of sound reflections as possible. To achieve this, the entire soffit above the lighting grid usually has a black, highly sound-absorbing finish. Walls require a physically robust sound-absorbing finish applied to as much of the area as possible (often 150–200mm thick mineral wool or fibreglass with metal perforated finish). This finish must be integrated with the extensive technical requirements for cable routes and facility panels.

For background noise and sound insulation, rock and pop studios utilise many of the principles found in television studios. The room acoustic finishes are often designed to have flexible elements, such as sliding or hinged panels that can be adjusted to tailor the sound of the space, depending on the type of music being played. Particular care is taken designing for the response of low-frequency sound, which often requires the use of tuned sound absorbers that can be of the order of 200–300mm deep, in addition to the depth of the wall construction.

Orchestral studios follow many of the principles of concert hall design in terms of requiring low background noise levels (around NR15) and significant sound insulation (often needing a box-in-box). Careful consideration is given to the ensemble conditions for the orchestra (often necessitating a suspended reflector array). They can be used in several different formats such as album recording, live radio broadcast (with or without audience) or television/film soundtrack recording (often with a projected film behind the orchestra from which the conductor takes cues).

Radio presenter studios are typically small (around 20–40m²), accommodating only three to five people (one or two presenters, a producer and any visiting guests). The use of high-quality large diaphragm microphones requires very low background noise levels of the order of NR20. Cooling is often provided by fan coil units positioned outside the studio and ducted in. This is not only to help control of noise, but to avoid the risk of any fluid leaks onto the technical equipment below.

Constructions are usually box-in-box, with a floating concrete floor, independent drywalls and lids, and lined entrance lobbies with sound-absorbing treatment. Floors are usually carpeted. A sound-absorbing ceiling is suspended below the lid, providing a zone between for the distribution of services. Cabling is generally distributed under a raised access floor or in box skirting.

Very small radio studios are sometimes 'self-op' units where the presenter also controls the broadcast systems. Where separate technical control is required, this is often from an adjacent control room with a visual connection via a high-performance acoustic window. These are usually two sheets of glass, each within an independent wall, spaced at least 200mm apart with a sound-absorbing finish in the reveals. To address sound and visual reflections in the glass, each pane is angled downward to the adjacent room by around seven degrees.

Voice-over booths are one-person spaces following similar acoustic principles to radio studios, but are used in television production with a high-performance acoustic window to an adjacent sound control room or dubbing suite. Some voice-over booths used for international language commentary for sports events require significantly lower acoustic standards, such as when the commentators use close-lip microphones.

Following similar sound insulation and background noise principles to other radio studios, radio drama studios are larger spaces. They often contain variable room acoustic finishes in the form of drapes or hinged panels to allow flexibility in the room response, depending on the scene in the drama. Actors usually perform standing up, but may sometimes sit or lie down in line with their character's behaviour, which affects the sound of the voice. Walking areas and steps made from different materials are often incorporated, as are kitchens, in order to allow the convincing integration of different sound effects. Some sound effects are recorded in a separate dedicated Foley studio.

Generally not used for recording sound, sound control rooms are spaces intended for critical listening – requiring low background noise levels (NR25 or lower) – and often take the form of a lightweight box-in-box construction with lobbied entrances. Sound control rooms are typically paired with a specific studio, but some are flexible and can be connected with multiple studios. They usually incorporate a high-performance deep cavity window to facilitate visual communication between artists and engineers/producers. Television sound control rooms do not usually have a direct view into the studio. They instead rely on a large bank of monitor screens. There is usually an acoustic window into the adjacent production control room, allowing visual communication between the sound engineer and the producer.

The geometry and finishes of spaces for critical listening must be carefully considered such that the distribution of room modal response is appropriate. Useful guidance on this and other room design properties is provided by the European Broadcasting Union. Spaces used for critical listening of music (rather than only speech) often require a deep zone for wall treatment, 200–300mm thick. This may be a combination of sound-absorbing and sound-diffusing.

Audio dubbing and mastering suites are used for post-production of sound and follow similar acoustic principles to sound control rooms, except that they are not directly linked to a particular studio. When working with film, these can be very large – similar to the size of a small cinema. For TV dubbing or mastering (the final stage of the music production process), suites tend to be smaller (of the order of 30–40m²).

Production control rooms are not for critical listening, but still require controlled background noise (around NR30) and room acoustics to aid the concentration of the production team working with the associated studio. Box-in-box constructions are not typically necessary, but sound-absorbing wall and ceiling finishes are required.

In terms of acoustic design, edit suites are comparable to private cellular offices. With a background noise level of around NR30, single-stud, slab-to-slab drywalls are typically appropriate. Carpeted floors, sound-absorbing ceilings and areas of sound-absorbing wall finishes (around 50mm thick) are typically incorporated.

An increasingly common feature of news broadcasting has been to present while located within much less acoustically controlled open plan areas. Often referred to as the 'hub and spoke' model, the broadcast space is at the 'hub', with support working spaces around it and often visible in frame. Major broadcasters (e.g. Sky, Bloomberg, BBC) have adopted this approach for some of their programmes. The use of close directional lapel microphones can allow presenters to work in spaces with a less controlled acoustic and higher ambient noise levels. The benefit of this approach is that it can facilitate a more dynamic and flexible backdrop, often with the news team in shot behind the presenters.

Future

While there will always be a need for highly controlled acoustic environments, it is expected that broadcast from open spaces will continue to develop – especially in the context of live news bulletins. The use of glass walls in radio and news studios has increased in recent years – these not only provide a dynamic backdrop, but also help to create a greater sense of openness within the workplace. With careful attention to the geometry of glass studios, these can be acoustically successful and are likely to continue to be popular in news applications.

Danish Broadcasting Corporation Headquarters

LOCATION: Danmarks Radio, Copenhagen, Denmark

ARCHITECT: Dissing + Weitling

COMPLETED: 2006

Segment two of this national facility is the focal point for daily sports and news programmes which are transmitted from the large newsroom, newsroom studio and TV studio.

The building features a circular glass news studio with a view out into the newsroom, and a sliding curved glass wall that can be opened out into the newsroom. The news desk is carefully positioned away from the acoustic focal point of the curved glass wall. There is integration of sound-absorbing finishes to the underside of the roof and to the fascia panels beneath the balustrades. The studio also features a powerful, sound-absorbing ceiling finish, a benefit from early acoustic modelling of studio response.

Close-up of circular glass recording studio, which presented a series of design challenges.

View of main working studio office spaces, with circular studio in the foreground.

Air Studios

LOCATION: Hampstead, London, UK

ARCHITECT: Alfred Waterhouse and
Heber Percy & Parker

COMPLETED: 1880, 1992

Associate Independent Recording was founded by
Sir George Martin and John Burgess in 1965 after their
departure from Parlophone records. In 1985 they moved
to the dramatic Lyndhurst Road Congregational Church,
a Grade II listed building located in the Hampstead
suburb of northwest London.

The main space, now Lyndhurst Hall, underwent
a historic renovation to preserve the original
architecture, with some upgrades to material finishes
for acoustic purposes, and improvements to the sound
insulation of the building envelope to mitigate noise
from road traffic. Most notably, this included the
addition of 25mm thick single glazing over an airspace
behind the existing stained-glass windows that were
refurbished and remain exposed to the exterior of the
building. State-of-the-art master control room and
vocal booths were also incorporated. By retaining the
acoustics of the main space with some modifications,
and the addition of suspended sound reflectors
and absorbers that can be deployed as needed, the
space is one of the most sought after in the world
for film score recording and can accommodate a full
symphony orchestra and choir.

Five additional box-in-box spaces make up the
remaining studios, accommodating writing and
recording spaces for popular music, as well as film
scores, television post-production, and dialogue,
sound effects and music for video games.

View from the balcony,
with visible sound-
absorbing panels
placed over pews for
some recordings, and
suspended element with
sound-reflecting, diffusing
and absorbing qualities.

Main control room; note
sound insulating window
with deep airspace.

Studio 1 has a main window
that is angled downwards, to
prevent strong sound reflections
across the room, sound-diffusing
surfaces to ceilings and wall areas
including convex inner windows,
and slatted and purple fabric-
wrapped sound-absorbing panels.

Control room for Studio 1.

BBC Pacific Quay

LOCATION: Glasgow, Scotland, UK

ARCHITECT: David Chipperfield Architects and Keppie Design

COMPLETED: 2006

This huge complex, situated on the River Clyde, contains two large television studios, a news studio, a rock music and drama studio, three dubbing suites, radio broadcast studios, voice over booths, digital audio workstations and around 40 edit rooms.

The technical and office spaces are arranged around a five-storey atrium or 'street'. With the exception of Studio A, which is structurally independent from the rest of the building, all of the other studios have resiliently supported concrete floors with either blockwork or drywalls.

At nearly 800m^2, Studio A has a full walkable grid at high level with a sound-absorbing ceiling above. Sound-absorbing wall finishes consist of 150mm thick medium-density glass fibre, with 50% coverage of 0.7mm thick Zintec steel sheet to achieve an appropriate balance of low and mid/high-frequency sound absorption. Wire mesh facing provides protection of the wall finish, with rubber spaces against the steel sheet to prevent rattling in response to high sound levels. While it has independent walls and an independent concrete lid, it did not need a concrete floating floor because there were no significant sources of vibration nearby, and there were no acoustically sensitive or noise generating spaces directly adjacent.

There is formwork for entirely separate concrete floating floors for the radio drama studio, which also features hinged acoustic panels. There is an adjacent control room, and a deep cavity acoustic window between the radio drama studio and the control room.

The 'street' is the main connecting element of the entire building, spanning over five storeys, and provides a space for meetings, collaboration and rest from studio environments.

Studio A is the main studio space in the building.

Detail of the spring isolators for the air-handling units above studios.

Sky Studios, Osterley

LOCATION: London, UK

ARCHITECT: Arup Associates

COMPLETED: 2010

Sky Studios is the most sustainable broadcast facility of its type in Europe, incorporating attenuated naturally ventilated studios and office areas under the Heathrow flight path, close to the M4.

Interior of one of the studios.

Technical facilities include eight TV studios and control rooms, 45 edit suites and four dubbing suites with associated voice-over booths.

All the studios are floating box-in-box masonry constructions with a one-metre-deep natural supply air plenum beneath, containing extensive attenuation to control noise intrusion from nearby vehicles and planes. Two of the studios are separated by two nine-metre-high operable walls, which can be opened to facilitate a 550m² live audience studio. It is a flexible building, which allows bulletins to be delivered from many different areas, including the open plan Sky Sports newsroom.

Construction of the studios commenced first; note the physical separation between adjacent studios.

Each studio can be ventilated naturally or mechanically. In natural ventilation mode, warm air rises by stack effect in the external chimneys. External air is drawn in from outside, through an attenuated plenum beneath the floating concrete floor, and into the studio through perimeter grilles. When it is too hot or noisy for natural ventilation, acoustic doors seal off the passive intakes and air handling units draw supply air at high level, with the return air path using the chimneys.

Office spaces above are also naturally ventilated via attenuated slots and large central chimneys. The studios have 200mm deep sound-absorbing wall finishes, black sound-absorbing lay-in tiles, and sliding acoustic get-in doors in both inner and outer boxes.

Studio steelwork erection.

Natural ventilation
concept diagram.

Studio precast concrete
panel erection.

View of the physical
separation gap at
ground slab.

Isolating pad for studio,
below steelwork.

BBC Hoddinott Hall

LOCATION: Cardiff, Wales, UK

ARCHITECT: Capita Symonds Architecture

COMPLETED: 2009

Hoddinott Hall at Cardiff's Wales Millennium Centre is the home of the BBC National Orchestra and the Chorus of Wales. It is not only the orchestra's base, where all its rehearsals and studio recordings are made, but also a concert hall seating approximately 350 people.

Because the auditorium is used for rehearsals and studio recordings as well as for public concerts, the BBC specified that they wanted a consistent reverberant sound quality for the hall when it was either full or empty of audience. To deliver this requirement, bespoke sliding acoustic panels were designed and installed at high level to form an acoustic 'duvet', controllable with a handheld remote unit.

The hall features timber sound-scattering finish at low level, side soffits providing useful 'cue-ball' sound reflections from the orchestra to the audience, whilst faux balconies provide distribution routes for supply ductwork. Sliding sound-absorbing panels can be deployed or stored in timber housings to change the room acoustic. Tuned sound-absorbing modular boxes are fixed to the soffit above the grid. There is a suspended reflector array with integral lighting, each row of which can be adjusted in height to aid orchestral ensemble. Resilient rubber bearings are used to support the precast concrete on a steel frame box-in-box construction.

The modular sound-reflecting and diffusing canopy can be seen above, with dark grey broad-band sound-absorbing panels on the walls, which retract from behind plywood panels. Pyramid sound-diffusing panels are also strategically located on the upper walls.

Designed as a recording hall with occasional audience, the studio is sized and designed like a traditional concert hall.

Issue	Priority	Comments
Room acoustics	M–H	Acoustics and noise have an important role to play in both patron experience and behaviour. Expectations and impressions are highly subjective. Patron experience, and to a certain extent behaviour, is driven by how noisy a restaurant is. Some owners feel that highly controlled acoustics are a mark of good quality. Others see lively and noisy environments as an indicator of fun and popularity. Understanding the proprietor's expectations is essential early in the design process.
Speech intelligibility	M	This can be important where the restaurant experience is intended to be one that prioritises conversation. There are rarely specific criteria to be achieved; it all depends on the expectations of the client, which should be ascertained early in the design. In food preparation areas, communication between staff is key.
Audio systems design	M–H	Sound system design is usually integral to the dining experience. The type and quality of the system, its sound levels and source content have a big influence on patron experience, and lend the space character. Advances in sound system design will also allow for dynamic changes in performance, potentially with the ability to selectively target certain sounds to specific locations.
Sound insulation – external	H	The noise environment around the building must be quantified to optimise the façade performance and facilitate appropriate interior conditions. The façade may also be an important aspect in controlling noise emission to the surrounding environs. Specific client and/or statutory requirements for noise should be understood early.
Sound insulation – internal	M–H	Requirements can vary widely based on client and establishment type. Separations between different functions (e.g. bar and dining room, dining rooms and private rooms, toilets and kitchens) are all important quality and perception factors, and requirements should be determined in the early planning phases. If the space is located in a mixed-use development, understanding insulation requirements to those functions will be an important consideration.
Speech privacy	M	If the ability to have discreet conversations at tables is important, it will influence planning, layout, furniture type and partition design approach.
Impact/vibration isolation	H	Footfall impact noise (both airborne and structure-borne) within and between spaces (vertically and horizontally) can be an important perception factor regarding quality. It should be considered early as it will drive the decision of floor finish and/or incorporation of impact isolation below, or in the final floor finish.
Mechanical and electrical noise	M–H	Mechanical noise is usually the primary consideration. The higher the noise level, the louder people will need to talk to be heard over it. It is important to select a noise target that is balanced against the perception requirements for the space.
Structure-borne noise	H	Sources might include transport systems or underground car parks. In more high-end spaces, ensuring that these noise sources do not impact function is important.
Environmental noise	M	Building systems equipment or venting located to the exterior are usually the main source of environmental noise. This issue is particularly relevant for establishments located close to residential buildings.

H – High   M – Medium   L – Low

Introduction

Acoustics have a significant impact on patron behaviour, and their impression of restaurants. This is usually (but not always) pre-considered by owners and operators to achieve their desired outcomes.

Architectural style

A wide variety of architectural styles and corresponding acoustics are found in restaurant, bar and dining spaces. Some retain their character for decades. Others change with the times, responding to fashion or branding shifts and evolving to better express the kind of food and culture they serve. Culinary 'experiences' are becoming increasingly important for both chefs and patrons. They mirror a growing interest in and awareness of where the food comes from, and how it should be served to experience it best.

In tandem with these developments, noise is becoming a more frequent subject of critique, included and rated in reviews by both critics and the public. Patrons are actively seeking out spaces that match their noise requirements for a quiet dinner, one-on-one discussion, or a lively atmosphere.

Acoustic features

Given the diverse range of eating and drinking establishments, there is no uniform approach to acoustics. Aims should be discussed early in the design process. Spaces with predominantly hard materials (or more utilitarian/modern in design) are easy to clean and maintain. These result in lively room acoustics and generate high levels of occupational noise (which increases with patron numbers). They also respond to other noise levels in the space (people speak more loudly to overcome the noise, making it noisier). Loud music and open kitchens/preparation areas are both sources of additional noise. Some owners prefer a noisy atmosphere as it gives the impression of energy – it also affects how quickly people eat and how much they drink, an important factor for table turnover time and revenue.

In high-end establishments, where pricing is less reliant on high turnover, good acoustics are often fundamental and project an image that combines refinement, privacy and high quality. In such spaces, it is typical to see combinations of more luxurious materials, including carpets, table furnishings, soft furniture, textured light shades, sound-absorbing ceilings and wall hangings, alongside the increasing use of green walls (which absorb sound), high quantities of textured materials to diffuse sound and high-quality sound systems, playing music at lower overall volume levels.

In many of these spaces, the sound in food preparation areas is also given a high degree of consideration, to ensure that inter-personal communication is optimised for best results and accurate preparation.

Challenges

Workplace noise is becoming an increasingly prevalent concern. Employers must comply with statutory noise-at-work regulations and provide hearing protection if appropriate. In the past this was considered relevant in more 'industrial' spaces but it is increasingly impacting restaurants and should be carefully considered.

Opportunities

As experience design goes beyond eating and drinking, and remote working practices mean that some eating and drinking spaces also double as working and meeting places, acoustic design and infrastructure for audio and data systems is changing. Patrons might seek a certain kind of background noise for working, along with access to WiFi, power outlets, etc. Anticipating and accommodating different user behaviours – and the way they sound – will become increasingly important.

Sound systems will become more sophisticated in quality, and in their ability to respond to the environment. For example, having the capability to adjust levels and programme different materials based on real-time measurement of activity may become focused to individual locations.

Marina Bay Sands

LOCATION: Singapore

ARCHITECT: Moshe Safde Architects, Aedas

COMPLETED: 2011

At the restaurant and bar environments in Marina Bay Sands, Singapore, acoustics have been a primary focus to ensure the right balance of occupied noise control, liveliness and sound system performance, aligned closely to the target audience.

Many acoustic control measures are integrated into the interior design, in soft furnishings behind metal mesh and timber-slatted grilles and as velvet and other fabric-wrapped panel insets, such that the visual character of the space is dominant.

Note the red velvet-wrapped panels used on walls and ceilings as sound-absorbing and textured sound-diffusing surfaces.

This bar has sound-absorbing treatment behind grilles, as velvet-wrapped panels and in soft furnishings.

Stack at the Mirage

LOCATION: Las Vegas, Nevada, USA

ARCHITECT: HLW International, GRAFT

COMPLETED: 2006

Stack Restaurant at the Mirage takes a combination of approaches. The canyon-like effect of the timber interior wall treatments is microperforated and sound-absorbing in some areas. It also has a significant sound-diffusing effect. The upper ceiling (black) is made from Tectum®, an aspen-based wood-wool product with high sound-absorbing performance.

Stepped timber provides sound diffusion, with a sound-absorbing ceiling.

Colonie Restaurant

LOCATION: Brooklyn, New York, USA

ARCHITECT: MADesign

COMPLETED: 2011

The use of living green walls is becoming increasingly widespread in many building types, particularly in restaurants. When well designed, these features provide significant sound absorption. Strategically located, they can be very helpful, not only in general occupational noise control, but also in creating transition zones and noise separation between otherwise visually connected spaces. This example, Colonie restaurant in Brooklyn, New York – separates the bar from the seated restaurant area.

A green wall absorbs sound between the bar and restaurant areas.

Issue	Priority	Comments
Room acoustics	H	This is an important factor driving patron behaviour. It has a strong link to branding and customer expectation. More utilitarian design can engender 'lively' acoustics and result in high noise levels, meaning that worker noise exposure can be an issue. When identifying surfaces for sound-absorbing treatment, it's important to consider retail layout. Treatment is sometimes incorporated into the fit-out details, or located at high level, away from usable display surfaces (e.g. tops of walls and on ceilings). These factors must be considered together to determine appropriate criteria.
Speech intelligibility	M	Localised speech is usually optimised through close-proximity customer-to-staff interactions. It may also be an important factor in large shopping malls where speech intelligibility of PAVA systems is important for emergency and evacuation situations.
Audio systems design	H	Sound system design is usually integral to the retail experience. The type and quality of the system, sound levels, and the source content have a big influence on patron experience and brand association, as well as providing the space with character. Systems may be zoned within a retail space so that different sounds can be played in different zones, or sound levels controlled separately in each zone. Future use of automated or digital virtual shopping assistants may have an impact on both system design and room acoustics design approach.
Sound insulation – external	M	This is usually driven by how the retailer wants the interior space to be perceived, and controls incoming noise appropriately. Since storefront design options are often limited, sound system zoning can be configured to play at slightly higher levels closer to entrances and façades. This can be especially important in busy urban areas or in malls, where there are lots of competing sounds. In residential areas, or mixed-use buildings, control of sounds to adjacent spaces can be important.
Sound insulation – internal	L–M	The key issue is usually to control sound coming from or propagating to the adjacent space. Some retail forms may require spaces where higher sound levels can be made (AV equipment or musical instrument testing, etc.). Coordination with services delivery can be important if they occur during operating hours and must not negatively impact the customer experience. This may impact spatial planning.
Speech privacy	L	This is usually an issue in high-end stores where dressing or fitting areas may require more privacy.
Impact/vibration isolation	L	Usually important in multi-floor environments with the same or different tenants, where impact noise might affect customer impressions of 'quality'.
Mechanical and electrical noise	M	Mechanical noise is usually the primary consideration; the higher the noise level, the louder people will need to speak to be heard over it. It is important to select a noise target that is balanced against the perception requirements for the space.
Structure-borne noise	L	This is usually not a high-priority issue for retail spaces.
Environmental noise		Building systems equipment or venting located to the exterior are usually the main source of noise. This can particularly impact shopping venues situated close to residential areas; requirements should be determined early to design appropriate noise control measures.

H – High   M – Medium   L – Low

Introduction

The relationship between acoustics and retail has as much to do with psychology as with sound or products. The factors that affect a potential customer's decision to make a purchase represent an area of study in themselves, and sound has been shown as a key influencer in this regard.

Architectural style

Sometimes stand-alone shops, sometimes concessions or tenant spaces within larger shopping mall complexes (some of which are historic and have a specific character), a wide variety of architectural styles – and associated acoustics – can be found in the retail space. Shifts in fashion, branding and advertising mean that many such spaces frequently change in terms of their aesthetics and spatial arrangement. Retail 'experiences' have become an important way for brands and owners to reflect a unique style or a particular aesthetic.

Sound can be a contentious issue in retail spaces, with some shoppers complaining of high noise levels in some (particularly youth-focused) stores, alongside the health ramifications of workers being exposed to loud sounds over a long period of time, which is becoming an increasing concern.

Acoustic features

Acoustic goals are usually driven by brand identity. They can vary widely, but should always be discussed early in the design process. Predominantly hard materials are typical in more utilitarian or modern spaces. These are easy to maintain and spatially reconfigure, but can result in very lively room acoustics and generate high levels of occupational noise, if patron numbers are high (often not the case in very high end and exclusive stores). Where these finishes are used in spaces of high patron density, sound-absorbing ceilings and sound-absorbing treatment high on walls will usually be present, as goods or other retail materials take up the remainder of available wall and floor space.

Music is popular in retail environments. In larger malls, tenant spaces may have one sound system and common areas another. It is important to consider how these interact with each other and plan accordingly. Common spaces often use sound-absorbing ceilings, planted areas, music, fountains and water features to intentionally create noise, which is added to by operational sounds from, for example, escalators. The music should be given due thought and is a choice that can be a particularly important focus for some brands.

Opportunities

As experience design begins to surpass the products themselves to include AR, mixed reality and other technology, this will have an impact on spatial design, especially if audio is required for communication or information transfer. This is already being seen with the introduction of virtual assistants, for example. It is to be expected that AI will increasingly be used to recognise patrons, know what they are looking for, and offer specific instructions on how and where to get it. This may change user behaviour and corresponding acoustic requirements in buildings, and increase the use of dynamic audio, visual and technology systems to guide the shopper.

Sony Flagship Store

LOCATION: Los Angeles, California, USA

ARCHITECT: Klein Dytham Architecture

COMPLETED: 2011

The Sony Flagship store at Century City in Los Angeles was designed as a modular concept for a potentially global rollout. With a wide range of products, many with audio, visual or interactive aspects, the concept needed to create contrast between lively, spacious open areas, and spaces with controlled light and sound to provide optimum display conditions for devices – without creating a din through the whole store.

Using a modular approach to sound absorption, and the creation of pocket environments within the room, sound-absorbing treatment is provided using recycled rubber panels covered in fabric in a variety of colours. Each colour also represents a specific product type in the store.

Sound-absorbing treatments are incorporated into fabric panels to match the store's visual identity.

Comme des Garçons

LOCATION: New York, USA

ARCHITECT: Amanda Levete AL_A

COMPLETED: 1999

The New York flagship location for Comme des Garçons is an interior fit-out of a 19th-century warehouse building. The dramatic tunnel entrance creates an audible and visual transition between the noisy street and the interior of the store. Inside there is very little in the way of sound-absorbing treatment apart from the clothing itself. Although only a small quantity, this makes a big difference in the reverberant space of mainly sound-reflecting finishes. The bespoke casework helps to create a variety of individual 'pocket' environments, allowing a discreet, individualised and quite private experience, within the large volume. It is a rare and particularly pleasing retail environment both when quiet and busy.

Casework separates the store into discrete acoustic environments, and clothing provides the majority of the sound-absorbing treatment.

The tunnel provides a dramatic entrance that also separates the store from the street, and creates an acoustic interlude between the two.

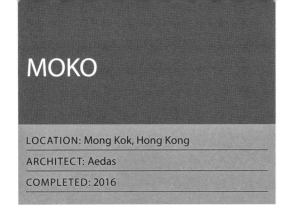

MOKO

LOCATION: Mong Kok, Hong Kong

ARCHITECT: Aedas

COMPLETED: 2016

MOKO in Hong Kong is a good example of how key acoustic features can be used in a large-scale retail shopping mall. The main circulation spaces have almost ubiquitous sound-absorbing ceiling finishes. Specific areas are used for transition or to create special environments where the use of sound-diffusing and transparent components (with sound-absorbing treatment behind) and green walls help control occupational noise and create aural comfort.

Sound-absorbing treatments to ceilings and the undersides of escalators are visible throughout.

In some areas, sound-diffusing elements coupled with green walls are used to provide acoustic contrast.

Issue	Priority	Comments
Room acoustics	H	The acoustic criteria and design approach for public spaces in airports should be specifically developed to control activity noise levels, while ensuring good speech intelligibility via amplified and natural sources.
		At person-to-person communication points, room acoustics must be optimised. The placement of materials to promote early sound reflections and reduce reverberance is essential.
		In large volume spaces, materials can be used to control activity noise levels while enhancing the passenger's visit with an aural experience that complements the visual one. In low-volume spaces, materials should be used to further control activity noise levels and sound propagation between connected spaces.
Speech intelligibility	H	Essential in all areas. High-quality, person-to-person, and one-to-many communication is required. PAVA systems are ubiquitous in most airports; they are a key management tool in emergencies and must be clear and intelligible.
Audio systems design	H	PAVA systems are crucial elements found throughout airport terminals. Live and pre-recorded announcements are frequent, and the primary method of communicating with travellers.
		The loudspeaker type, location and aiming design should complement the room acoustic design strategy to provide uniform coverage at output levels that are comfortable.
		Intelligibility relies on good acoustics to ensure that the output signal is free from late reflections and noise.
Sound insulation – external	M	The noise environment around the terminal must be quantified to optimise the façade performance. Aircraft movements on the ground and during take-off and landing are primary external noise sources. The distance between public spaces and aircraft operations areas (e.g. runways) must be considered in terms of background noise criteria. Sound insulation is more critical in certain spaces (e.g. airline lounges and control towers) where specific criteria will apply.
Sound insulation – internal	M–H	Close attention must be paid to noise propagation from circulation spaces, security checkpoints and retail vendors into areas where high-quality person-to-person communication is required.
Speech privacy	L	This is a key requirement in specific spaces such as security, police interview rooms and crew rest areas. These should be identified during the planning phase and located sufficiently far away from noise producing spaces where possible.
Impact/vibration isolation	H	Footfall, rolling luggage and service equipment (both airborne and structure-borne) within and between spaces (vertically and horizontally) must be considered, with impact isolation incorporated as needed. The use of softer flooring finishes can also help control activity noise build-up from impact sources.
Mechanical and electrical noise	M–H	A target range should be set and achieved as high noise levels negatively impact communication and increase passenger stress, while low noise levels increase annoyance from sound generated by other travellers and sources outside. This aspect should be considered in conjunction with the façade design to produce optimum results.
		Operational noise from automated people moving systems (e.g. escalators, moving walkways) and baggage handling systems should also be considered.
Structure-borne noise	H	Sources might include transport systems, baggage handling infrastructure or underground car parks. The location of existing or future transport systems – at grade or underground – is important. Noise mitigation may require vibration isolation for either part of or the entire building.
Environmental noise	M	Building systems equipment located on or venting to the exterior are usually the main source of noise from airport buildings. Ground operations (engine run-up and run-down) and flight operations are major sources of environmental noise. They are a key element of airport planning.

H–High   M–Medium   L–Low

Introduction

Airport terminals are often a traveller's first experience at a new destination, and the last upon departing. They are also visited in transit between locales, with different airports competing to be a transfer location of choice. The importance of traveller experience in these spaces is being recognised as crucial by passengers, airlines and operators alike. Positive acoustics play an essential role in creating an atmosphere of calmness, efficiency and safety.

Architectural style

Early airports were open fields without terminals. In 1925, Ford Airport in Dearborn, Michigan became the first to offer a waiting room and ticket office for passengers. Post-WWI and WWII, the aviation industry grew exponentially, which led to the construction of dedicated passenger terminals, initially limited to just a few principal airports. These were typically less developed in terms of their service function, with priority given to essential operational facilities.

As demand increased, designs improved, allowing passengers to be covered from arrival to departure, in a similar fashion to a rail system. The 'pier finger' and 'star' terminal shapes congregated passengers within a central area, before moving them into the fingers or points for departure. Security and safety began to drive design in the 1970s, increasing distances between airside and landside areas. Consequently, security, immigration, customs and baggage areas became the compression points in the journey through the terminal.

Initially, acoustic design approaches were relatively basic. Carpeted floors and sound-absorbing ceiling tiles became ubiquitous, while PA systems were deployed throughout the building. Both measures often suffered from lack of optimised design and poor maintenance, resulting in poor passenger experience, especially during periods of travel disruption. This was often exacerbated by overlay of competing entertainment systems and screens (unmuted during PA announcements) and multiple competing airlines making announcements. One reaction was the introduction of the 'silent terminal' where no announcements are made at all – information is instead delivered visually – implemented with varying degrees of success.

Passengers are now required to spend extended periods of time in some spaces, while others they move through more quickly, depending upon passenger congestion. Staff must occupy these spaces for even longer periods, so acoustic conditions are important for their wellbeing and task performance. This has usually been handled via the provision of large volume spaces and plenty of light. As the modern terminal evolves, the creation of an acoustically appropriate journey that is calm and stress free, while also able to impart information efficiently in normal operations as well as during service disruption or safety situations, is increasingly crucial.

Acoustic features

The wide range of physical spaces found within the modern airport requires various approaches to acoustic design.

Control towers have very specific acoustic needs and require the assistance of a design specialist.

Many workplace and office areas need to accommodate staff during both active and passive operations (for example, sleep and rest areas for flight crews). Some building systems, such as baggage handling, may need to be located in ceiling voids and service areas above these sensitive spaces. This requires careful consideration when it comes to space planning and noise mitigation.

Terminals are often large volume spaces encompassing a variety of functions. For maintenance purposes, sound-absorbing treatment cannot be directly applied to surfaces, such as floors, and are therefore located mainly on the ceiling. In security, immigration, customs and baggage retrieval areas, journey times can vary greatly. Sound-absorbing treatment to ceilings, some wall areas and – in certain cases – carpet, is usually relied upon to keep occupational noise and reverberance low, thereby minimising stress to passengers. As passengers often need to travel some distance between spaces in the airport, noise and vibration control of equipment (e.g. moving walkways, escalators or elevators) is important for promoting a calm atmosphere. Beyond internal sound, the building envelope must mitigate noise from air traffic while idling, taking off and landing, although usually some controlled incoming noise is helpful to set the context of the space; a complete absence of air traffic noise is rarely required or expected by passengers.

As air travel has become more accessible, airline operators have increasingly used the passenger experience as a means of differentiating their brand. The sonic quality of the airport terminal can influence the perceived quality of both the airport authority and airline operator's brand – another reason why acoustics matter.

Opportunities

In the future, it is possible that airports will become destinations not only for the traveller but also for the local and regional community. Facilities for arts, culture, entertainment and shopping are and will increasingly be located within them, supporting a broader live/work/play model. One can expect that an increase in mixed use will further the need for attention to acoustic design.

Transit to and within the airport may require an increased dependence upon personal mobile devices, with some of this infrastructure already implemented for serving hearing or visually impaired passengers. While this shift might see a reduction in the number of general announcements via PA, it is likely that audio systems will continue to play an important role in emergency situations.

Environmental noise from air travel has always been problematic, and is an increasing concern as traveller numbers increase. Improvements in ground-based radar are allowing steeper approach angles for some aircraft. This can reduce noise impact in some areas. While this will bring potential relief to nearby residents and increase the value of land around airports, it will be some time before the technology is fully realised and implemented. New aircraft technology, such as next-generation supersonic aircraft, offer the possibility to further reduce the impact of environmental noise.

Personal aviation transport such as vertical take-off and landing (VTOL) and other 'flying-taxi' technologies are undergoing rapid development and testing. At present, although many of these technologies are electric, they are not silent. The noise they produce is very different in character to existing aircraft. If widely deployed, this technology will dramatically change the noise environment and have an increasingly widespread impact on building acoustic design (especially sound insulation). It will also potentially change the kinds of buildings located within airport complexes if, for example, widespread parking infrastructure is no longer needed.

Changi Airport, Terminal 4

LOCATION: Singapore

ARCHITECT: Benoy, SAA Architects

COMPLETED: 2017

The fourth terminal of Singapore's primary international airport, situated about 15 miles from the commercial centre of the island.

Acoustics play an important role in creating a low-stress or stress-free environment. One of the notable aspects of the design for many terminals at Singapore's Changi Airport is that the terminal buildings are not generally large volume spaces (with some notable exceptions); this means the acoustic design is less challenging than many large volume check-in and arrivals halls that are often found in international airports.

Particular attention has been paid to the finishes. Sound-absorbing ceilings are ubiquitous and vary in type and form to suit the architecture. Carpet can be found extensively throughout, which is unusual for such a high-traffic building. It makes a noticeable difference to the quality of the spaces. Audio-visual systems are used in an ambient way; to enhance the serene experience, many spaces play soothing natural sounds (water, birdsong), and create light and visual interest. Sound insulation of the terminal buildings from landside and airside operations is generally high. In most locations, these activities are barely audible within passenger areas.

View of check-in area; note the sound-absorbing treatment behind the ceiling slats, and carpet in the kiosk area.

Rest and waiting areas have sound-absorbing ceilings, carpet, and environmental audio and visuals to create a sense of calm.

JFK Terminal 4

LOCATION: Queens, New York, USA

ARCHITECT: Skidmore Owings Merrill

COMPLETED: 2001, 2013 (Delta expansion)

JFK Terminal 4 serves as an international arrivals terminal and major hub for Delta Airlines long-haul flights.

During the design of JFK Terminal 4, a significant step change was occurring in speaker design with the introduction of the phase array loudspeaker. These digitally controlled devices consist of long thin arrays of multiple 100mm or 150mm diameter loudspeaker drivers, in various overall lengths. They allow the directivity of sound to be controlled in the vertical plane – meaning that sound can be directed in a wide horizontal 'slice' directed to the listeners, while limiting sound going towards the ceiling where it creates unnecessary reverberation. In the first installation of its kind in the USA, these loudspeakers liberated the design team of some prior constraints of acoustic design, allowing for a large, single-volume space, without technology trees or columns to provide loudspeakers on a regular grid. The main ceiling still requires sound-absorbing treatment for control of noise from people, and to help the speech intelligibility of the public address system, but it also allows much of the technology to be arranged along a single strip in the terminal building.

Close-up of the consolidated technology block; the highly directional thin phase array loudspeaker, six of which cover the entire check-in area, can be seen to the right of the image.

View of the main check-in area, with the sweeping roof incorporating sound-absorbing treatment into solid areas.

Issue	Priority	Comments
Room acoustics	H	Good room acoustics are essential for a pleasant customer experience and are often equated with quality, reliability and safety. Incorporating sound-absorbing treatment is crucial to achieve appropriate speech intelligibility and control of occupational and train-generated noise. The range of spaces makes this challenging, from large volume concourses and foyers with long reverberance, to tunnels and platforms with constrained shapes and multiple strong early reflections (that propagate easily along platforms). Surfaces are typically hard-wearing and sound-reflecting, while rigorous operational requirements (fire, smoke, maintenance, etc.) limit material selection.
Speech intelligibility	H	Appropriate speech intelligibility from PAVA systems is essential to public safety, and for the delivery of passenger information, which is particularly important at rush hour or during service disruption.
Audio systems design	H	A large number of loudspeakers need to be integrated into the architecture, and given the room acoustic challenges, they must be carefully selected and placed for optimum performance. There can be significant variations in type, shape and form that need to be accommodated within the design aesthetics. The infrastructure design approach must also be flexible enough to account for future variations.
Sound insulation – external	L	This is generally not a concern except in above-ground stations where the transmission of occupational noise, PAVA sound levels, and train noise to surrounding areas may need to be controlled.
Sound insulation – internal	M–H	Good planning should avoid locating noise producing spaces (e.g. equipment rooms) close to noise sensitive spaces such as operations, control and PA announcer rooms, ticket offices, and – in larger international stations – customs and immigration areas.
Speech privacy	L	Not a primary consideration except in some customs and immigration areas.
Impact/vibration isolation	L	Impact noise control is important for spaces listed as critical in terms of internal sound insulation (see above).
Mechanical and electrical noise	M–H	Of particular importance to noise sensitive areas as listed above. In public areas, noise usually needs to be controlled to deliver environments that ensure comfort and reduce stress. Noise levels associated with emergency smoke extraction systems are a critical concern in public areas, and should be controlled to maximum NR70 in operation to ensure PA announcement sound levels are not too high (to avoid shock or confusion in an evacuation process). When transit systems are included within other buildings (e.g. monorails inside airports) or open to functional public spaces, equipment-generated noise may require further consideration.
Structure-borne noise	M	Train movement on rails generates significant vibration. If the transit system is located close to buildings (horizontally or vertically) this vibration needs to be controlled, often requiring track isolation.
Environmental noise	H	Building systems equipment or venting located to the exterior are usually the main sources of environmental noise to be considered when systems are close to homes and workplaces. Environmental noise impact from operations of any transit system (the system itself and associated buildings) requires attention, and is usually covered as part of the environmental impact assessment.

H – High   M – Medium   L – Low

Canary Wharf; an acoustic scale model of the upper entry concourse with scale model loudspeakers visible (metal).

reduce the active acoustic volume, improve airflow, allow segregation of occupied platform and train in the event of a fire, prevent people from jumping or falling onto the track and stop litter, which contributes to track fires.

A uniform approach was taken to the industrial design of the loudspeakers, lighting and other fittings throughout. There are six different loudspeaker types on the system, all following the same design approach but with varying sound directivity characteristics, to respond to the challenges of different acoustic environments in the stations.

Canary Wharf Station is monumental in size. In certain areas, five levels of the station are connected acoustically. This presented design challenges in ensuring that speech intelligibility targets for the PA system could be met, and that sound transfer between the spaces was limited.

In the main concourse, an acoustic scale model determined the locations for sound-absorbing treatment, working on the JLE directive that loudspeaker coverage design should be optimised with the minimum amount of sound-absorbing treatment required to achieve the speech intelligibility target. Specially built ultrasonic loudspeakers were built for the scale model to simulate the performance of the expected loudspeakers.

Below: Canary Wharf; upper entry concourse. Black expanded metal mesh panels with black tissue-faced mineral fibre behind (left middle). Either side of the central columns there is detail developed for incorporation of sound-absorbing material behind an array of 25mm diameter stainless-steel tubes.

St Pancras International

LOCATION: London, UK

ARCHITECT: William Henry Barlow, HS1 PPP

COMPLETED: 1868, 2007

St Pancras Station was renamed St Pancras International Station following its redevelopment in 2007 as the main arrivals terminal for High Speed 1. Originally designed by William Barlow in 1863, it is one of the largest enclosed spaces in the world.

The stunning train shed is 210m long, 30m tall and has arches that span about 70m. The redevelopment in 2007 included a 200m extension to the train shed, renovation of the architectural elements using original materials and an addition of eight platforms, giving a total platform count of 13.

Sound-absorbing treatment was required to control sound reflections from the PA loudspeakers, particularly from Barlow's shed roof down to the lower-level concourses, which are open to the main volume. Heritage requirements necessitated careful navigation. In the previously timber areas of the lower roof section that needed replacement, microperforated sound-absorbing panels with 50mm mineral fibre behind are incorporated to closely match the appearance of timber, including the joint system. In the deck extension, the curved sail structure provides acoustic treatment in the form of perforated metal filled with 50mm mineral fibre.

Acoustic treatment beneath the platform undercrofts, within the cast-iron arches, are perforated metal with mineral fibre. Distributed overhead loudspeakers are suspended over the platforms within the structure, also housing lights. The platforms are not occupied except when boarding or exiting trains, and announcements in these areas are infrequent, but potentially critical in emergency situations. At the historic end of the Barlow train shed (closest to the Midland Hotel), column loudspeakers are installed at the sides and covering the old platform forecourt, mounted on drop-poles and painted to match the architecture.

The solid areas of the Barlow shed roof are perforated sound-absorbing panels, designed to match the original timber.

Loudspeakers are generally located in the catenary structure between the lights. Some areas at the ends of the station are covered with thin column loudspeakers with high directivity, visible here in the far left of the image.

Areas of the undercroft under the historic arches have an integrated element with lights and loudspeakers in the spine, and sound-absorbing wings either side.

2nd Ave Subway Stations

LOCATION: New York, USA

ARCHITECT: Arup and AECOM

COMPLETED: 2017 (Phase 1), and ongoing

This is a new subway line being introduced into an already developed neighbourhood, with some significant noise and vibration-sensitive spaces along the route.

The focus of this project was two major acoustic design challenges: ensuring good-quality speech intelligibility in stations for public address/voice evacuation functions, and designing vibration mitigation to the track system.

The acoustic design of the stations drew on the Jubilee Line Extension (London, UK) as a key benchmark. The first part of the project assessment was to analyse challenges with speech intelligibility on the existing system, which was particularly important as the new and existing systems had to be integrated. Every aspect of the signal chain was investigated, from acoustic conditions in the announcer's booth to the signal chain from the microphone through amplifiers and cabling to the loudspeakers, and the loudspeaker layouts and sound-absorbing treatments in the stations – most stations on the existing system have no sound-absorbing treatment integral to the design. The design team used an auralisation process to demonstrate the design issues to the client, as a starting point to introduce changes to key aspects of the PA system that were network wide.

High background noise from ventilation systems, high noise levels generated by trains moving through stations, and high levels of reverberance were all key challenges in the existing system. Sound-absorbing finishes were integrated into the station design, the most widely used being perforated ceramic and metal panels backed with a fibreglass core, inset into the concrete tunnel form. Sound-absorbing finishes are also applied at track level to reduce noise from train wheels on rails, and at the ends of stations to reduce train entry noise at crossovers and switches. Silencers were placed at each end of the ventilation system fans; many are large units approximately two and a half metres high, so they had to be designed into the ancillary facilities early to ensure that there was space for the rest of the ventilation equipment. The acoustic comfort, sense of calm, and speech intelligibility are significantly improved when compared to the rest of the New York subway network.

The area surrounding the new line has high-density development of every type. The most sensitive on the route are hospitals, many of which are located in key areas along 2nd Avenue and have a range of vibration-sensitive equipment within them. Before Phase 1 was built, site measurements were conducted to capture source vibration levels from existing lines, and this data was used to predict potential vibrations from the new line. It was determined that vibration mitigation of the track form would be required. Various schemes were considered, with the implemented solution being a Low Vibration Track (LVT) consisting of individual concrete blocks that fasten the track to the ground, but are separated from the trackform concrete by rubber boots, to reduce the amount of rail vibration transmitted to the tunnel invert and buildings above. This was considerably more expensive than using traditional timber sleepers, but provided better mitigation, with long-term maintenance advantages.

Rails are fastened to the ground via concrete blocks that are separated from the trackform by rubber boots, to mitigate the rumbling as trains enter and leave stations.

On the platform at 96th Street Station, the sound-absorbing panels made from ceramic, metal and fibreglass are clearly visible, inset into the wall.

There are two silencers at either end of each station to mitigate noise from the ventilation fans.

Washington Metro

LOCATION: Washington, D.C., USA

ARCHITECT: Harry Weese Associates

COMPLETED: 1976–1991

Learning from acoustic challenges of other subway systems that pre-dated it, addressing acoustics issues was fundamental to the design of this metro system from the beginning.

The main station volumes are much larger than is ideal, acoustically. The coffered structure is designed such that sound-absorbing panels could be inset within them as needed, on a station-by-station basis.

The PA system uses distributed loudspeakers located close to occupied areas of the platform to broadcast messages at sufficient sound levels for passengers, without contributing a significant amount of sound energy to the reverberant field (which would reduce speech intelligibility). Announcements are relatively infrequent, the most regular being a reminder to step back as trains approach (which is also indicated through the floor lighting varying in brightness). Passengers are aided by comprehensive visual signage throughout the station visible from most occupied areas, giving clear indication of train arrival times.

Detail of the coffers, with sound-absorbing panel inset.

The view of Union Station from the mezzanine level.

Issue	Priority	Comments
Room acoustics	H	Room acoustics need to balance the needs for intelligibility of speech with those required for worship music. For example, traditional unamplified choral or organ music may require greater reverberance than more contemporary amplified music.
Speech intelligibility	H	High-quality speech intelligibility is a key consideration for spaces where talks, readings and sermons are frequent.
Audio systems design	H	Most spaces require voice amplification systems to allow congregations to hear the spoken word. Contemporary worship music is also typically delivered via an audio system, requiring amplification of singers, musicians and choirs. The use of video, within the main worship space and for simulcast to overflow rooms, satellite worship spaces, and for web streaming and television broadcast may be a requirement.
Sound insulation – external	H	Noise ingress through the building façade should be considered in the design of the overall worship experience. If the space is also to be used for broadcast or recording, then requirements may be more onerous.
Sound insulation – internal	M–H	Consider the placement of higher-noise spaces (e.g. MEP rooms, youth activity rooms) and, where possible, avoid locating them directly adjacent to acoustically sensitive spaces, such as those used for worship, counselling or audio recording.
Speech privacy	M	Spaces used for prayer or private discussions may necessitate a greater level of speech privacy; requiring walls with a higher sound insulation performance, and/or the increasing of HVAC background noise level to boost the masking effect.
Impact/vibration isolation	H	Footfall impact noise (both airborne and structure-borne) within and between spaces (vertically and horizontally) must be considered. Incorporate impact isolation below or in the final floor finish as needed.
Mechanical and electrical noise	M–H	Set a target range and achieve it; understanding that high noise levels negatively impact concentration and communication, and increase stress. Low noise levels increase annoyance from people around you and from outside. Also consider this carefully in conjunction with the façade design to produce optimum results.
Structure-borne noise	H	Sources might include, for example, transport systems or underground car parks. Determine whether existing or future transport systems are located at grade or under the building. Mitigation may require vibration isolation for either part of or the entire building.
Environmental noise	M	Sound emission from worship spaces, its audibility at surrounding properties, and compliance with noise ordinance limits need to be considered. This can impact the roof and façade sound isolation design. Noise emission from building systems equipment should also be considered.

H – High   M – Medium   L – Low

Introduction

Worship spaces encompass a wide range of acoustic design approaches, from highly reverberant temples and cathedrals emphasising the ethereal and mystical, to modern worship spaces that place high importance on speech intelligibility, amplified sound, broadcast and recording.

Architectural style

There are myriad building styles depending on the type of worship. Within any given type, there is potential for wide variations based on surrounding context and societal conditions at the time of construction. In the pre-Reformation West, Solomon's Temple provided the basic dimensions that were replicated in early worship spaces. As the technologies of architecture, building and engineering developed, the benefactors and builders of worship spaces were often the first to embrace them, creating ever more monumental spaces.

Acoustic features

Places of worship increasingly became wider, longer and especially taller, with predominantly hard sound-reflecting materials – wood, stone, glass. The result was long, rich reverberance that contributed to the sense of wonder.

Curvature was also used extensively and precisely to focus sound to particular locations – often to accentuate height, thus emphasising sound coming from the gods. Composers of music in these spaces, initially writing choral, but later also organ works, used these features to intertwine music with architecture. Intelligibility of the spoken word was not a high priority (e.g. in the West, as most congregations were not able to understand the Latin used during services anyway).

The advent of the Gutenberg printing press increased literacy, meaning that sermons were increasingly delivered in local languages and dialects. This in turn placed a greater emphasis upon the importance of congregations understanding their meaning. In some parts of Europe, Catholic churches were converted to Protestant and simplified to bring more focus on spoken sermons. Icons were removed and interiors painted white. Gradually, as Protestantism evolved, emphasis on better speech intelligibility developed in tandem. This resulted in smaller spaces with lower ceilings, which were less reverberant.

The advent of speech and music amplification systems over the last 60 years has allowed worship venues to grow without sacrificing the intelligibility of the spoken word. This is true for many types of spaces, including Jewish and Buddhist temples, Islamic mosques and Christian churches, where spoken word is a dominant part of the worship experience.

The use of amplification has also changed the spatial relationship of musicians and choirs to the physical worship space; historically they were placed in specific locations to best project their sound through the worship space.

The change in styles of worship, from the use of organ and choral music, cantors, etc. to contemporary worship music, with the use of amplified singers and bands, has also driven a change to rooms with much more controlled acoustics.

Challenges

Room acoustics in places of worship need to balance the varying requirements for speech and music, and the needs of musicians and congregations. This must be identified and discussed at the very outset of a project. If amplification of speech and/or music is a possibility, this should also be evaluated early in the design process. These considerations will affect both the physical volume and the materiality of the space. It is also increasingly important to understand what other activities might take place in addition to the services themselves.

Unamplified music, especially organ and choral music, benefits from more reverberant acoustics. Many spaces geared towards this function make use of predominantly sound-reflecting materials (wood, stone, glass, treated wood), with sound-diffusing detailing and relatively large dimensions, especially height. These characteristics typically create challenging room acoustics for speech, so careful consideration is required at the outset. Improvements in sound system design may one day mean implementing technology that can adequately amplify spoken word and provide good speech intelligibility in reverberant conditions. However, amplifying music in these spaces is significantly more challenging.

Where amplified speech and music is a core requirement, minimising room dimensions to control reverberance while providing the appropriate spatial impression is crucial. In addition, a significant amount of sound-absorbing and sound-diffusing surfaces on wall and ceiling surfaces will be required.

Room reverberance is also often beneficial in allowing congregants and audiences to feel supported in their own singing and worship. This is a key acoustic differentiator between worship and performance spaces; worship services are inherently interactive, where audience participation needs to be acoustically supported. This requirement needs careful consideration in the case of mostly amplified services. Variable acoustics (deployable banners and curtains) can be used to change room reverberance, typically to control sound in more reverberant situations (see concert halls and opera houses). To make spaces sound more reverberant, 'electroacoustic enhancement' or 'electronic architecture' systems can be used. These can also assist audiences by providing acoustic support for congregational singing. In either of these situations it is fundamental to understand what the natural acoustics should be designed for and what the

variable mechanisms are expected to achieve. These systems have cost and space implications (for deployment and storage) which must be considered to create the most acoustically and spatially appropriate worship area possible.

Opportunities

In contemporary venues where the use of technology is already widespread, its continued incorporation should be expected. The aforementioned electronic architecture systems may play an especially important role by being able to recreate spaces of the past, or to transport congregations aurally to different environments, based on the type of service. The potential for creating spaces that can be multi-denominational could offer profound opportunities for mutual understanding, and the establishment of positive places for community interaction.

St Mary's Cathedral

LOCATION: Sydney, Australia

ARCHITECT: William Wardell (1900) and Arup (sound in 1996, AV in 2003)

COMPLETED: 1900

Like many historic churches and cathedrals around the world, the greatest acoustic challenge was balancing the modern requirements for high speech intelligibility with the long natural reverberance for choral and organ music, the mainstay of traditional church repertoire.

Loudspeakers are integrated into the structural columns to the left and right.

These buildings, where budget has allowed, have often been at the forefront of adopting new sound system technology in a bid to resolve this issue. It is only since the early 21st century that a robust solution was developed, thanks to significant improvements in computing power. The phase array loudspeaker is specifically designed to create very directional horizontal sound, with limited vertical dispersion, to deliver high speech intelligibility in reverberant conditions. They are generally best suited to speech applications, as they are most directional at speech frequencies, so by no means a solution for poor room acoustic design in all situations. At the altar end of the room, two loudspeakers are integrated into the structural columns left and right. Moving further back, covering the nave and aisles to the left and right, loudspeakers are integrated into the structural columns above the visual display panels.

Loudspeakers seen here are also covering the trancepts.

Cathedral of Our Lady of the Angels

LOCATION: Los Angeles, California, USA

ARCHITECT: Rafael Moneo and Leo A. Daly

COMPLETED: 2002

An impressive structure constructed of poured-in-place concrete, with a seating capacity of 3,000 on a single floor covering the length of a football field from pulpit to Baptistery.

The altar is 24m away from the nearest congregant on either side of the transepts. The ceiling rises from 18m above the floor at the rear of the sanctuary to almost 28m at the front of the cathedral. The design was required to last 500 years and to withstand a magnitude 7.1 earthquake.[2]

The cathedral is sited immediately adjacent to the 101 (Hollywood) Freeway with five lanes of traffic in each direction, producing sound levels in excess of 75dBA at the façade of the building all day and night. Natural light coming into the sanctuary was a key goal and required a double-glazed translucent alabaster window system with more than a foot of airspace separating the two panes, to create a tranquil interior space.

The sanctuary is a huge volume – approximately 93,450 cubic metres. The floor of the nave is covered completely with limestone pavers. The traditional wood pews have no cushion; walls are poured-in-place concrete. The untreated natural reverberation time at critical speech frequencies would have been in excess of 12 seconds. Auralisation was used to demonstrate the impact of this from a design perspective, indicating optimum mitigation measures.

Approximately 60% of the wood ceiling is slatted with fiberglass behind, and a series of heavy Belgian tapestries is backed with glass fiber and spaced 15cm away from the concrete walls to control late reflections and reduce reverberance.

The rear solid concrete wall has openings and is angled upwards to send sound reflections to the sound-absorbing ceiling, rather than back to the front of the church where they would be perceived as echoes. The resulting mid-frequency reverberation time of the sanctuary is 3.75 seconds.

The view towards the organ and sound-absorbing ceiling, with natural light coming through the 30mm thick sound-insulating assembly.

A dense array of suspended ceiling loudspeakers aimed downward onto the seated congregation, and a relatively high level of reverberance, results in a cathedral-like natural acoustic environment – good for congregational singing and organ music. It can also deliver a high degree of clarity for sermons and other related functions requiring speech intelligibility. This often hard-to-achieve balance is due to the way acoustic energy is distributed in the room. The organ excites the cathedral's long reverberation time and the sound system does not.

View to the rear, with sound-absorbing ceilings and tapestries visible, as are the rear wall openings (to reduce the sound-reflecting surface). Loudspeakers are located in the trumpet-shaped brass fittings, also integrated with lighting in some locations.

Kericho Cathedral

LOCATION: Kericho, Kenya

ARCHITECT: John McAslan + Partners

COMPLETED: 2015

The aim was to develop acoustics that combined the divergent themes of: 'family at table' (curved seating around the altar, common in the African Catholic tradition); a single, unifying volume; clarity of speech delivered from anywhere within the cathedral; and a lively acoustic ambience to encourage participation in the service.

The resulting design limits the room volume relative to a European cathedral of similar capacity but creates a space that naturally provides an appropriate acoustic environment without significant intervention to the form or materiality. The ceiling is sound-diffusing at mid to high frequency as a function of the form of timber slats, with airspace and clay tiles behind, which creates a good blended sound and avoids strident sound reflections.

A sound system was essential for two reasons: even the strongest voices struggle to carry past 20–25m, and the cathedral is more than 50m in length; plus, the clergy wanted to be able communicate with crowds of worshippers in the surrounding landscaped gardens when the building was full, on special occasions. Sound systems for cathedrals and large traditional churches are typically based on tall directional column loudspeakers. However, to protect the aesthetic simplicity in the cathedral, the team selected smaller units that could be hidden in the building finishes.

Rows of loudspeakers are located behind the slatted timber ceiling, with distributing speakers down the length of the building for even sound coverage and good speech quality. Ceiling speakers in the transepts are intentionally located near open doors to spill sound into the grounds to serve larger crowds, and additional connections are provided to extend the system to temporary external loudspeakers, if required. To keep costs down, the design was based on widely available products that could be installed by local contractors. A digital processor is provided to time-align the output of each row of loudspeakers, and manage levels, and the system generally operates automatically, though it can be operated wirelessly when required for larger services.

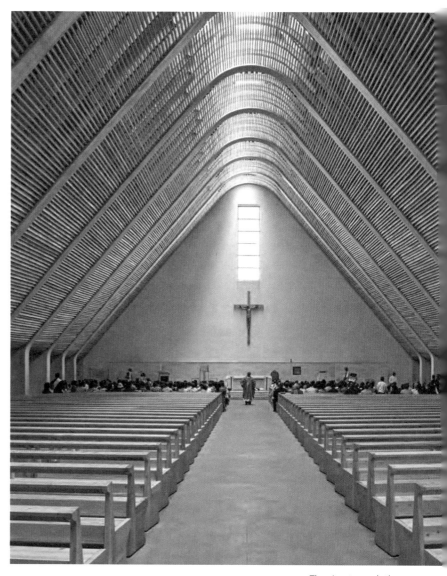

The view towards the altar of the cathedral.

Diagram of the loudspeaker coverage strategy; all loudspeakers face in the same direction, pointing towards the audience and away from the front of the room.

Bibliography

Acoustics, Sound – General Interest

Apfel, Robert E., *Deaf Architects & Blind Acousticians?*, New Haven, CT, Apple Enterprises Press, 1998

Byrne, David, *How Music Works*, San Francisco, CA, McSweeny's, 2012

Cox, Trevor, *Sonic Wonderland: A Scientific Odyssey of Sound*, London, UK, The Bodley Head, 2014

Hale, Susan Elizabeth, *Sacred Space, Sacred Sound: The Acoustic Mysteries of Holy Places*, First Edition, Wheaton, IL, Quest Books, 2007

Horowitz, Seth, *The Universal Sense: How Hearing Shapes the Mind*, New York, NY, Bloomsbury USA, 2013

Krukowski, Damon, *Ways of Hearing*, Cambridge, MA, The MIT Press, 2019

Krukowski, Damon, *The New Analog: Listening and Reconnecting in a Digital World*, New York, NY, The New Press, 2017

Levintin, Daniel J., *This is Your Brain on Music: The Science of a Human Obsession*, New York, NY, Plume/Penguin, 2007

Thompson, Emily, *The Soundscape of Modernity: Architectural Acoustics and the Culture of Listening in America, 1900–1933*, Cambridge, MA, The MIT Press, 2004

Soundscapes, Sound Art

Dia Arts Foundation, *Max Neuhaus: Times Square, Time Piece Beacon*, Beacon, NY, Dia Arts Foundation, 1997

Hayward Gallery, *Sonic Boom: the Art of Sound*, London, UK, South Bank Centre, 2000

Oliveros, Pauline, *Deep Listening: A Composer's Sound Practice*, New Jersey, iUniverse Inc., 2005

Schafer, R. Murray, *The Soundscape: Our Sonic Environment and the Tuning of the World*, New York, NY, Destiny Books, 1993

Smith, Mark M., *Hearing History: A Reader*, Athens, GA, University of Georgia Press, 2004

Auditorium and Venue Design

Barron, Michael, *Auditorium Acoustics and Architectural Design*, Taylor & Francis, Oxford, 1993

Beranek, Leo L., *Concert and Opera Halls – How They Sound*, Acoustical Society of America, 1996

Forsyth, Michael, *Auditoria: Designing for the Performing Arts*, London, UK, The Mitchell Publishing Company Limited, 1987

Hammond, Michael, *Performing Architecture: Opera Halls, Theatres and Concert Halls for the Twenty-First Century*, London, New York, Merrell, 2006

Izenour, George, *Theater Design*, Second Edition, New Haven, CT, Yale University Press, 1997

Izenour, George, *Roofed Theaters of Classical Antiquity*, First Edition, New Haven, CT, Yale University Press, 1992

Steel, James, *Theatre Builders*, Great Britain, Academy Editions, 1996

Acoustics Textbooks

Adams, Tyler, *Sound Materials: A Compendium of Sound Absorbing Materials for Architecture and Design*, Amsterdam, the Netherlands, Frame Publishers, 2007

Ballou, Glen, Editor, *Handbook for Sound Engineers – The New Audio Cyclopedia*, Howard W. Sams & Co., 1987

Bergmann, Heinz, *Praktische Bauphysik*, Fourth Edition, B.G. Teubner GmbH, Stuttgart/Leipzig/Wiesbaden, 2001

Bies, D.A., Hansen, C.H., *Engineering Noise Control*, Boston, London, Prentice-Hall, 1988

Cremer, L., Muller, H.A., *Principles and Applications of Room Acoustics, Volumes 1 and 2*, Applied Science, 1982

Davis, Don, Davis, Carolyn, *Sound System Engineering*, Second Edition, Newton, MA, Focal Press, Butterworth-Heinemann, 1997

Egan, M. David, *Architectural Acoustics*, Plantation, FL, J. Ross Publishing Classics, 2007

Everest, F. Alton, *Master Handbook of Acoustics*, Fourth Edition, The McGraw-Hill Companies, Inc., 2001

Fahy, Frank, Gardonio, Paolo, *Sound and Structural Vibration*, Second Edition, Oxford, UK, Burlington, MA, Elsevier, 2007

Grueneisen, Peter, *Soundspace, Architecture for Sound and Vision*, Birkhäuser, 1st Edition, Basel-Boston-Berlin, 2003

Heller, Eric J., *Why You Hear What You Hear: An Experiential Approach to Sound, Music, and Psychoacoustics*, Princeton, NJ, Princeton University Press, 2012

Long, Marshall, *Architectural Acoustics*, Second Edition, Cambridge, MA, Academic Press, 2014

Nunes, Ze, *Sustainable Acoustics: Sustainable Acoustic Scheme Designs from Mach Acoustics*, London, Mach Acoustics Ltd, 2011

Parkin, P.H., Humphries, H.R., Cowell, J.R., *Acoustics, Noise and Buildings*, F.A. Praeger, 1958, 1979

Rossing, Thomas D., *The Science of Sound*, Second Edition, Addison-Wesley Publishing Company, Inc., 1990

Sound Research Laboratories Ltd, *Noise Control in Industry*, Third Edition, London, UK, Chapman and Hall, Boca Raton, FL, CRC Press 1991

Webb, J.D., B.Sc.(Eng), Ph.D, C.Eng, M.I.Mech.E., Bramer, T.P.C., B.Sc.(Eng) C.Eng, MIEE, Cowell, J.R., B.Sc, B.Arch, M.Sc, et. al., *Noise Control in Mechanical Services*, Great Britain, Sound Attenuators Limited and Sound Research Laboratories Limited, 1972

Zürcher, Christoph, Frank, Thomas, *Bauphysik, Bau und Energe*, vdf Hochschulverlag AG, ETH Zurich (*Constructiion and Energy – Guide to Planning and Practice Editor: Ch. Zurcher*), Stuttgart, 1998

Chapter 1

1 Seth Horowitz, *Universal Sense: How Hearing Shapes The Mind*, USA, Bloomsbury, 2013

2 Liat Clark, Listen to the ancient sounds of Stonehenge: app transports you back to 3,000BC, https://www.wired.co.uk/article/stonehenge-acoustic-app-listen-to-history, 2017, accessed 31 October 2019

3 Philip Ball, Mystery of Chirping Pyramid Decoded, https://www.nature.com/news/2004/041213/full/041213-5.html, 2014, accessed 31 October 2019

4 George C. Izenour, *Roofed Theaters of Classical Antiquity*, New Haven and London, Yale University Press, 1992

5 *De Architectura*, Libri X, Volume V, http://www.vitruvius.be/, accessed 31 October 2019

6 David Byrne, *How Music Works*, San Francisco, McSweeney's, 2012

Chapter 2

1 https://www.who.int/docstore/peh/noise/Comnoise-4.pdf, accessed 31 October 2019

2 https://lighthouse-sf.org/, accessed 31 October 2019

Chapter 3

1 Margaret Carrigan 'Museums Make Space for Sound Art This Fall', *Observer*, <https://observer.com/2017/10/3-new-york-museums-make-space-for-sound-art-exhibitions-this-fall/>, 2017, accessed 30 October 2019

- *Sonic Arcade: Shaping Space with Sound*, Museum of Art and Design (MAD)
- *Transformer: Native Art in Light and Sound*, (the National Museum of the American Indian (NMAI)
- *The World is Sound*, The Rubin Museum

2 Juliet Kinchin, 'Sound and Vision: A *Making Music Modern* Virtual Tour and Playlist', *Inside/Out A MoMA/MoMA PS1 Blog*, <https://www.moma.org/explore/inside_out/2015/01/08/sound-and-vision-a-making-music-modern-virtual-tour-and-playlist/>, 2015, accessed 30 October 2019

3 Tara Drinks, 'NBA Creating Sensory Rooms at More Than Half of Its Arenas', Understood, < https://www.understood.org/en/community-events/blogs/in-the-news/2018/05/04/nba-creating-sensory-rooms-at-over-half-of-its-arenas>, 2018, accessed 30 October 2019

4 Umberto Bacchi, 'Can Dubai go green with flying taxis and 'rooms on wheels'?', Reuters, < https://www.reuters.com/article/us-cities-future-emirates/can-dubai-go-green-with-flying-taxis-and-rooms-on-wheels-idUSKBN1WW0EG>, 2019, accessed 30 October 2019

5 Arup, *Cities Alive: Green Building Envelope*, Berlin, Germany, Arup, 2016

Chapter 6

1 Sandy Brown Associates, 'Evelyn Grace Academy', <https://www.sandybrown.com/case-study/evelyn-grace-academy/>, 2010, accessed 30 October 2019

2 Paoletti, D.A. (2011) 'What's So Special (Acoustically) about a Cathedral?' 3rd Architecture, Culture and Spirituality Symposium, Focal Press, Waltham, 1–12.